DIVISION OF THE SOCIETY OF ST. PAUL, STATEN ISLAND, N.Y. 10314

"The bishops should present Christian doctrine in a manner adapted to the needs of the times, that is to say, in a manner that will respond to the difficulties and questions by which people are especially burdened and troubled."

> Second Vatican Council: Decree
> *Christus Dominus*, 13.

"One should not be surprised that there are many forms of theological study and teaching . . . In fact, this multiplicity of forms is desirable. It indicates the richness of our doctrinal heritage."

> Pope Paul VI:
> Address on the Magisterium of the Church,
> December 4, 1968

a Contemporary Theology of Grace

by CHARLES R. MEYER

Imprimi Potest
William P. Le Saint, S.J.
Pres., Pont. Theol. Faculty
St. Mary of the Lake Seminary, Mundelein, Ill.

Nihil Obstat
Edward Higgins, OFM Cap.
Censor Librorum

Imprimatur
Joseph P. O'Brien, S.T.D.
Vicar General, Archdiocese of New York
November 20, 1970

The nihil obstat and imprimatur are official declarations that a book or pamphlet
is free of doctrinal or moral error. No implication is contained therein that those who
have granted the nihil obstat and imprimatur agree with the contents, opinions or
statements expressed.

Library of Congress Catalog Card Number 70-158567
SBN: 8189-0202-7

Designed, printed and bound in the U.S.A. by the Pauline Fathers and Brothers of
the Society of St. Paul, 2187 Victory Blvd., Staten Island, N.Y. 10314 as part of their
communications apostolate.

CONTENTS

CHAPTER I

Methodology

In our day man has landed on the moon. He has even exceeded the biblical injunction to dominate the earth. In the future he may well see religion as totally superfluous and his own power of self-transcendence as the one single value to be cultivated. But as he begins to conquer space man comes more and more into confrontation with the vastness, splendor and awesome beauty of creation. This may well open him up to a new consideration of religious truths. Both alternatives are possible. What will happen depends very much on what teachers of religion and theologians will do.

For those charged with the proclamation of the Gospel message the present may be the kairos, the moment of truth for religion, the time ripe for the harvest. But one thing is certain: if there is a great opportunity now to promote religious values, it will be totally lost unless some means of expressing them relevantly to modern man is found. Until the diehard devotees of the past come to realize that they are making sense only to a species of man that is rapidly becoming extinct, theology is in trouble, for our own day has witnessed a giant step in the evolution of man. *Homo sapiens* is on the wane; *homo cyberneticus* is emerging.

The Catholic theology of grace which we have inherited from the past was conceived and elaborated in the context of the philosophical system known as Scholasticism. Science today has not simply rejected this philosophy. Most of the truths it proposes are simply taken for granted and have become presuppositions for thinking and acting in everyday life. But its methodological approach to thought, highly rationalistic in structure, is too tedious for modern man to appreciate. Today's philosophical reflection tends to be more holistic. People today are apt to rely more on insight, intuition, feeling and experience than on pure logic. As a consequence there has been a psychological repression of formal theological thought in our society. People today shy away from the overtly theological. But as in all cases of repression, what has been consciously rejected, what is not able to be borne reflexively, is still largely influential in the establishment of thought and behavior patterns. Disguised theological forms constantly pop up in everyday life. Overtly secular preoccupations have been cathected with religious significance. Religious meaning has been transferred to less threatening symbols. Our banks have become temples, our school-texts catechisms, our moon-probes pilgrimages and our football games liturgies. We give no second thought to the fact that even the names of the days of the week honor Teutonic and Roman deities. Even the great religious festivals of Christmas and Easter have significantly undergone a secularizing metamorphosis.

Despite society's incessant drift away from the obviously religious, there is a clear-cut reluctance to abandon religion entirely. The theological has been so much a part of our culture, has been so intricately woven into the warp and woof of it, that total eradication is impossible. There is no such thing as instant culture. But to purge society of theological and religious elements would require the immediate creation of a new totally secularistic substitute. The failure of the French Revolution in its attempt to do this is an historical case in point.

The existence in our culture of what might be termed an anonymous or larval theology, then, is the pivotal point around which any current methodology must be constructed. Advocates of secularization like Harvey Cox might well point out the futility of any attempt to explicitate theology again. They see the task of the theologian today as being centered not in any counter-current swim, but in further enhancement of the secularization tide. Yet the fact is that there is a demand, articulately voiced by many educated Christians today, for a relevant theological renewal. Many religious people are admittedly adrift, but they refuse to be entirely cut loose from their moorings. They look to the theologian for help when addressing themselves to the basic question about the ultimate meaning of human life. Such help will not be forthcoming from a mere reiteration of past theological formulas. But it might well emanate from a careful analysis of the contextual framework of modern religious and quasi-religious feeling.

Modern life is energized by the critical and empirical attitude engendered by the scientism of the nineteenth century. In our time much of its theoretical montage has proven false and been rejected. But its basic tenets have borne fruit in the re-evaluations and resultant technical advances of our day. Its presuppositions have found increased viability in the current cultural milieu. Fundamentally it is idealistic. It highlights the subjectivity of the thinker. Its central insight is that reason itself is historically conditioned. There can be no such thing in science as eternally valid principles. Even the abstract truths of mathematics and logic are conditioned by the formulas in which they are enunciated and the understanding with which they are invested. A fortiori subjectivist criticism becomes valid when it is applied to other forms of thought. Wherever it is employed it has a relativizing effect. In Catholicism conciliar decrees and papal documents have to be contextualized, given a Sitz-im-Leben, as much as the Bible was in Protestantism. It is the softening, eroding effect of contextualization in life that has given rise to the repression of dogmatic formulations of thought. But the principle of dogmatism is never itself fully rejected. It is merely transferred to more acceptable areas. While formulations cease to be dogmatic, the principles of subjectivist or historical criticism are dogmatized.

The scientific world today insists that nothing is absolute. Yet it has absolutized the principles of empiricism. Everything must be verified by experience or experiment. And still both in theory and practice empiricism has to be contextualized. It is a principle that cannot be lived. $E = mc^2$ has become as absolute a principle for today's science as the statement that God is triune was for the thirteenth century's theology. But Heisenberg's principle of indeterminacy indicates that mass-spatial and kinetic parameters of sub-atomic particles cannot be simultaneously measured with absolute accuracy. Thus $E = mc^2$ cannot be empirically verified. Before a flight a scientist does not insist on checking for himself the air-worthiness of his plane. In the real world empirical principles have become as irrelevant as theological ones. But in the world of thought they are sacralized and exist as larval forms of theological dogmatism.

The philosophical world today subsists on existentialism. Yet existentialism is the cocoon harboring pupal forms of imaginal theological concerns: the nature of man; his freedom, his possibilities for self-transcendence, his limitations. Is Camus' *The Fall* a modern treatise on original sin? Is Eliot's *The Cocktail Party* a description of an up-to-date liturgical celebration in which a psychiatrist has replaced the priest?

If larval theology pervades the intellectual world today, it is even more in evidence in the interests of people at large. Everywhere from the White House to the ghetto one experiences today a fascination with psychology. No other single academic discipline has acculturated itself to the extent that psychology has in American society. The cant of this field has become the *lingua franca* not only of the bourgeoisie but also of the deprived classes. Yet in no other area is the transference from overtly theological concepts as much in evidence as in the field of psychology. The father of modern psychology Sigmund Freud has made four great contributions to the science. His notion of intra-psychic conflict, largely between the conscious and the unconscious, with the ego as arbiter between the id and the superego, certainly reflects Augustine's theological elucubrations on the two cities or the two *pondera*: *pondus mei et pondus Dei*, and the choice between them that is man's eternal challenge, and the source of his life-tension. Freud's concept of anxiety as the root of all human drives hides theology's quest for the explicitation of man's thirst for the transcendental. Freud's proposal of the unconscious as highly influential on human behavior is reminiscent of the medieval theologian's interest in the supernatural and mystical. And Freud's greatest contribution to psychoanalytic theory—his doctrine of transference—can be seen as no more than a larval form of the theological notion of grace and the hypostatic union, its root, where the healthiness *(salus)* of God rubs off on weak and sick man.

It is the task of the theologian today to explicate these forms of larval theology, to make men aware of the religious ideas and values ingrained in their daily life and interests. To be sure, in doing so he must make use not only of scholastic theology, but of many other varieties of theological discourse. In his book *God-Talk* John Macquarrie points out different forms of theological methodology employed by St. Athanasius in his treatise *De Incarnatione*. He singles out mythological, existentialist, ontological, authoritarian, logical, pragmatic, linguistically analytic and analogic or symbolic procedures in various passages. Indeed all these ways of pursuing the theological enterprise are possible to the modern student as well. But naturally today those methodologies must be preferred which are most influential in moving people to accept and act. Among them for obvious reasons the most effective will be seen to be:

1. The existentialist approach. This is certainly the method which great theologians like Rahner and Tillich have employed with profit. Theology is seen as centered in man. Man's being is limited, but is endowed with an awesome potential for self-transcendence. This power is rooted in human freedom. Man is the only creature that can completely dispose of his own being.

Man's potential to transcend and his use of it tells us something about God, for man is the image of God. The widespread assimilation of this view of humanity is attested to especially by the current civil rights movement.

2. The evolutionary or revolutionary approach. Our time has been very much affected by the process philosophy of Whitehead and a greater awareness of salvation history as a process of development. The evolutionary ideas of Teilhard de Chardin have permeated the works of theologians like Schoonenberg and Hulsbosch. Man's existence is played out in a series of actions that have significance to the extent that they manifest transcendence of former states or retrogression to more primitive ones. Evolution itself from the Alpha point of creation to the Omega point of final consummation is evidence of God's saving work among his people. Man strives constantly to negate his imperfections and so transcend himself. His very being is a structure of hope, a hope rooted in his power to deny, to protest, to throw off structures of the past. Demonstrations, sit-ins, campus unrest and the hippie movement give ample evidence of the motivating force of this world-view in contemporary society.

3. The approach of linguistic analysis. Philosophers like Wittgenstein believe that language is prior to thought. As far as others are concerned I am what I say. My thought is crystallized in communication. But communication has to be given a meaning. And there are meanings and meanings: personal meanings, cultural meanings and universal meanings. In the age of the analog computer the significance of meaning in communication is easily perceived to be paramount. Though computers work marvels, only man can assign meaning; only he can program them.

4. The approach of historical criticism. Theologians of our time more than ever have become aware of the need to concretize propositions in the setting of the era in which they were formulated. Theologizing for Catholics is conditioned essentially by a credal commitment. Progress made outside of the framework of the past may not really be valid. More than ever in the past today's theologian is in possession of wider and more accurate

information about the sources from which his theology has emanated. In reaction to gross radicalism educational institutions today are pointing up the fact that the world of the present is through its advanced technology in a much better position to appreciate and savor the wisdom of the past. But it cannot abandon that heritage.

If the theologian is to explicitate larval forms of theology indigenous in modern culture, he will have to employ, each in its own proper place, all these methodologies. But his act of explicitation itself must be seen essentially as a kind of communication. He must feed back to society in undiluted form the formal theological findings of his investigations. He must do this with a minimum of distortion. In communication it is necessary that the transmitter exhibit a high degree of fidelity so that its modulation be relatively distortion-free. The most important work of the theologian is to formulate clearly and precisely the message of the past. For this historical criticism is necessary. Next, the transmitter has to translate the message, whether it be sound or picture, into another medium to establish contact with the receiver, and it must be locked in with or in tune with the receiver. The theologian must analyze, both linguistically and ideationally, the value-patterns of the society in which he lives. Once he is locked in with his audience, he must then effect through a painstaking analysis of both the message and the situation of his would-be receptors the conversion that is necessary to produce a strong, clear signal. The result of such communication is bound to be creative. People will be galvanized into action or reaction. They will provide feedback which will either strengthen or weaken the signal and thus be instrumental in further reducing distortion. Where there is no resonance between transmitter and receiver there can be no feedback. This is the reason why theology has become stagnant, why it has become the private preserve of an esoteric few. It is the aim of this book to re-establish in one area of theology, at least among those who have some familiarity with the subject, a feedback link.

CHAPTER II

Grace

What is grace? Our catechisms respond: 1. the supernatural gift of God bestowed upon us for our salvation through the merits of Jesus Christ; 2. a spiritual quality which changes sinner to saint, makes us friends of God, his heirs and adopted sons, deserving of heaven, and temples of the Holy Spirit; or simply, 3. a share in divine life.

Undoubtedly this last definition of grace as divine life was most widely used in the recent past. It is not only a traditional concept, but one based upon Scripture. It seems to present best the description of grace St. John gives in his gospel. This gospel was, as we know, not only a response to the difficulties created by the Nicolaites, but also an attempt to address the basic religious questions of its own cultural milieu.

Ancient peoples were preoccupied perhaps much more than we with the problem of the meaning of human life. What is life all about? Is this earthly existence the be-all and end-all of everything for the individual? Or is there any hope for some kind of immortality? Religious leaders and savants among the ancients were almost unanimous in their response to this last question. Yes, there is hope for some kind of life after death. The religious myths of the time indicate that man by placating the gods and ingratiating himself with them might be able to obtain from them the immeasurable gift of immortality. The ancient philosophers point out that the human individual, resplendent with knowledge and graced with self-mastery, is just too precious a cargo to pass through the grave into extinction.

The next question that the peoples of old asked about life was this: "If we can hope for some kind of life after death, what will it be like?" We encounter a great divergence of opinion in the response given to this query. In the literature of the affluent, like the ancient Egyptians, we see life after death described in terms of earthly life. The Egyptian hoped after death to be taken to a heavenly Egypt. When Ra, the sun-god, made his daily trip in his fiery chariot across the sky, he took with him the double-images of those who had died in the Two Kingdoms to the land of the West. There they would find a better, a more perfect Egypt. We find in the tombs of the ancient pharaohs evidences of this persuasion. The king was provided for his new life in the West with the things he had used in the former one on earth: his Nile boat, his jewelry, cutlery, foodstuffs and, in the most ancient graves, his wives. The *ka*, in so far as it was possible, was given for its life all the things that the *ba* had used and enjoyed on earth.

Quite a different response to this question was given among the poorer civilizations of the ancient world, particularly among the island peoples of the East. They experienced nothing but squalor and misery on earth. They had to look forward to death as a merciful release. For them heaven had to offer just the opposite of what they endured in earthly life. So very often their religious literature would tell them: "What is east here will be west there, and where the feet are here the head shall be there."

These two basic questions about immortality were asked by the ancient Christians as well. The first, of course, was answered in the affirmative. There is hope for some kind of life after death. But surprisingly enough, considering the fact that early converts to Christianity were principally from among the 'anawîm, we find the second answered much after the fashion of the Egyptians.

In several of the catacombs are to be found frescoes representing what scholars have presumed to be the central ethos of the life of the *ekklēsia,* the people called out from among others to form the Christian community, the Church. Around a table are seated five or seven figures, some veiled as women were in ancient times, some shabbily, others well-dressed. On the table is a plate with a fish, a basket of loaves and a flagon of wine. What is the significance of this symbolic drawing? Does it represent the Last Supper? The Mass? The presence of women at table might incline us to answer no. Was it then the agape-meal or love-feast, commemorated by St. Paul, in which not just the priestly caste but the whole community realized its pastoral, that is feeding *(pascere),* duty by calling into its celebration the poor and downtrodden and providing them with a meal? Or did it represent the heavenly convivium, the goal of the Christian life? Certainly from its situation in the burial grounds of the ancient Christians we might be tempted to give an affirmative answer to the last question even if we leave the others in doubt. But archeologists inform us that we must answer yes to all these questions. What is represented is the Christian life as such in all its aspects. The Last Supper was the source or authentication of that life. The Eucharistic banquet is its symbol or sacramentalization. The agape-festival was its realization on earth. The heavenly convivium is its consummation in eternity. But in reality it was all just one life.

The third question that ancient peoples asked about immortality was how it was to be achieved. The answer was clear. Man is mortal. Only the gods are immortal. If one is to become immortal, he must get that gift from a god. And the only way to obtain it is to placate one's god, to identify oneself with him, to put the seal of one's approval upon that god by acting out, by imitating the mysteries of his life; in a word, by doing his "thing." There was cabbalism in the rites to be performed; they were kept secret from the uninitiated. But to those who believed, those who had the gnosis, the symbolism of the ritual was apparent. If one sought immortality from Dionysus, he was in luck. The "thing" of Dionysus was wine. By imbibing one transcended oneself, the distress or misery of the moment, and obtained a foretaste of what eternal life with his god would be like. If one's goddess was Aphrodite, the course of the ritual was obvious.

Certainly, someone will say, the crudity of such a procedure would preclude the possibility of this having been the Christians' answer to the third question. But the fact is, it did not. The Christian too had to obtain eternal life by identifying himself with his God, with Christ. He had to do the "thing" of Christ. But what precisely was the "thing" of Christ? The paschal mystery, of course, the mystery of Christ's passage through death to a resurrected life.

But there was, obviously, an essential difference between the pagan and the Christian view. If we analyze it, the Christian notion will be seen to be the exact opposite of the pagan. Men are mortal; it cannot be otherwise. It would be blasphemous to seek immortality from God. Man must pay the debt of sin. He must die. What is promised by Christ is resurrection, not immortality, that is, escape from death. But it is precisely through death that man attains eternal life. Animals pass away; they do not die. Angels cannot die. Only man can die. Death is the epitome, the perfect realization, of human life. It is only in accepting one's humanity, in avoiding the pride of Adam's sin manifested in his desire to be like God, that man can pass to eternal life, to participate actually in God's own life. It is in humanity itself that one can achieve true transcendence. To ask God for what he has already given man is to show one's lack of faith.

Thus there was introduced into Christianity right from the start over and above the eschatological element in life an incarnational or this-worldly one. And these elements were not viewed as completely distinct, but intimately connected and interwoven, in a sense, identical.

The Christian identified himself with Christ in the sacraments. He initiated the paschal mystery in his life by baptism. The real significance of this ritual is lost in our society. In the ancient mid-

dle east water was seen as the most appropriate symbol of both
life and death. The Greeks and Romans knew how to swim; their
prowess in the Olympic games showed this. But the Israelites,
unless like Peter they happen to live on the seashore, generally
did not. They lived in an arid land, one largely bereft of deep
bodies of water. To be immersed in water was for them tantamount to dying. To be pulled out of a deep pool of water by a
minister of Christ was, in their symbolism, to have accepted death
and been rescued from it, given a new life, by Christ. They
thought of how their fathers had passed through the waters of
the Sea of Reeds by the power of God, while the pursuing Egyptian army perished. But water was for them also a symbol of life.
They believed, according to the story of Genesis which is not too
far removed from modern scientific conceptions, that all life began in water. They had witnessed new life emerging from the
waters of the womb. They had experienced the life-giving effect
of water on their travels through the desert lands. So they com-
prehended how in the baptismal ceremony, by anticipating their
death, by accepting it and the human condition it implied, they
identified themselves with Christ in his death. And they saw the
very vehicle of death was also a sign of resurrection and new life.
They were one in symbol with the resurrected Christ.

Many of the early Fathers of the Church do not speak of
grace, God's life-giving gift to man, in abstract terms. By grace
they mean baptism. And of course they understand that what
baptism symbolizes is new life, Christ's resurrected life, the Christian life. It might seem then that in accordance with our historical analysis we can best pursue the real notion of grace by
seeing it, as St. John and the latest catechisms did, to be life,
divine life under its eschatological aspects, and the Christian
way of life in its incarnational ones. Perhaps this is the way one
of the most outstanding catechetical instruments of our time
chooses to view grace. The index of the new Dutch catechism
indicates that the word "grace" occurs only on six pages of the
rather extensive text. There is no separate treatise on grace. The
reason for this, seemingly, is that the whole book is about grace.
It is all about God's life, his relation to man as concretized in

Christ, and the way in which man ought to respond. It is all about the Christian life. It is all about grace.

But as we said in the introductory chapter, in addition to historical analysis there is another limiting factor to be taken into account in elaborating contemporary theology. It is the question of current relevance. To speak of life to people today means to speak in abstraction. There are many kinds of lives that people live in today's world. Some live in Sybaris; others in the ghetto. For some life is a rat-race of enervating daily toil to provide future security for children who eventually become hippies. For some life is an alienated existence; for others, total self-centeredness; for still others ecstatic and thrilling self-fulfillment. It may be that everyone today as in the past must ask what life is all about. But in the ultimate analysis it proves to be a mystery that experience of it does not clear up. And when one begins to speak of divine life the mystery is compounded. If the more familiar analog is obscure, the less familiar one becomes utterly incomprehensible.

Certainly we cannot abandon the conception of grace as divine life. It is a notion clearly enunciated in the gospel of St. John and found from the earliest times in Christian tradition. But is it possible to specify that life more, make it more concrete—and this too in accordance with Scripture? What concrete aspect of human life most clearly points out what precisely is meant by grace? What area of human life today conceals a larval theology of grace?

Perhaps a clue to the solution of this question is given by St. Paul. The Christian life is like married life. The union of man and woman symbolizes perfectly the union between Christ and his Church. In the Christian life God stands in relation to man as husband to wife. And the relationship is one of love. Love is life. Love is God's life, as St. John, too, says, and love is man's life. Grace is God's loving presence and man's transformation in it.

In describing grace as love we may seem to have parted ways with the scholastic tradition. St. Thomas sees grace as inseparably connected with charity, but as formally distinct from it. (We are speaking here only of what has been known as sanctifying grace;

a later chapter will be devoted to questions about actual grace). He would define grace as a quality or habit infused by God into the essence of the soul which justifies the sinner and gives him a participation in the divine nature through adoption. But he alludes also to what theologians have called the uncreated grace, that is, God himself who abides with the just man and whose presence is both the cause of and effect of (in different orders of causality) created grace. And, of course, with St. John, St. Thomas recognizes the fact that God is love. We must also be aware of the fact that the scholastic system is not totally to be identified with the Thomistic one. In proposing the idea that grace is love we may have broken directly with the Thomistic tradition, but we are actually following another scholastic view, the Scotistic one.

The word "love" itself creates problems for many people today. The English language is impoverished in having only one word to describe human situations for which the Greek has at least four. Does the word we are using mean erotic love *(erōs)?* In a sense, yes, for sexual love is the paradigm from which radically all other types have emanated. As we shall see, the understanding of God's love for Israel was so associated with patriarchal life that even in begetting offspring the nation was constantly reminded of Yahweh. Are we referring also to familial or brotherly love *(philadelphia)?* Yes, to the extent that we are, through grace, adopted sons of God and because of this brothers of one another. Do we mean love as experienced among friends *(philia)?* Indeed, inasmuch as Christ called his followers no longer servants but friends. Is the love to which we refer charity *(agapē)?* To be sure, and this primarily, for grace as divine love is precisely the love that God has for himself communicated to men and enabling them to commit themselves fully to him and to their fellow-men who are his images. We use the word "love" formally and properly in this last sense when referring to grace.

The English word "grace" signifies attractiveness, charm, comeliness, seemliness, beauty, congruity, harmony of features, pleasurable or winning ways, endowment. St. Thomas points out various meanings of the corresponding Latin word: that which makes

a person likeable or lovable; an endowment or gift, recognition
or acknowledgment of a gift received. Various words in the Hebrew text of the Old Testament have been rendered as "grace"
in English translations: *'ahēb* from the root *'hb* which means to
desire, to breathe after, long for, love; *hēn,* favor, good will,
gracefulness, *hesed;* desire, ardor, love.

The idea of St. Paul that the union of man and woman in
marriage symbolizes the relationship of man to God has its roots
in very ancient Old Testament lore. The primitive revelation of
God to man as explicitated in the book of Genesis emphasizes
man's similarity to God. Man is the image of God. Adam names
the beasts. He becomes a creator, for to give meaning to reality
is to complete and perfect the work of creation. But among the
beasts he finds none similar to himself. From his own substance,
according to the story, there is produced an image of himself,
woman. Her he can love. He can unite himself with her. She is
like him. She reflects him to himself, and so he can commit himself totally to her. The basic Narcissism of all love, already appreciated by the writer of this passage, demands that the beloved
be an image of the lover (so that in loving the beloved the lover
fulfill himself) and that he be able to bestow upon the beloved
something of himself in the very act of love. The story of the
creation of Eve may have social and legal significance regarding
the status of women in Jewish culture. But it also has theological
import. It concretizes what has already been said in the creation
story in a number of different ways. Because woman has emanated from man, because she is an image of him, because like
him she is free to respond in kind, man can love her and commit his entire being to her. But exactly the same relationship
exists between God and man. Man emanated from God by creation. Other creatures did too, but man is different. Man like
God himself is a creator. He dominates the rest of creation. Like
God he is free. Like God he can love. He stands in the same
relationship to God as woman does to him. He reflects God to
himself. He can respond in kind to God's offer of love. So he is
the object of God's desire, of God's ardor, of God's passion. God
seeks union with him. And when he responds, he becomes, like

all beloved persons, beautiful in the eyes of his lover. He is graced.

In God's primitive revelation to man the whole theology of grace is epitomized in one sentence:

na'ăśeh 'ādām běṣalmēnû kidᵉmûtēnû

"Let us labor to make man into a reflection of ourselves so he might become our image" (Gen. 1, 16). Man is different from the other creatures. God simply produced them. In relation to them the word *bārā'* (made, created) is the one most often used. But here the verb is *'āsāh*. Perhaps it signifies that God must be at special pains to produce the reflection of himself he desires in man. Other beings were simply made by God what they are. Man has to be constantly influenced by God's loving act to become what God wants to see in him. God's action produces a *ṣelem*, a cut-out, a paper-doll image *(Schnitzbild)*, a replica, an idol of God like those found in pagan temples (Von Rad), or according to an older and perhaps less reliable philological tradition, a shadow of himself (Tregelles). The word "shadow" is particularly significant theologically, for a shadow has no being or movement of itself. Its every motion follows the action of whatever produces it. If man allows himself to become the shadow of God then he can perfectly image God and his action. And if God's act in regard to man is love, man can reflect it perfectly in his own love.

The Fathers of the Church have seen man's imaging of God whereby he can become the beloved of God in six areas of human endowment or activity. Substantively, they say, man reflects God in his reason, his freedom and his dominion over other creatures. Participatively man models God in his holiness, incorruptibility and divine sonship.

This primitive revelation was developed by Israel in its concept of the covenant relationship. Israel had a contract with God. It was like a marriage contract. Initiated by the rite of circumcision, it was fulfilled by fidelity to God's word and law. It was violated by the adulterous action of setting up or following other gods. Constantly in the Old Testament in the sayings of Yahweh and the remonstrations of the prophets God is

portrayed as a jealous husband who pursued Israel with relentless ardor, encouraging her, defending her, giving her a share
in his own possessions, while Israel remained a cold, unresponsive, adulterous wife. The symbolism of Hosea's marriage with a
harlot cannot be understood except in this context. But the fact
is that, despite her frequent lapses, Israel did remain essentially
faithful to this relationship with Yahweh while the pagan nations did not. Israel always believed that she could be the
spouse of Yahweh, that she could have direct dealings with him
as a wife with her husband, that Yahweh was in her as a
husband is in his wife through his love of her. But such a
belief was too much for the other peoples. They, too, had evidently received the primitive revelation about the all-high
God who created them. But they could not believe that they
were called to love him. They could not accept the fact that
the one who was above all could also be within them. Transcendence and immanence could not be reconciled in their
thought as these concepts about God were in Israel's theology.
While they acknowledged their own power to transcend themselves and become like their gods, they could not see this power
as imaging God's own power to transcend himself and be like
them, become immanent in them.

Mircea Eliade highlights what he calls the doctrine of the
primitive pair which is evidenced in almost all aboriginal cultures outside of Israel. Among the Chinese it is Yin and Yang;
the Egyptians had Nut and Geb; the Indians Koni and Lingam;
the Maori Rangi and Papa; the Toradja I-lai and I-ndora; the
Yoruba Orolun and Oduna; the Norse Frigga and Thor; the Japa-
nese Izanagi and Izanami; the Hittites U and Im, and so on. This
universal belief in a pair of gods solves for ancient peoples the
theological problem of the transcendence and immanence of the
divine. In the pair, one is the sky god, the transcendent god who
is almost always male; the other is the earth god, the immanent
god, usually female. Primitive religious books say: "The earth is
our mother; the sky is our father." The sky fertilizes the earth
with rain, and so life is produced. The only exception to this al-

most general rule is the Egyptian sky god Nut who is female, while the earth god Geb is male.

Outside Israel a goddess is substituted for the people as the spouse of the all-high god. The marriage concept, to be sure, is retained. But the primitive revelation is distorted to make it more bearable, to make people less responsible, to soften the stark reality of God's word, to erode the idea that God could really love man or man God in such a way, and to simplify the theological problem created by a God who could be both transcendent and immanent, who could be far above and still at the same time in his people.

This is not to say that Israel's concept of God was not to some extent subjected to the same dynamic. Israel often forgot her duty as the spouse of Yahweh. Israel tended to have the same problem as the other nations about the transcendence and immanence of God. But among the Jews the question was solved by a theological stratagem quite different from that of creating a goddess to stand between God and his people. Israel had two names for God. El was the generator-god, the source, the power, the God who was transcendent. Yahweh was the clan God, Israel's own proper God, the immanent God. *Yahweh* from the Hebrew verb meaning to be present was the special name revealed to Moses by God when he asked for a sign to authenticate his leadership of the people. "Tell them: I shall be present who am present. The one who is presence sent you." (Cf. Ex. 3, 14). But for Israel the transcendent and immanent God was always one and the same identical divinity. El was the name used for that God in his role as creator and dominator; Yahweh the name used for his role as lover, husband and guide.

Charis is the word that is usually translated "grace" in New Testament texts. It is akin to the Latin word *charitas*, whence is derived the English "charity." The Greek term like its Hebrew counterpart signifies beauty, charm, attractiveness, wholesomeness, talent or gift in the sense of endowment. It is also used, as the corresponding word in Latin *(gratia)* and the Romance languages in general, to mean thanks. This secondary meaning is easily derived from the primary, for thanks is the response in thought and feeling that one makes in appreciation of a gift or endowment. One is grateful for being graced. A person who is unaware of or unresponsive to his charm cannot really be charming. The English word "thank" like the German *danken* is akin to the word "think" (German: *denken*); it denotes a state of reflection, of mindfulness, of awareness, directed toward a gift or endowment. So while the Romance languages like Greek relate even etymonically and metonymically the gift or endowment and one's reaction to it, the Teutonic tongues, given more to hendiadys, not only employ different words, but in course of time have tended to become oblivious of the relationship that exists between them. The northern European languages stress the subjective or reflective element in the reaction to a gift that we call thanksgiving while the southern European languages emphasize the objective element, seeing the gratifying reaction as part of the gift itself. An understanding of this fact is important if we are to comprehend the relationship between grace (*charis*) and the Eucharist (*eucharistia*) the great act of Christian thanksgiving. Only a Eucharistic people can be graced; the Eucharist is grace *par excellence*. The reason for this will become apparent later when we discuss the meaning of the Mass in relation to grace.

Outside of the writings of St. Paul, New Testament literature does not pursue the paradigm of the man-woman relationship with reference to the God-man relationship as the Old Testament did. The reason for this is obvious. By the time the New Testament writings began to appear the real meaning of Christ's existence had at least larvally been apprehended by the Christian community. In New Testament literature one encounters often more than just the first glimmerings of a truth that far out-strips in awesomeness and significance the notion of God's immanence proposed in the ancient covenant writings. God is now not just the husband of his people loving them from on high. God now is himself incarnate. Fixation on the metaphysical aspects of such a stupendous fact led later writers away from a description of it in terms of marriage. Undoubtedly this was due also to the fear that an expression already used of the relationship between God and his people in the Old Testament would be totally inadequate to capture the almost ineffable significance of the new one set forth in the Gospel. But the fact that St. Paul recognized the old model as still valid emboldened some of the Fathers of the Church still to make use of it. A significant number describe the Incarnation as the marriage non-pareil between God and humanity.

The New Testament does propose with the greatest force possible its central theme of love: God's love for man and man's obligation to love God in return. And the love that is emphasized is precisely familial love. God is a Father and men are his children. While this idea, of course, is forever valid, and, as Harnack has indicated, the very essence of Christianity, it would not seem as appropriate today as it was in New Testament times to explicitate a theology of grace in terms of it. The sense of family solidarity witnessed in the patriarchal society of those times whereby father, mother and children were seen as objects of one and the same all-pervasive love, one shared love, is not everywhere in the same degree and with the same understanding perceptible in the modern world. By reason of the prevalence of divorce, the ever increasing use of birth control and a growing preoccupation with sexuality in marriage our society has been forced to make a clear-cut distinction between love of a wife or husband and love of children. They are different kinds of love as we understand them. This fact prompts us in explicitating a larval theology of grace for our time to explain grace not in the New Testament terms of love of children for a father, but rather in the Old Testament theme of the love of a wife for her husband. As we understand it, marital love is more intimate, more exciting, more engaging, more involving than filial love. It is love in a more radical and fuller sense. The moral theologians of the past few centuries seemed to be aware of this fact in their musings on the so-called order of charity (*ordo charitatis*) when they put in first place love between husband and wife, and love between father, mother and children in the second.

Of course, it may be objected that the very reasons given for the breakdown in our society of the idea of familial love—the prevalence of divorce, promiscuity, sexual license—can be adduced also in witness of the erosion that has taken place in regard to marital love itself. This is true. But despite the problem, there seems to be still operative, especially among young people, an ideal of romantic love which normally leads to marriage. Certainly in ancient times marriages were not based on this notion of love. Today this ideal is not sustained in the temporary liasons that are becoming more prevalent and is indeed shattered in the many marriages that do not work out. But it still does exercise an influence on many. There is always in evidence a romantic quest of an ideal partner, one to whom total commitment can be made, even by the philanderer and sexual dilettante. In fact, the prevalence of divorce today may very well be largely attributed to the failure to realize in the concrete the expectations of this ideal. In explicitating the larval theology of grace contained in human love then, we will not, as St. Paul and the ancients did, use precisely the paradigm of married love, but rather that of the current ideal of romantic love.

To understand more fully and explicitly the love of man for woman as a larval form of the love of God for man, we must consult the writings of the psychologists and existentialist philosophers of our time. If grace is the love of God for man, and the pattern for this love is to be found in the love of man for woman, then by understanding the full significance and operation of this human love we can come to a better appreciation of what the grace relationship implies. We can more easily reject the prevalent notion of grace as a thing and come to see it precisely as a relational reality and one that is not at all ethereal and abstract, but concrete and vitally dynamic. Psychology and existentialism are largely concerned with the problem of human love. A careful examination of selected texts in these fields will cast light on the subject of our interest.

Arnold Toynbee's version of *ad astra per aspera* is in a sense a key idea in existentialism. Man today has found out what his real treasure is because of the historical attrition and eventual destruction of presumed values. Man's life is essentially a protest. Man must inveigh against the obliteration of his idols, the upsetting of his value systems. As history sees it, man's life is basically one of protest against the encroachment by the world man was ordered to subdue, the inferior world, into what was considered the private preserve of humanity. Protest achieved the status of a formally organized movement under Martin Luther. He complained that the Roman Church had substituted scholastic philosophy for the gospel and canon law for love. He turned the spotlight away from institutional existence where personal values had to yield to societal ones toward the individual whose conscience was seen as completely autonomous under God. The industrial revolution was carried on under the aegis not of religion but philosophy. The sacral nature of individual labor was threatened by the greater capabilities of machines in supplying the market from which profits were to be realized. Man's dignity was affronted in what had been the principal area of his human operation. Retrenchment was in order. Personalist philosophy redirected attention to other values in human life not affected by industrial machines. After all machines could not think, create, lead and guide. But then came the cybernetic revolution. The very human values salvaged during the industrial revolution are now being placed in jeopardy again. Will the day come when computers will completely outstrip man in thinking and guiding? The new threat to man's dignity is being met once again by retrenchment. The alogical aspects of human life are now being put to the fore. Can computers have an experience? Are they conscious? Can they take delight in deliberately making a mistake? Can they go on a psychedelic trip? The attention of philosophers shifted from the intellectual to the volitional aspects of human existence. In all the revolutions man has thus far experienced, revolutions which sometimes tend to strip him of his dignity, he has retained one power, one capability which no one or no thing can ever take from him—his ability to protest, his freedom to deny, to say no. Man's freedom is what is seen by the existentialist philosophers as the ultimate constitutive element of his nature.

A man who protests demonstrates that he possesses something of ultimate value in the pursuit of which he is willing to sacrifice all else. Basically protest is the admission of some kind of subconsciously operative larval theology. Protest implies that one can freely commit the ultimate value that one sees in one-self where and when and to whatever cause one wishes. Protest then implies love. It indicates that man can have an ultimate value which can be committed to an other.

Existentialist philosophers like Heidegger belabor the idea that being (*Sein*) is in reality nothing, that is, no thing, but rather the common explanation of all things. However, of all things, only human reality has to face the question of being. Man may be defined as the only creature for whom his own being is an issue. Man can separate himself from his being, question it and do something about it. Man's being is never fully possessed. It is always, as it were, out in front of him. It is not given to him entirely; it is to be achieved. It is a to-be-made. Human reality is most appropriately described by the German word *Dasein*. Man is being-there, located being, being whose proper place is out there, projected being. Sartre distinguishes two kinds of being in man. Being *en soi* is that which man holds in common with other beings: it is what one is. Being *pour soi* is the projected being of man: it is the being to be made; it is this being that characterizes and distinguishes, sets apart, human reality.

The being of man, then, essentially implies the power to transcend, to bring the actual locus of one's being to the projected locus. And transcendence is achieved through a never-ending investment of one's being in free projects. Through freedom man has the power entirely to dispose of himself within the limits of his located being. An individual's personality is phenomenologically perceived by others as the sum total of all his projects, achieved or to be achieved. His individuality is noted by others in terms of the ways in which he has made use of his freedom. He is seen as the sacrament of the ways in which he has chosen to exist.

As *Dasein* man must be continually outside of himself. He becomes human and witnesses his humanity to himself only when he transcends. Yet to transcend he must nihilate himself as he is. He must protest his being where he is, and identify himself with his being where it is-to-be. In this process he becomes aware of his humanity for himself, but he has not yet bridged the gap between his own subjectivity and the world that seems to exist outside of himself. His objective human existence can become a fact for himself only through confirmation by another. It is only by transcending himself in relation to another and by perceiving the similar transcendence of another in relation to him that he can objectify his own human existence.

The fact is that though freedom, the ability to dispose of oneself, is man's greatest asset, to certify its objective existence and exploit its possibilities he must surrender it. This is the most awesome fact about man's limited, localized existence. His most precious self must be alienated in transcendence. Complete self-fulfillment can be attained only in love. And love is impossible without the total investment of that which a man values the most, that which founds his very selfhood and subjectivity, his freedom. Certainly the lover does not want it so, but as a matter of fact the real goal of a lover's enterprise has to be the alienation of his own freedom. The power to free oneself is proved only in its use. To use that power is to choose. And to choose is to limit oneself by being no longer free to choose the contradictory or opposite of what one has chosen.

The existentialist view of man is one that has permeated every area of our society. But basically it is not a new idea. Its roots are to be found in the humanistic ideals of the Renaissance period of history. Cardinal Nicholas of Cusa who died in 1464 hit upon what became its basic tenet when he singled out the distinguishing characteristic of human existence as freedom. All other beings, he taught, have an immutable essence; man has no essence. His essence is to have no essence. He makes himself what he wants to be. He creates his own entity. Thus he becomes a creator like God precisely because he is free. Unlike God's, however, man's creative power is not absolute. It is limited by the circumstances of his being. But when the opportunity presents itself, man can transcend himself and truly become a creator. So Nicholas defines man as a God according to circumstance, a *Deus occasionatus*.

In his *Being and Nothingness* Jean-Paul Sartre analyzes existentially the process of falling in love. It begins with seduction. By this is not meant anything deceptive or evil. Seduction is simply a call to love and the manifestation of a desire to be loved. The other, the potential object of love, is first seen as a look. The one who would venture being loved must risk being seen. The objectivity of his own being can be established only if it is apprehended and held captive by the other. The prospective lover must present himself to the other as an attractive prey; he must be seen as a fascinating object. He must be apprehended as possessing the fulness of being, at least in some area. He has to be able, in a sense, to present the world to his beloved. He is a great athlete. He has money, position, connections. His self-assured mien is characterized by *politesse* and *élan*. As far as the prospective beloved is concerned, he seems unsurpassable. He does not want to appear insincere or hypocritical. He strives in every way possible to live up to the ideal of himself he presents to his beloved. As Heidegger points out, he becomes what he says. He is the word he reveals to the other. Projecting himself into the position of the other, he perceives how true this is. He senses an even greater incentive to be what he says. He is what he says.

At this point the lover's attention has shifted more directly to the subjective. Originally he saw himself as only an object, although an engaging and fascinating one, in the eyes of his beloved. He saw himself no more prized than the doll she played with as a girl and still treasures in a prominent place in her room. Even if he were to become the object she treasured the most he would still be just an object, a thing to be used, in her eyes. His subjectivity would not be confirmed. The ambivalence he has about himself as a person would not be resolved. When he begins to attend to what he is saying, however, when he becomes aware of himself as a word, when he becomes sensitive to the discrepancy beween what he perceives himself to be and what he proclaims himself to be, his focus becomes more subjective. What he says is more directly linked to the subjective, but still not directly enough. What the lover really wants is that the beloved possess his very subjectivity. And in turn he wants to possess the subjectivity of the beloved. He must overcome the subjectivity of the other. It is an obstacle to love. Only in securing from the beloved the total surrender of her subjectivity can the lover validate the objective existence of his own subjectivity. Only if he can assimilate her precisely as looking at his subjectivity can the basic question about his own being, about his objective existence, be answered.

The lover must bridge the gap between the objective and the subjective. Ultimately he must as far as possible eliminate all objective elements from his proposal. He must present to his beloved that which is most representative of his subjectivity itself, his freedom. He must, as Sartre says, eventually abandon seduction and take as his project *being loved*. Love is really a demand to be loved. The other's most precious selfhood, the other's freedom, must be alienated. This cannot be done as long as the lover is perceived as just an object. To capture the consciousness, the freedom of the other, the lover's project must be freed of all instrumentality. The lover must be prepared to surrender his own freedom.

It has to be noted here that at this point we must part ways with Sartre. His purpose in analyzing what happens in love has a purely philosophical orientation. He is not precisely interested in the ideal of romantic love as such. He wants to show how love can be used to validate existence. This is his primary intent. One's own subjectivity can be confirmed merely by capturing the consciousness of another in love. The act has to be reciprocated by the true lover, who wants also to love, but not necessarily by the philosopher, who wants only to see his own objective existence confirmed in this manner.

Sartre points out that the subjectivity of the beloved must be captured without crushing it or violating it. The lover's own being can be authentically confirmed only if the consciousness of the beloved is left intact, not distorted in any way. That is why the offer of the lover has eventually to be freed from all kinds of instrumentality. Love is cheapened, imperiled or destroyed by violence or deceit, or even by demands in justice.

To work its charm love has to be freely given and freely received. Once the lover has projected his pure subjectivity, his desire only to love and to be loved, objective considerations no longer have any part in the relationship. Total subjective involvement is of the essence of the chemistry of love. It brings about the magical transformation of both the lover and the beloved. In the eyes of the partners, in their subjectivity, each undergoes a change in respect to the other. Though the lover may, as Sartre says, actually be ugly, small, misshapen, cowardly and wishy-washy, he is no longer seen as such. These facts about him are no longer important for him. He is loved. His defects are swallowed up in the overriding power of his joyful loving personality, in the totality of his commitment and the commitment that has been made to him. He is idealized in the mind of the beloved. A child who truly loves his mother is blind to her defects though they may be very obvious to others. In the eyes of the beloved who freely responds to his offer of love the lover achieves the self-transcendence he desires. He fulfills his most basic human need. He begins now to exist. In confrontation with this thrilling and exhilarating fact all else ceases to have importance. But, paradoxically enough, the more he loves the more the lover loses his being. The more he loves the more the lover is cast back on the possibilities of his being, on his power to be. The more the lover loves, the less he is, but the more fully he exists. His transformation is not merely a subjective one, existing only in the eyes of the beloved. Through love he has really been endowed with a new power and with a new incentive for further self-transcendence. Love enables him to do things he could not have done before he committed himself to his beloved. To be sure, he seems to have lost some of his freedom. He is no longer at liberty to do anything that will offend his beloved or harm love itself. He is held in a kind of thraldom. But it is the kind of thraldom that brings him satisfaction and complete self-fulfillment. We shall discuss this point at greater length later when we consider the nature of human freedom.

Essentially love is an ecstasy that invites further ecstasies.

It is a power given to fulfill the expectations of the beloved, to be actually what the beloved perceives one to be, to measure up to the image the beloved has projected upon the lover. This projection is what transforms each of the parties in the eyes of the other and in reality. But the most marvelous thing about the operation of love is that it transforms the parties involved precisely by leaving them what they are. It is an invitation to measure up; it is a demand for further ecstasies; it is a power given to be more; but love itself cannot be totally conditioned upon the fulfillment of this expectation or demand or the actualization of that power. One must be loved for what he is. Otherwise true love would be impossible: it would become instrumental. Thus love can really exist where there is no empirical evidence of it, no external manifestation of it. It is normal that love be expressed, but failure to give any sign of it does not necessarily deny it. The transformation it produces is so deeply rooted, so inward, that it cannot be perfectly externalized.

Love involves risk. It demands faith on the part of the lover. The lover can never be absolutely sure except through faith that the beloved really means what she says. One can never through empirical evidence be certain that the other has responded in kind to an offer of love. Ultimately the lover must trust that he is not being deceived, that his partner is not play-acting. Without faith and trust love cannot exist, or, if it does exist, it will soon be eroded by suspicion.

As we have seen love requires an alienation of freedom. It involves committing the ultimate value of selfhood to another. It implies a surrender of being. It demands fulfillment of the expectations the other has projected upon his lover. But at one and the same time love can be seen as the conferral of true freedom, as a new kind of freedom. The lover surrenders his freedom in relation to the beloved. But he thereby acquires a different kind of freedom he could not have enjoyed before he committed himself to love. This new freedom is a shared freedom. The lover's freedom is now deeply involved with that of the beloved. The freedom they both surrendered is now returned to them validated, strengthened and augmented. Whatever of strength existed in the freedom of the lovers as individuals is now to be found in their common freedom. Whatever of weakness existed before they loved is now strengthened by their mutual commitment, by their encouragement and support, one of the other. And if freedom is the being of man, lovers have thus acquired a new being, a new form of existence. Their very being is now intermingled. So through love, and through love alone, one becomes truly human, accomplishes and fulfills the basic drive of his humanity itself. He truly achieves the state of being at one and the same time fully himself and yet truly other to himself. He experiences in his own being the immanence and transcendence of love. He comes truly to exist and so truly to be free.

Love is essentially creative of being. The common freedom of the lovers is focalized on a project. In marriage this project is the augmentation and solidification of love in the production of new life. The child is the outward sign, the image, the concrete realization of the love of the spouses. In the child the lovers have a reflection of themselves in transcendence. The authenticity of their own self-surrender is established for good, and the facticity of both their objective existence and common freedom is signalized. The project of love is its sacrament.

Existentialist philosophy, then, has much to say about love. But so also does psychology. It would, of course, not be possible to consider all of the different theories of love advanced, nor would this be to our purpose. But it might be helpful in understanding the complex relationship that love is to supplement the basic ideas proposed by the existentialist philosophers with the more concrete applications of a noted and influential psychologist like Carl Gustave Jung.

One of the most important features of the psychological theory of Jung is his idea of the archetypal image. An archetype basically is a matrix or form which assists the individual in assimilating, organizing and coordinating his experience. It is essentially a subliminal or unconscious image in the light of which and in reference to which empirical data are appropriated and understood. It may be the result of a personal childhood experience or simply a given of what Jung calls the collective unconscious, that is, the myths or idiosyncratic behavior patterns of a given culture or civilization as a prepersonal conditioning of the lives of its adherents. The legend of a people and its ways of life begin to exert a subconscious influence on an individual from the dawn of his consciousness. He will make them a part of himself often without even reflecting on them, and take for granted the fact that he is to live in accordance with the norms and customs of his clan.

Indigenous in every family or at least in every society are its sexual archetypes, the *animus* and *anima*. In normal family life at a very early age the child becomes aware of psychological as well as physical differences between the sexes. He forms for himself from contact with his father an idealized, generalized notion of what masculinity means. This idea will be the future reference point for judgments about masculinity. As it recedes into the subconscious it becomes the male archetype (*animus*). A similar process characterizes the child's relationship with his mother and results in the formation of the female archetype (*anima*). As the child becomes more aware of his own sexuality, he tends to identify more and more, if he develops normally, with the proper archetype. Both archetypes are instrumental in establishing the behavior patterns of the child in relation to sex: his own proper one as a point of identification and the other as a point of reference. After puberty the sexual archetypes become focal areas in the individual's psychic activity. The normal person uses his archetypal image of the opposite sex as a guide in the selection of a marriage partner. A boy in his encounter with girls will project upon each of them his own *anima*. He will become aware of areas of correspondence and divergence. It may be that he notes that this girl or that has deep-sunken eyes, a bad complexion, fat legs, or is too intellectual, argumentative, vapid or fatuous. He does not know why, but somehow he dislikes these qualities very much. But when the boy finds a girl that most perfectly reflects to him his *anima* the chemistry of love will be set in operation. She will become the realization of his *anima*. In fact she will be his ideal woman. He will be truly identified with her. Though he is not fully conscious of it, because she is really his *anima,* he will regard her as part of himself. He will tolerate no criticism of her. He will be blinded to her faults or defects. Many a concerned parent or anxious counsellor has experienced the futility of trying to dissuade such a boy from pursuing the promptings of his love. But he has only one intent: to be one with his *anima* again.

The implications of these notions for the work of explicitating a larval theology of grace are by now, presumably, quite apparent. Of course, God cannot really be equiparated with a human lover. He in no way needs to establish his own being by a love directed outside of himself. But apart from this and other considerations there are many striking similarities that cannot be ignored.

The possibility of having such a thing as the grace-relationship between God and man is ultimately rooted in the Christian doctrine of the Incarnation. It is the most astounding of all the Christian mysteries. Even though he is most complete and totally fulfilled in his own being, the notion of the Incarnation indicates that God as a matter of fact desired to be other to himself. He willed as it were to transcend himself. His transcendence may perhaps be better described in terms of the Pauline concept of the kenosis, the emptying out as it were, or the concealment of what he was to enable him to appear in different guise. But howsoever it is described, the fact is that God moved from being just what he was to being what formally he was not. Not because he himself needed it; but because his creatures did need it to attain the purpose he had in mind for them, he, as it were, sought confirmation of his existence outside of himself. He willed to extend his love outside of himself. He created beings capable of knowing and loving him. He created subjectivities whose existence could be fully established only in his being, and who would by their commitment to him confirm his being outside of himself. But there is only one being outside of God who can do this most perfectly: the Incarnate Word, in whose personality are united both creatureliness and divinity.

In him all other beings were created. He is both the reason for and goal of all existence outside of God.

In his essay entitled *"Zur Theologie der Menschwerdung"* Karl Rahner defines man in terms of the Incarnation. This definition has been instrumental in spurring Catholics today to reconsider old distinctions between the sacral and the secular, the supernatural and the natural. The view of man it presents has undoubtedly sparked the phenomenal spread in the Church today of a doctrine of Christian humanism. It founds our own concept of larval theology. It is precisely this definition that leads us to believe that a comparison of God with the lover of the existentialists might not really be as far-fetched as it might seem at first blush. It and it alone captures the full theological significance of the primitive revelation of God that man is created as his shadow so that he might become in truth an image of him.

Man according to Rahner is what arises when the communicative element in God, his Word, appears as an instrument of love in the void of nothingness outside of God. This Word appears as man. Man then is to be seen as a kind of code-word, a cipher, for God. Man is a kind of abbreviation for God. When God sought to be other to himself, man arose—not just any man, but *the* Man. Because of him other men also come to exist.

St. Thomas was very much at pains to elaborate an intricate theory of participation in order to explain how through grace man could in some real sense possess the divine nature. Rahner has cut through the tangle of metaphysical intricacies created by Aristotelianism by invoking the simple existentialist idea that the exercise of freedom is self-limiting. If God sought some good outside of himself—indeed because of himself and for himself— he instituted a project in which he invested his freedom and total love. This project had to be divine, for in God too freedom is identified with being. But precisely as an exercise of freedom, it was self-limiting, for, as we have explained, choice limits absolute power. But precisely as an act of love, this project had to be open to participation by others. This project is man, not, as Rahner says, any man, but *the* Man, the man *propter quod unumquodque tale et illud magis,* the paradigmal or model man, the man who was in the fullest sense the image of God, the divine Logos made man.

God, then, is a lover. St. John tells us that his very essence is love. His goal like that of any lover was to alienate his freedom in regard to another. When he freely decided to create man, he was no longer free not to create. His act was divine in its subjectivity, but limited in its object. When God sought confirmation of his being outside of himself, man arose. But because all love is basically Narcissistic, man had to arise as a contraction, a limited expression, a shadow-image of God. Endowed with a limited participation in God's own intelligence and capacity for love, man was able to respond to God's offer and commit himself fully to God's own project.

God's seduction is concretized precisely in the full revelation of himself in Christ. Christ possesses and offers to man the fulness of being. He has as God total power. He is truly unsurpassable. He has overcome the world and can lay it at the feet of his beloved. As the divine Word Christ is truly what he says. The evangelization and catechesis of the past has belabored this fact. But unfortunately it has rarely passed beyond the stage of seduction. It tended to remain totally objective. Christians consequently sought to possess God in Christ merely as a fascinating and valuable object. They saw God principally as a need-fulfiller, as an object of the greatest utility, the source of their own well-being and salvation. But the real goal of God's enterprise, like that of any lover, was to alienate his own subjectivity. He wanted to be loved. He projects himself in Christ simply as a to-be-loved. Thus he wishes to alienate the very subjectivity of man, to overcome his freedom. God desires ultimately to free his love of all instrumentality. He wishes to capture completely the consciousness of man and thus, as it were, transcend himself in man. If man responds in kind he too becomes a lover. He transcends himself. He can no longer appear in the eyes of God as insignificant, weak and sinful. His defects are swallowed up in the totality of his commitment of himself to God. He is given the power of love. He is internally transformed. But he is transformed precisely by being left what he is in himself. What transforms him is the capacity he receives, and can receive only from love, for additional self-transcendence in the order of love. He is given in the most concrete way possible an invitation to further ecstasy. It is the presence of God the lover that we call uncreated grace. It is the beloved's transformation in that love that we term created grace.

When man responds to God's offer of love and is transformed by it, he alienates his freedom to God. He gives to God his very being and humanity. But since according to Christian revelation he sees that God has first alienated his own freedom and being in Christ, man knows that what he surrendered will be returned to him, as in the case of human love, enlarged, strengthened and validated. Man's bent is for self-transcendence. He must be other to himself. This is the only way in which he can authenticate his humanity. But when he finds his transcendence, his self-otherness, his being and humanity in Christ, when he identifies himself in love with Christ the project of God's own love, he experiences an ecstasy beyond his wildest dreams. He has attained a state of self-otherness in which he now holds in common with God himself his freedom, his love and his very being. God's love and his own love meet, are identified and become objectively indistinguishable in their common goal or project, Christ. Man becomes truly other to himself in Christ. Through his act he participates in God's own freedom and being in Christ. Because he was created in love by God, his being already participated in some sense in God's own. His being is a shadow of God's. But through his commitment to God in love, he participates in God's being in the fullest possible way, after the fashion of Christ's own participation. He becomes, as Christ, truly an image of God. In the dynamic of love Christ is concretely the common self-transcendence of both God and man, the link between the human and the divine. He is the first grace, the prime analog of all grace.

So it is that by his response to God's love in Christ man becomes divinized in a very true sense of the word. He becomes in the fullest possible sense an image of God for he identifies himself with Jesus, the image of God *par excellence*. He recognizes in himself in the most complete way possible to man the fulfillment of Rahner's definition of humanity as self-alienated divinity.

Whatever men make of themselves through the investment of their freedom in other loves, whether of persons or other projects, it is not possible for them to be in such a full and true sense other to themselves. They are and will still be in such love just human. They will always have to fall back on themselves, for the human appetite for self-transcendence is insatiable. As long as they remain just human they must continually seek to alienate themselves and never completely succeed. They will always perceive themselves as not enough, their being as nothingness, their humanity still as a to-be-made. The graced person alone has contacted in the fullest way possible to man what lies beyond his own being, his *Dasein*: Being as such, divinity. He alone through his commitment to God in love has, while still remaining what he is, become truly other to himself. He alone has truly transcended himself. He alone has become fully free. He alone is able to experience the fact that grace is freedom.

Were we further to explicate this idea in terms of Jungian psychology we would see Christ as God's archetypal image of man. When through God's loving presence Christ's own self-giving and love for the Father are reflected in a man's actions, the Jungian love-dynamic would become operative. The image of Christ is projected upon that individual. Basic correspondence is noted. New being is created. He becomes in the eyes of God identified with the divine archetypal image of man. Given still his own limitations and faults, that person is essentially remade in the image of Christ. He is truly transformed in God's love.

We have already indicated that the early Church fully recognized the Christian's basic identity with Christ and celebrated the fact in her liturgy. In the baptismal ritual the Christian publicly acknowledged his belief in this doctrine. He manifested it by doing the 'thing' of Christ, by acting out the paschal mystery. After appropriating the death and resurrection of Christ, after accepting his own humanity as a concrete link with Christ now actualized through love, he was anointed with chrism. Ritually he now became a "christ," an anointed one. He had Christ's job to do in the world. For him the ascension too was a part of the paschal mystery. Today it may be meaningless because we do not know where heaven is, whether it is above, below, within or outside. The word itself turns us off. But we would be one with the early Christians in belief if we understood the ascension to mean that in his humanity Jesus identified himself with us, and so made it possible for us to project ourselves as one with him, to form one body with him and so to prolong his presence and his work in ourselves.

In a sense the ascension is the most important and yet the most neglected element in the paschal mystery of Jesus. Why is it important? Because it means that the Jesus who walked the streets of Jerusalem two thousand years ago is no longer with us? That therefore we cannot really get to know him? In a sense, yes. The flesh with which he accomplished his mission two millenia ago is no longer visibly with us. In another sense, no. The flesh by which he is accomplishing today, right now, what he came to do for the whole world is with us. And his ascension and our celebration of the paschal mystery tells us that it is our flesh!

Baptism can occur only once in the life of the Christian. In it he identifies himself once and for all with Christ. But it is difficult, nigh impossible, for him to believe what he has done, that he has really identified himself with Christ, that he is really graced. So the paschal mystery has to be repeated again and again under another ritual form, the Mass. Baptism is birth into the life of Jesus; the Eucharist is nourishment of it.

Many Catholics still view the Mass as the great expression of their faith. Some think this is true because on Sunday in the Mass they recite the propositions of the Nicene creed and in community signify their assent to them. They believe that in the Mass the Eucharistic bread and wine become the body and blood of Christ, and this requires great faith. But it might well be suspected that many Catholics do not at all appreciate a deeper significance of the Mass. In its basic symbolism the Mass does not attest to the Christian's belief in and love of God as much as it does just the opposite: God's faith in and love of man.

Symbolically the Mass presents again the great mysteries of salvation history, the Incarnation and Redemption. Of course, these mysteries are themselves an astounding revelation of God's faith in, trust and love of man. Particularly, however, the Mass symbolizes the trust of God in the people who participate in it. In procession at the offertory representatives of the congregation bring up their gifts of bread and wine. These gifts are symbols of the people present—what they are, their lives, for human life is sustained by food and drink. But these gifts themselves in the course of the Mass according to Catholic belief become the body and blood of Christ. This, of course, happens for a purpose. And the purpose is not exactly, as many think, just to have Christ present in sacramental form. It is rather to impress upon the congregation in the most dramatic way possible who they really are, that through their belief and love, through baptism, they have been converted into the very body and blood of Christ in the world. If the Church were not in reality the body of Christ, this ritual action would not have any meaning, no real effect. The words of the priest: "This is my body; this is my blood" are pronounced primarily over the congregation and only in a secondary sense over the gifts which represent the people present. It is only because the Church, a segment of which they are, actually constitutes the body of Christ, and because Christ is personally present in his Church, of which the priest is the official spokesman, that what they are can be reflected in the gifts which are symbols of them, and Christ can become sacramentally present under the appearances of bread and wine. Thus the identity between Christ and Christians initially expressed at baptism is proclaimed again at Mass. Later on when those present at Mass receive communion they introject those gifts presented to God in lieu of themselves, gifts that now have been transformed according to their belief into the body and blood, that is, into the whole person of Christ. Thus once again they indicate their belief and understanding that God is counting on them to continue and perfect the work initiated by Christ himself. This is the responsibility of Christians in the world. Unless they manifest Christ and his works in their flesh, the world will not know him. So the liturgy itself is really an effective proclamation of the Pauline doctrines of the mystical body and the *anakephalaiosis*, or recapitulation of all being in Christ.

The early Christians called the Mass the Eucharist. For them the liturgical rite was the memorialization of grace, of God's grace non-pareil, Jesus, and of God's grace in them, his identification of them with Jesus through his loving action. The Eucharist is the great act of thanksgiving: Eucharist means thanksgiving. We have already explained how the word "grace" is related to the word "thanks." English-speaking people see the Eucharist formally as the recollection of and memorialization of grace; the Greeks and Latins view the Eucharist formally as grace.

The liturgy then is the first and primary ecstasy of the Christian's love, of his graced condition. It is the first externalization, celebration and sacramentalization of it. But it is more. It is also a source or cause of it. The sacraments of the Church effect grace or its growth in the Christian, and this *ex opere operato*. Here we are confronted with a special difficulty.

In general the *ex opere operato* working of the sacraments does not pose as great a difficulty in regard to the idea of grace as love as might first be suspected. Theologians have never understood the sacraments to operate in some kind of magical way. They always presuppose some response in those who are able to react. They can never be effective in the absence of some minimal disposition in the recipient. This minimal disposition must be at least evidenced in an habitual intention of doing what God wants. In particular, however, special problems may arise when we consider the operation of the sacrament of penance in conjunction with motives of the penitent inferior to charity and, secondly, the question of infant baptism.

According to the Council of Trent contrition or sorrow motivated by love of God in himself and for himself is not required for the reception of grace in the sacrament of penance. Attrition, or sorrow arising from a supernatural but inferior motive, suffices. How then does the person graced in this sacrament become a lover of God? St. Thomas has provided an answer to this question. Through the operation of the sacrament itself attrition becomes contrition. The sacrament itself is a concretization of God's love, of God's grace and all that it implies. In embracing the sacrament the penitent at least implicitly signifies, if he at all understands what the sacrament means, his intention to love God in the way God wants him to. So though he may not formally advert to the fact, his concrete action in the sacrament is actually a response of love.

A more difficult proplem arises in the case of the baptism of infants. Here the recipient of the sacrament is not able to make a responsible return of God's offer of love at all for he is not even able to ratify the sacrament himself. The infant, of course, by the same token, has never rejected God's offer of love through personal sin. If the sin of which he is guilty, original sin, is viewed in the light of modern theological explanations as the *Weltsünde,* that is, the prepersonal conditioning of this individual to live in a sinful world, a world alienated from God's love, the baptismal rite itself can be seen as a guarantee by the Christian community to remove this difficulty and rear the child in the atmosphere of God's loving presence. He is thus prepersonally conditioned, disposed to the extent he can be, to make a loving response to God. His sponsors in particular and the Church in general vouch for the fact that from the dawn of his personal consciousness he will know God's love. Through the sacrament he is given the power to love, to know with whom he has identified himself. This power of self-transcendence in relation to God in Christ is essentially what grace is. And it is effected in regard to the individual infant through God's loving presence in the sacrament. The power to love that the sacrament gives will, of course, be actualized only through the fulfillment of the pledge made by his parents and sponsors. Perhaps this

point is not sufficiently emphasized in current sacramental catechesis.

In discussing this question, of course, we must be careful
to avoid the Lutheran and Quesnelian views of grace. Grace is
not just God's loving presence or regard. This is only one aspect
of it—what theologians call uncreated grace. But they have always insisted upon another aspect of grace; there is also a
created grace, that is, the real transformation of man in and
through that presence. In the adult that transformation is
effected through an actual self-transcendence and commitment
to God as well as an at least minimally conscious self-identifi-
cation with Christ, the project of God's love. In the infant that
transformation is effected through the capacity, the ability, the
power to love guaranteed by the vectoring from the start of his
gradually developing subjectivity toward God through acceptance of him by the Christian community.

The implication of the views of grace we are proposing for
the ecumenical movement of our time can be seen, for instance,
by comparing them with the notions of Protestant theologians
like Karl Barth or Jewish Hasidists like Martin Buber. In his
The Humanity of God Barth shows how Jesus is the focal point
of divine and human freedom. At this point one encounters the
closest communion of God with man. Barth insists that men
can identify with Jesus the man as their brother. Hasidic doctrine makes a basic distinction between God's internal (En-Sof)
and external (Shekinah) glorification. The task of the hasidim
is to manifest through their piety and good works God's glory
in the world. They must identify themselves with God as his
Shekinah and he in turn will become immanent in them. Thus
in their lives they presage the day when the En-Sof and Shekinah will again be united.

Those who are open to the explanation of the Eucharist and
baptism which we have presented will see that there can be no
valid objection from a theological point of view to intercommunion among those who have been baptized. To be sure, there
are many disciplinary, psychological and sociological deterrents

to the practice at present. But from a strictly theological viewpoint, if the Eucharist is the nourishment of the initial union
between Christ and Christians effected by baptism and not the
sign of a more perfect kind of union, there is no real problem
about intercommunion. If the Eucharist as a sacrament is the
sign of the inner union of grace rather than of the external bonds
of church or ecclesial community, the chief objection against
intercommunion vanishes. Opponents of this practice who challenge it on theological grounds must consider the bond it effects
a more perfect one than that of baptism; but tradition ac-
knowledges only one bond: that of baptism, which the Eucharist
refurbishes and nurtures.

Liturgy is the first ecstasy or externalization of the love relationship that grace is. Community is its second. Love is diffusive
of itself. As we saw, it is creative. It involves all who love the
same Father into a fraternity. Even among the pagans this was
seen to be so. Among the Chinese we find the brotherhood of
the tong. The Babylonians at the summit of their ziggurats built
a bridal chamber for their gods and goddesses. Votaries emanated from this room as offspring of their union. They looked
upon themselves as brothers in the spirit. But especially in
Israel was the communitarian aspect of religious life emphasized. Normally Yahweh dealt with the people as a whole. His
covenant was with the nation as such. No individual man
looked upon himself as the spouse of Yahweh: his nation was.
To experience salvation it was sufficient to be accepted into
the community by circumcision. If God had dealings with individuals like patriarchs and prophets, it was only in relation to
the people as a whole. When the people showed themselves
to be deaf to his words, he had to speak to those who could
still hear. Only they could represent his cause again to the
people. When they opened their ears to his word there was no
need for prophecy.

The early Christian Church was highly conscious of the
communitarian aspects of its life. There is reason to believe
that at times even property was held in common. Eucharistic

celebration welded individuals into a union. They were one with Christ and consequently one with one another. Less stress therefore was placed upon the grace life of the individual as such than upon that of the community as a whole. Perhaps this was true at first because of the roots of the Church in Israel. But as it grew in self-awareness the Christian community developed its own ethos. It became more conscious of various implications of the Incarnation. Christ was a human being, but not a human person. God's relationship to man in Christ, the most perfect imaginable, was established on the basis of humanity as such, not on that of human individual person to individuals. Then, too, the identification of Christ with Christians was better revealed in the life of the community as such than in the life of any of its individual members. While it was only symbolized in the life of each individual Christian, the mystery of birth and death was constantly being actualized in the community. Though it is obvious that most individuals who made up the Christian community in the early days were not martyrs, the community did have a constant experience of this witness of Christ. The corporate holiness of God's people was much more impressive than that of any individual. In community the defects of certain individuals in one area or another were seen to be compensated for by the virtues of others. No individual could have perfect faith or perfect love. Yet the Church at large displayed perfect faith and perfect love. In the Church relative to the stage of its own development there was always observable a more perfect achievement, from the human point of view, of the common project of God and man, the representation of Christ in the here and now.

This is not at all to say, however, that in the course of history the Church itself did not at times become guilty of error or blame. Even the Christ of the gospels would not escape flawing if he were judged in the light of later standards. We might today ask hard questions about his apparent insouciance in regard to such fundamental and pressing questions as slavery and war. Would not his treatment of the money-changers in the temple raise difficulties in the minds of many people today, especially when we try to reconcile it with the question Judas asked about the poor. If the basic message of the New Testament is one of concern and love for and forgiveness of others, did not Christ at times appear as guilty as the Pharisees in not practicing what he preached? We cannot be surprised at the fact that there always were and always will be defects in the Church. Christ predicted that scandals would come. O. Hobart Mowrer has implied that in our own time the Church has lost its power to heal psychic wounds—one that it should have as a graced institution. He shows how Protestantism through its doctrine on justification by faith alone has offered men what Bonhoeffer calls "cheap grace." Therapy requires the cooperation of the patient: a laborious and painstaking exertion and marshalling of psychic force. Catholicism on the other hand has substituted authority for the real medicinal power of divine grace. The Church, he says, has tried to guarantee the future by use of legalistic means rather than by reliance on faith. The Church of our time does not seem at times to believe or act upon its own doctrine. Thus it cannot be apprehended as a model of grace. The weak and sick have to seek a doctor who engenders confidence by evidencing his own balance and health, a doctor who has first cured himself. We must honestly acknowledge defects in the Church as well as in individuals. The Church is formally a human institution since it is composed of humans. It is graced and consequently divine only in certain aspects of its life and function. The only point we are trying to make is that in the general course of events Christianity and, consequently, the life of grace, is better witnessed in the community than in the individual.

We have identified grace with freedom. The graced person is one who is freed from the bondage of his own humanity and comes to enjoy a share in God's own freedom through Christ. Yet in fact the Christian often appears to be the most unfree of all human beings. He is enslaved by law. We shall explore the roots of this problem further when we come to consider the real nature of human freedom. It will then become more apparent why we can say that the observance of what the law commands is one of the further ecstasies of the graced condition. It suffices now just to remark that love prompts one to fulfill the expectations of one's beloved. The true lover performs this task most freely and willingly. His delight is in doing the will of his beloved. He understands fully the meaning of the dictum of St. Gregory the Great: *"Probatio charitatis exhibitio est operis."* Love is proven by deeds.

There are obviously many other ecstasies of the graced state. Some like joy, zeal and mortification pose no special problem. But one seemingly self-evident effect of love does today. Though there is greater devotion to the liturgy, there is indication of a definite disinclination and disaffection for personal prayer. It is clear that there ought to be some form of strictly personal communication between a lover and his beloved. Union, life shared, begets dialogue. But in our day we witness a dwindling of that dialogue especially among young people. Some thinkers are of the opinion that a redefinition of prayer is called for. This is the case particularly with prayer of petition. Since God does not seem to respond to prayer, they would envision it as necessary monologue rather than true dialogue. The individual needs to pray for himself, for his own benefit; he cannot expect that it affect God. They would define prayer of petition as Kierkegaard did when he said that prayer is not so much founded on the idea that God should come to the realization of what the one who prays wants or needs from him, but that the one who prays should come to the realization of what God wants or needs from him. Others, rejecting the idea of prayer of petition entirely, would allow only for some kind of reflection on God's revelation to man whence some enlightenment or inspiration might emanate as to how a person concretely is to carry out his Christian responsibilities.

But basically today's problems with prayer do not stem so much from its conception as from a loss of the presence of God. Neglect of personal prayer is directly connected with the Orestean or death-of-God movement in theology. God's presence is not felt. Hence it is useless to pray to him. But if we have defined uncreated grace precisely as the loving presence of God, it seems necessary to uphold the idea of God's presence by explicitating the larval theology of it. This we shall attempt to do in the next chapter.

CHAPTER III

Presence

In his *The Future of Belief* Leslie Dewart states that what
is absolutely fundamental to the Christian experience is that
which is conceptualized when we talk about grace. He shares
with Rahner the conviction that grace ought not remain just
a kind of mental construct to serve as an explanation of the
problem of how God can deal with men. Grace has to be related in some way to experience. And experience presupposes
presence. In defining grace in the first instance as the loving
presence of God we have by that very fact implied that it has
something to do with experience. It remains for us now to explore at greater depth the significance and parameters of that
relationship.

Dewart's book shows that there has been too much stress
in Catholicism on the rational and too little on the experiential.
And the rational elements in our faith have been examined
almost exclusively in the context of an outmoded philosophical
system. In focussing upon the importance for the man of today

of the experiential and the basic unreliability of rational argumentation in coping with that which is totally Other, Dewart calls for a shift of emphasis from the ontic to the presence-dimension of divine reality. Reason is not primarily concerned with presence, but experience is. What is really needed more than anything else today is a theology of presence.

But it is certainly an appalling and seemingly self-defeating task to try to come to grips with such a basic notion as that of presence. There is nothing more real and engaging than presence when one experiences it; there is nothing more elusive than presence when one assays to analyze it.

In theological literature there is certainly no dearth of material descriptive of ascetical and mystical experience. The writings of St. Teresa and St. John of the Cross are wellsprings of information on Christian mysticism. More recent investigations like those of Poulain and Mouroux deal with more ordinary and commonplace phenomena of the graced life. But attempts to integrate this area of theology with systematics, few as they are, have generally resulted in the over-rationalization that is so characteristic of the scholastic methodology. The deficiencies of an essentialist philosophy in attempting to describe a common experience like that of presence become very apparent.

When one first thinks about presence he is apt to describe it in terms of the local and temporal proximity of one body to another. But the very use of the words "local and temporal" casts some doubt upon the validity of such a definition. If there were no one to sense it, would the mere juxtaposition of bodies in space-time create a presence of one to another? Can there be such constructs as space and time without a mind? Does presence then necessarily imply a subjectivity? It would certainly seem that presence is primarily a kind of knowledge and not a purely objective relationship at all. The word itself, from the Latin *prae-scientia,* knowledge of something at hand, involves consciousness. Even if presence were measurable or definable in terms of the parameters of space and time an intelligence would have to intervene. For as Sartre points out in reference to time, the present really is not. It makes itself present precisely by fleeing. Before I can articulate the word "now" what I tried to express has already passed. Time itself is a construct of human consciousness. Nor is proximity in space necessarily the chief significant factor in considering presence. A gunman, for example, knows well that the mere positioning of his weapon next to my temple will not effect the result he desires. He has to call my attention to it. I have to be aware of its presence. This is not to say that temporal and local considerations do not at all figure in ascertaining how presence is to be described. The Greeks made a point when they used the word *parousia*, being-with, for presence. Time and space as such do not constitute presence, but they can embellish it.

Neither is the essential factor in presence to be explicitated only in terms of sense knowledge. Certainly sense awareness is more important in the perception of a presence than the scholastic theologians seem willing to admit. In fact, there can be no real experience of presence without some kind of sense knowledge. But though it is necessary for the experience, it is not the chief element in it. We must admit with the scholastics that presence ultimately has to be described in terms of an intellectual awareness.

But it seems that the scholastics were wrong in setting presence within the framework of a purely passive intellectual experience. The fact is that presence is not just a given. It is not the experience of an external reality forcing itself on my consciousness. I am not acted upon by a presence. Rather I create presence. Things outside do not extend their presence to my subjectivity. I make myself present to them. Presence is a function of my subjectivity. I direct my consciousness to things outside of me and so invest them with, endow them with presence. Before I can be aware of a presence outside of me, I must be a presence to myself. And normally it is in relation to some particular facet of my own self-awareness that I categorize and appreciate the presences that I create outside of me. My own self-image, with all that concept implies, is the essential reference point for establishing contact with reality

outside of my subjectivity. Once contact is made, the basis for
the experience of presence is at hand. The apprehension of myself in a particular relational way gives meaning to my contact
with what I see as located outside my own subjectivity either
actually or through my own projection. This significance or
meaning enhances my desire to create a presence for myself.
A verification of the contact made through additional reflection
will produce in me a feeling—depending on how I apprehended
myself in relation to the presence I created—of dread, uncanni-
ness, horror, mystery, awe, fascination, rapture, dependence,
etc. The total and perfect experience of presence will involve
all these elements: the proximity in time and space of some real
object; my awareness of myself as a self; my apprehension of
myself in a particular way as the result of my sensing of the
object; a feeling of contact with the object coming from my
relating it to a particular facet of myself; the creation in my
subjectivity of this object as a presence; the special feeling
I have because of experiencing its presence. The absolutely
essential elements in this percept, however, are only: my self-
awareness concretized in a particular way in relation to at least
a projected object outside my subjectivity and the resultant
feeling of contact.

Presence is an exclusively human experience precisely because it essentially involves an awareness of self. Sartre captures this idea most trenchantly when he describes presence as
that which defines the reflection for the person reflecting. But
it is not just the apprehension of self in any general way that
provides the basis for the experience of presence. The focal
point in the whole percept is the awareness and feeling of contact. It is the tailoring of self-awareness, the gearing of it, the
direct relating of it to a definite object that is the necessary
condition for the establishment of contact. The object toward
which self-awareness, so honed, is directed may, as we have
stated, be real or it may be projected. There is no doubt that
a better experience of presence will usually be had if its object
is actually sensed in the process. But a projected object can be
fully instrumental in triggering the experience. No one doubts

the fact that soldiers in Viet Nam can live almost constantly in the presence of their loved ones at home and experience the most excruciating anguish of homesickness.

The particularization of self-awareness in relation to the object to be contacted can occur in two ways. The object can be referred to a very definite, clear and concrete image of the self. This image can be formed in connection with a family relationship, a role, the mood of the moment, recollection of a past experience, etc. An example or two will bring out this point. You and I are watching a ballet on television. You see yourself as a person of culture. You have fine sensibilities and a deep appreciation of the arts. Your every remark to me is about the beauty and gracefulness of the dance. The performers for you are real people. You do not seem to be aware of the room we are in, its lights, the chair you are sitting in, the television set itself. You talk about the dancing figures as if they were actually in the room with us. You, however, have concentrated upon a presence that completely eludes me. I am a television repair man. When you ask me about the *prima ballerina*: "Isn't she just great?" I note that the set does not seem to have a full four megacycle IF bandpass. The picture is not as well-defined as it might be, although the fine tuning control is correctly adjusted. Perhaps a shunt damping resistor has open-circuited and raised the Q of one of the transformers. Then too the relationship of light to darkness in the picture is not pleasing. The contrast control is set right, so it must be that the engineer at the TV station has not properly fixed the pedestal level. The set itself, however, does have some other defects. There is a ten degree tilt on the raster. There are evidences of Barkenhausen oscillation in the horizontal flyback circuit. I feel very uncomfortable. I cannot at all appreciate your delight with the program. Or take another example of how we really create presences in relation to our subjective dispositions. I am lying on a beach. I am very much aware of the warm, invigorating rays of the sun. My mind is lazy and inactive. I am merely exulting in the reassuring presence of Old Sol. Next to me is a physicist who has created an entirely different presence. He is aware of the fact that solar radiation is actually exerting a measurable pressure on our skin and on the beach. The presence of the radiation for him is capsulized in the formula:

$$E_\lambda = \frac{8\pi hc}{\lambda^5 (e^{hc/\kappa\lambda T} - 1)}$$

The energy emitted in radiation is to be calculated in integral multiples of energy quanta which vary in direct proportion to the oscillation frequency. Surely I must admit that he had a much fuller and deeper awareness of the presence of the sun than I.

The second kind of reference point for presence that can exist in the subjectivity is one that is vague and subliminal. It emanates more from the lower, more primitive areas of the brain than from the cerebral cortex. Yet it can actually produce a more real, engulfing, moving experience of contact than the cortical images can. When a subliminal image is referred to an object that even is just suspected of being present, it can leave me paralyzed with dread and horror. It can make my hair stand on end. It can cause me to break out in a cold sweat. It can produce an experience that I will never forget, or one so threatening that I will repress it and become neurotic because of it.

This type of image lends itself more directly to the experience of a feeling of contact which, as we have said, is the chief element in the idea of presence. The clearer image about which we spoke before tends to establish more of an ideational relationship as the basis for a feeling of contact. The subliminal image can be composed entirely of sensible elements. It would in the scholastic system of philosophy be ascribed to the operation of what is called the *sensus communis*. It is said that monkeys in Zamboanga have no tails. At least they do not have prehensile tails as the South American varieties do. Yet without this added safety and guidance factor they perform a most remarkable feat. They have no anemometers or tape measures. They are not equipped with theodolytes. They lack laboratories for ascertaining the resiliency or tensile strength of different species and sizes of living wood.

Yet on the appearance of a predator even the smallest of them can execute with utmost perfection an extremely accurate thirty-foot leap from branch to branch in varying wind conditions. Each leap requires an absolutely correct estimation of distance, branch strength and sway, wind velocity and direction, as well as the muscular flexion required to cover the necessary distance. Moving into the area of human activity, we see similar feats accomplished by professional tennis players and golfers. Good golfers do not take a truckful of measuring equipment out to the course with them. They know that the secret of their success lies in a good feeling about their swing as it brings clubhead into contact with the ball. They try to cultivate this feeling and make their swing as automatic as possible. Obviously, however, their memory must retain at least a subliminal image of what a perfect and effective swing feels like. This is used as a reference point, as a kind of shibboleth, according to which they judge their actual swings as good or bad.

In other areas of human activity too subliminal or archetypal images are used as a basis of contact. They are especially significant when the object contacted is not sensed, when it is projected by the subjectivity, or when it is postulated by faith. The zodiacal signs, for instance, are very ancient and primitive archetypal images considered significant in relation to certain types of behavior by those who put some trust in them. The daily horoscope in newspapers and the vast sale of books on this topic support the conclusion that these ancient archetypal images effect some kind of mysterious presence for large numbers of people even in our sophisticated society.

The archetype has been described as the most deeply rooted and universal reaction of the developing subjectivity to itself and its environment. It exists in the form of a vague and yet at least generally categorized image. It is not, however, precisely a concept, a sense-image, or a logical construct. It is an undefinable catalyst of feeling. It is the counterpart in the affectivity of the concept in the cognoscitive faculties. It is the immanence of the subjectivity perceived as transcendent in what is vital and yet other to it. It serves a unifying purpose in regard to affective experience, enabling the subject more easily to relate individually diverse contacts with reality to one another. It is characterized by an aura of wholeness, completeness, for it is seen as possessing the fulness of which other related being participates. Thus it is essentially numinous, awesome, endowed with sacral power. Though not clearly defined, it seems complex and ambivalent: it is often regarded as being able to unite within itself opposites in the same order of reality. It is projected as absolute and permanent. It is so identified with the ego that it is not readily distinguishable from it. Simply it can be defined as the self of man perceived as affectively one with the numinosity of other beings.

While there are many different kinds of archetypes, it should be quite obvious that one of the most basic and influential is the archetype of person. The numinosity of human beings is concentrated in their personhood. Personality as such is not in any formal sense empirical. In the final analysis the personality of others has to be an object of faith. In his early development the individual gradually comes to see himself as different from his environment. He begins to see that he is unique and irreplaceable. He eventually will perceive himself as a true subjectivity. He encounters others whom he recognizes as persons like himself. But ultimately this perception has to be regarded as a projection. In his encounter with others every person observes in them the same kind of output he is sure he is presenting to them. He sees their bodies, their eyes, their facial expressions. He hears and understands their speech. He reads in their communications, verbal and non-verbal, signs of logic, emotion and exercise of freedom. Empirical evidence, seemingly, forces him to conclude that behind these phenomena there exists a person totally distinct from, and yet exactly like himself. But can he ever lay hold of that person? Can he define him? Can he ever come to know just who he is? He must acknowledge that he cannot fully comprehend his own personality. He cannot explain to others just who he is. How then can he ever grasp the personality of another? How can he be sure that the person he talked to last night is the same one he meets in the morning? The body is the same; the output seems to be the same: it is what one would expect from such a person; but how can he be sure that the person himself is the same? The problem becomes more acute when the separation is one not of twelve hours but, say, of twenty years. The existence of schizoid personalities further complicates the issue. *The Three Faces of Eve* and other accounts of split personality give one pause in being too apodictic about the possibilities of complete dissociation. Experiments with animals where the two brain hemispheres are surgically separated even down to the pons show that the two halves of the organism can be programmed quite differently up to the point of being set in total opposition to each other. The dominance of one cerebral hemisphere over the other in the human being can, at least in some limited way, be affected by selective input to the largely unprogrammed area of the brain in the non-dominant hemisphere. Everyone has met a person who, even without any previous practice, can move his arms in an exactly opposite circular motion. Lobotomy in humans has proved that quite different personalities can emerge as the result of surgical intervention. And every psychiatrist can testify that the moment of *Entschlossenheit* in the psychoanalytical process can produce radical alterations in personal behavior patterns.

All of this may signalize the fact that ultimately our feeling of contact with another personality may really be more a matter of projection and faith than of demonstrable fact. If this is true, the idea of an archetype of person may be much more important than one might at first suspect in the dynamic of establishing contact among persons.

Besides the generalized archetype of person, some psychologists postulate many other personal archetypal images. C. G. Jung mentions some of the more familiar ones: father, mother, wise old man, king, shadow, etc.

The importance of the father archetype in psychological research as well as in the psychoanalytic process is only too well known. Very often the success of psychoanalysis depends upon the ability of the analyst to displace in his own direction a repressed feeling of the subject toward his father. The analyst finds out about the subject's father and tries to play his role in the hope that perfect transference will eventually occur. Through word association, dream analysis and other means the psychiatrist attempts to ascertain the symbol-system of the patient, to discern definite relationships among his ideas and feelings about those who were associated with him particularly during his infant life. Then it will be possible for the doctor to reflect to the patient characteristics of those who were most influential in forming his self-image. If a neurotic's father was instrumental in the creation of his disturbance, when the psychiatrist images that father in his own attitudes and behavior in regard to the client, through his projection of his father archetype upon him the patient will tend to react to his doctor in the same way he responded to his father, and thus reveal some of his repressed feelings. The client's father becomes present to him once again in the person of the psychiatrist. And central to the dynamic of this presence is the functioning of the archetypal image of father.

The various personal archetypes then are of the utmost importance in any consideration of the question of presence. Actually a complete and perfect experience of presence can be achieved only when two or more personal consciousnesses attempt to stand in relationship to one another. The essential difference between contact among persons and that between persons and animals or things is brought out by Martin Buber not only in his use of the terms "I-Thou, I-You, I-It" in describing these relationships, but—and perhaps more clearly and definitely—in his German text also by the use of different words for "relationship" in these different cases. Between persons and objects there can be only a *Verhältnis,* a static, given condition of one relative to the other, whereas between persons there is a *Beziehung,* a drawing out of one in relation to the other.

We encounter the great significance of personal archetypes in establishing presence in psychic life also in the common experience known as personification. Men generally tend to create a personal presence where it actually does not exist. People are apt to talk to their pets as if they were persons and understood the meaning of words. The dog owner may know that his pet is able only to perceive sounds which through conditioning will trigger a trained response. But he does not seem to act in accordance with this knowledge. There are some people who tend to personify everything, their work, their tools, their organizations. In law, corporations have the status of legal persons, enjoying some of the rights and privileges of individuals. The doctrine that the Church is the mystical body of Christ is a time-honored, revelation-based example of personification. The dynamic of personification has profoundly influenced the development of language. Words themselves are endowed with personal qualities even though they do not refer to persons. Many languages, unlike English, do not have a neuter gender. Words have to be either masculine or feminine. Even those that are epicene in meaning are either masculine or feminine in form. Even if his accent is perfect, very often it is easy to spot a foreigner simply because he tends to fall back on his native idiom when using English and refers to objects as "he" or "she." In literature the apostrophe and other forms of personal address in respect to things are a commonplace. All these phenomena dramatically point to the pervading numinosity of some kind of personal archetype. They witness the relentless strivings of the human subjectivity to create in as many ways as possible the fullest and most satisfying kind of contact with reality.

We have said that one of the unique characteristics of an archetype is its ability to sustain within itself a union of opposites. If personification is due to the functioning of personal archetypal images, it might well be suspected that they are capable of producing also the reverse process. The reification of persons is also traceable to the operation of personal archetypes. Society tends to institutionalize its heroes. People try to preserve the memory of their loved ones. The ashes of a cremated father or mother may be kept on a mantle over the hearth in a family home, or a devoted son will place a picture of his deceased parents on his office desk. In this world of sense the memory of the dead can be made permanent only by some kind of reification or institutionalization. This is the only way the impression they made on others while they were living can be preserved for posterity. The phenomenon of reification is exemplified in its deepest religious sense in the Christian doctrine of the Eucharist. At times the dynamic operates in less obvious ways, for example through the creation of myth. Popular accounts of the exploits of the great through the intervention of the archetypal image tend to become stereotyped. Heroes are robbed of their individuality and isolated from their real temporal and cultural milieu. They become types, models, paradigms for all ages and all peoples. They are apprehended as ideals more than real persons. At times reification is made to serve ulterior purposes, as for instance in the case of the Stalin myth in Soviet Russia. The development of Christian hagiography, particularly in the middle ages when such writings as the Golden Legend catered to the popular craze, luculently attests to demand for reified heroes. The Mass liturgy reflects the fact that the Gospel itself was eventually regarded by the Christian community as a reification of Christ. When the sacred text is read, the congregation rises to greet Christ while the priest incenses and kisses it. And in the commentary, if not in the homily, the presence of Jesus in the word is always linked to his presence in the sacrament.

At times, as for instance in the examples we have adduced: the Eucharist and the mystical body, it is difficult to ascertain whether the process influenced and inaugurated by an archetypal image is one of personification or reification. Is the Sacrament, the Eucharist, as it has been reflected in the development of Christian theology, the result of an attempt to emphasize the special presence of Christ in his memorial meal, or does it rather stress the concern of the people of God to focalize their realization of Christ's presence in the community in this objective way? Is the Sacrament a personification of the ritual Supper or is it the reification of the mystical body? One could argue for both views by appealing to tradition. It is clear that Christ is personally present in the Eucharist, but he is present under the form of an object, bread and wine. Personification and reification really constitute one and the same process. They are apprehended as distinct only if one vectors his attention in opposite directions, either starting with the personal and ending with the objective, or vice versa. Thus both can emanate under the aegis of one and the same archetypal image, that of person.

In discussing the experience of presence thus far we have appeared to lay stress on the classical description of the archetype as it is advanced in certain schools of psychology, particularly that of C. G. Jung. This description, to be sure, is rejected by many modern psychologists. But for the purposes of larval theology we need not insist on the classical definition of an archetype: we used it only to clarify the notion of a subliminal influence on behavior, a notion which might well be obscure in the minds of those who are not adept in psychological science and lore. It would be better now before we proceed any further to widen the concept of archetype to include all types of mental or psychic symbols which, even though subliminal or repressed, exert an influence on behavior, in particular that behavior which results from perception of a presence. It really makes no difference how these symbols are viewed or described, whether as latent concepts, sense-images, feelings or percepts. The important fact about them as far as we are concerned is that they are instrumental in creating presence; and this fact, I think, is admitted in all schools of psychology, even those outside the psychoanalytical and Jungian tradition. For convenience' sake, however, we shall continue to use the word "archetype" in referring to them.

We have stated that the most significant element in the experience of presence is the feeling of contact it implies. When this contact is felt between persons it is properly called empathy. As we have explained, all empathy presupposes a certain faith in the actual presence of the other person even in the most ordinary and pedestrian sensible contacts. But the faith-element has to be more especially stressed in extra-sensory contacts. The data of ESP are well known because of the efforts of researchers like Rhine. The psychic phenomena of mysticism and voodoo have been popularized by Thurston and Williams. Everyone has been held spellbound by "true ghost stories," many of which are attested to by intelligent and reliable persons. Everyone has heard accounts of experiences with the psychic. Usually the story is set in an old house or hotel in a far-off city or foreign country. The subject has some apprehension before retiring, but manages to fall into a deep sleep. Suddenly he is wide awake. He is not aware of what woke him up. He looks around, but can see or hear nothing out of the ordinary. But what startles him is that he can sense some kind of presence in the room. It is a gripping, awesome thing. He breaks out into a cold sweat. He is completely terrorized because he is not able to explain his experience. He may hear a door slam, or a rustling or some other noise. The thing seems to be moving. Then almost as abruptly as the whole episode started it ends. He no longer feels under the influence of that mysterious presence. The experience is over, but he will never forget it.

Experiences and stories like this highlight the numinal element of empathy. But only faith can correspond with the numinal. But empathy also presupposes transcendence. Only by projecting oneself psychically into the other person can true contact with him be established.

The craze for psychedelic drugs among college students today may well point to a deepening thirst in our society for some kind of transcendent empathy. Interest is mounting too in the less bizarre but nonetheless transcendental phenomena of oriental asceticism. The doctrine of Zen Buddhism has proven itself particularly fertile along this line. The followers of this way seek an enlightenment, an experience of the transcendental called *satori*. The novice works under constant supervision by a master whose presence itself seems to be something of a catalyst in the attainment of a state where extra-sensory perception predominates. The master will very often provide tyros with an insoluble problem called a *koan* which is to be used as a subject for concentrated and continuous meditation. Here is a commonly employed *koan*: Think of the sound made by the clapping of hands. Describe the sound made by the clapping of one hand. The novice spends weeks and sometimes months concentrating on the problem. Finally he is exhausted and experiences a deep sense of defeat. But precisely when he is in this state of psychic exhaustion he most often attains a flash of *satori* or inspirational enlightenment in which he sees a perfectly satisfying solution to his problem. Eventually after working on a number of problems he is able to treat all reality in this manner. While strolling in a garden he may experience a feeling of full transcendence. He may become aware of his identity with the earth, sky and flowers. He may say: "Last night I dreamed that I was a butterfly. How do I know that today I am not a butterfly dreaming he is a man?"

The experience of the hero of Sartre's novel *Nausea*, Roquentin, while seated on a bench in a city park may also be an example of a kind of *satori*. He contemplates an ancient, gnarled chestnut tree. Its roots are deep in the earth. Its branches extend threateningly overhead. Its leaves rustle in the wind. But he sees all the phenomena of this situation as totally insignificant. He penetrates to a vision of being-in-itself. He feels an overwhelming disgust for it. It is *de trop;* it is too much. He has a similar experience in the municipal library while looking at pictures of the town's founding fathers and heroes. They are just memorialized faces. They really signify nothing. The whole of their being is captured as far as on-lookers are concerned in these pictures. Is this all they are as persons? Is this all that can be said about them? Is this their presence?

A reverse kind of empathy, a counter-empathy is scored in the existentialist literature of our time. Take, for instance, Camus' *The Stranger* or Sartre's *The Wall*. They stress the total lack of meaning in human life. Existence, they say, is totally absurd. Man cannot seek the numinal in it. There is nothing numinal about it. There is no Logos, no intelligibility, in life. The need of man to explain himself to himself is what causes the projection of Logos upon nature and the inexorable process of history. What man wishes were presence is really absence. But in reality novels like these presuppose what they try to destroy or debunk. The fascinating element in the stories of *The Stranger* or *The Wall* is to be found in the meaning they give to non-meaning, in the magical, fatal presence they create by denying other presence. If Logos is absent, its place is taken by Fate. The plots themselves become numinous by denying the existence of numinosity. They establish contact with their reader by denying that contact is possible.

Empathy, the feeling of contact between persons, is the essential element in the experience of presence. It is produced in the human subjectivity through the instrumentality of a correlating self-image, an archetype. But it is re-enforced, amplified and extended by feedback from the emotional state which results from it. Such a state, as we have said, can be one of fear, awe, joy, love, etc.

Theology itself has created the problem it experiences today when dealing with the question of the presence of God. Theology has been too antiseptic. It has too easily dismissed the importance of feeling. Theologians have practically submerged the genus in their zeal to cultivate the species in their own definition of man as an *animal rationale*. If they treat of feeling at all, their discussions are jejune and adversative. And yet feeling pastorally is the most significant of all elements in the religious experience. In its attempt to define what it held to be totally Other and hence indefinable theology took no cognizance of Tersteegen's reiteration of a basic theological principle of St. Augustine. A God who can be conceptualized is really no God. It failed to heed James' description of the fabric of religious experience. There was no comprehension when he spoke, much after the fashion of the mystics, about darkness. Darkness, he said, precisely because it is darkness can hold a presence that can all the more be felt because it is not seen. For scholastic theology it did not seem possible that a presence that could not be rationalized could be a real presence. It was incomprehensible to this way of thinking that anything that could not be conceptualized could be real.

How then could a presence that is indefinable be perceived as more real than that of the perceiver to himself? But it is a fact that even the presence of the perceiver to himself cannot in the ultimate analysis be rationalized.

It is no wonder that medieval theology could only smile benignly at the words of the mystics. They were poets, not philosophers. Their language was metaphorical, not scientific. Theology could not really concern itself with them because it could not understand them. Science is always at a loss in coping with feeling. Feeling cannot be taught; it can only be awakened. And it cannot be awakened by reason; it can only be aroused by the Spirit. And pneumatology is the weakest area of theology.

As Dewart points out, for centuries theology has incubated in the matrix of Greek thought. First it was dominated by Platonism, then Aristotelianism. But the overriding characteristic of both of these philosophies is that which it holds in common with Stoicism. Ultimate perfection is achieved in apathy. Emotion is the talisman of change, corruption, mortality. The unchanging, absolute spiritual idea is the harbinger of the divine, the permanent, the immortal. Thus in the Greek frame of thought the key attribute of God had to be his *apatheia,* his being totally unaffected from without and consequent unchangeableness. Today's physics sees change as a perfection: the more a body reduces its mass to motion, the more energy it puts out; the less static it is, the more power or force it exhibits. But the Greeks held just the opposite. Complete passivity, complete unchangeableness was their ideal of perfection and power. The world today might better appreciate the reality of God if he were described in terms of a being who is total change, all motion, than in the way he is in accordance with our Greek heritage as one who is immutable, static, absolute. The God of revelation in no way corresponds to the God of the Greek philosophers. Scripture portrays an angry, jealous, passionate, loving, concerned God. Yet theologians have preferred the God of philosophy to the God of the bible. A God who does not experience passion is certainly the unmoved mover of Aristotle; but is he the living God who revealed himself most fully in Jesus?

Following out its philosophical concept of God, Christian theology explicitated the essentials of the religious life of man also in terms of *apatheia*. The goal of the spiritual life is vision, passive experience. Yet can man really be fully happy if he is not creative? To be virtuous and thus attain to vision, man has to tread the middle ground between excess and defect. But does not Scripture say that the Lord vomits from his mouth the ones who are neither hot nor cold?

Martin Luther rebelled against this apparent departure of theology from its roots in revelation. His sermons vilify apathy and brand it as unbecoming God or man. He bewails the fact that theology has made God look like a silly yawner, an open-mouthed idiot, a fatuous cuckold who lets another lie with his wife and pretends he is not concerned about it. The Christian life of those who really come to know the God of revelation, he says, abounds in dancing and leaping for joy, while those who reject that God are ridden with fear and guilt. Luther did not hesitate to call reason a whore. And the German philosopher Hegel knew what he meant. He saw the disasterous effect the apotheosis of the rational was having upon religious life in his time and reacted by stating that the only organ man has capable of contacting divinity is his power to love, not his power to reason.

Our society today has largely lost all awareness of the presence of God. We can lay part of the blame on theology's insouciance about feeling as a wholesome and necessary part of religious experience. Thought has choked out emotion; rationalization has resulted in sterilization. The current liturgical revival with its emphasis on the familial aspects of worship ventures to set the scales in balance once again. But it is not likely that harmony will be restored by any direct attempt to resurrect the long buried religious feelings of the older generation. Sincere feeling can be aroused only indirectly. Feeling is the last in the train of psychic processes that is drawn by personal archetypal images. The key issue is that of the archetype. Archetypes found the experience of presence; the awareness of a personal presence engenders empathy; empathy arouses other feeling. Once the problem of the archetypes is settled, the rest of the process will be automatically insured provided the theology of the future will not try to scuttle emotion as a legitimate and valid form of religious expression.

Seemingly the theologian who bends his efforts in today's Christian society to recoup a sense of the presence of God starts from a position of advantage. He is dealing with an actually graced people; he addresses himself to persons who are committed Christians. He is plying his trade among a people who at least one time have felt in a significant way the presence of God. If grace really is what we implied, the total surrender of one's subjectivity to God, the complete transformation of self in God's loving presence, then at least at the time this surrender was made or ratified, one must have had an experience of the presence of God, howsoever crude or rudimentary it may have been. No person commits his total subjectivity to a merely conjectured presence. Nor is the problem of God's presence centered in the lack of even an occasional sense of contact with the divine. Once in a while people do feel God is present. The liturgy certainly should offer Christians a daily opportunity for an experience of God. Yet, as we said before, the full and involving sense of it is not widely appreciated, and people are bored rather than excited by it. Often it is poorly executed. Many regard it as a drag, as something one has to suffer through in the hope that God will accept the sacrifice made in enduring it as a pledge of faith and devotion. Now and again one does experience good liturgies. At a guitar Mass (surprisingly well attended even by the older folk), at a particularly meaningful burial service, some may actually sense the presence of God and respond to it as a graced person should. I have heard participants in some of the Masses at conventions of the Liturgical Conference attest to the fact that these were the most moving experiences of their lives.

At other times awareness of the presence of God occurs in a totally different context from the overtly religious. Several priests attending T-group sessions at a western university related that they had a fuller experience of God's presence and operation in the group than they ever had before in retreats, spiritual exercises or even at Mass. Mothers tell how they really feel the presence of God in dealing with their children. And even sports celebrities, presumably not just to say what their public might want them to, bear witness to the presence of God they sometimes experience in the game.

The real problem stems not from lack of an occasional contact with God, but from failure to have an abiding and overriding awareness of God's presence, one which the doctrine of grace we have proposed should inculcate. Only this kind of awareness can guarantee personal prayer and the actual implementation in daily life of the commitment made in the grace-contract to be Christ in the world. And this problem exists in our society because of the absence of a homogeneous archetypal image to instigate that continual awareness.

The archetypal image around which Christ constructed his own preaching of the word to the Israelites was a particularly significant one to them. He spoke of the kingdom. And unlike other nations they had no kingdom. No king, no national leader ruled over them. They were under the domination of foreigners, under the Romans. All of their expectations, all their hopes seemed doomed. The promises of Yahweh to make them into a great nation appeared inane. Yet they still had confidence in the word of Yahweh. But they also felt an abiding sensation of injury and frustration. Yahweh himself had been their king in times past. Their salvation history showed them how countless times in the past Yahweh himself had rescued the nation from perils of all sorts. They lived in expectation of a new saving act of God. But today the era of kings is gone. The king-archetype is no longer viable, though some preachers do not seem to have realized it.

One of the archetypes employed in the early Christian evangelization of the pagans was that of the *kyrios-doulos*, the master-servant. It was particularly apt because most of the converts at that time were from the slave class, or at least from the lower

echelons of society. Numerous slave rebellions and social up-
heavals rocked the empire and unsettled it. The audience of
the evangelizers of that time longed to hear of the paradox
of the cross. They needed assurance that the one who died as
a slave was really the triumphant one, the only one who attained a state of immortality proper to gods and heroes about
which their former religion so greatly concerned itself. They
exulted in the fact that by imitating him in his sufferings they
could participate in his glory.

During the time that patriarchal society was in vogue, an
era which extended from the pre-Christian age perhaps well
into the renaissance period, the archetype of father-son was also
dominant. It was exhilarating to realize that the Christian was
in fact an adopted son of the heavenly Father. Thus that divine
Father was continually rendered present to the Christian people because they thought often of their earthly father. He dominated their lives. From him they received life itself. From
him they learned all they knew. He protected them, fed and
clothed them. He arranged their marriages. At every important
juncture of their lives he made his influence felt. But they could
not think of him without becoming aware also of their heavenly Father, who was for them the idealization of all the good
of fatherhood.

In certain quarters in our own time stress is laid on the
archetype of community, the *koinonia* of the New Testament.
True enough, our society today is greatly threatened by fragmentation. Black separatism looms large in the consciousness
of all today. The ghetto and its atrocities, urban riots, failure
of integration and white insouciance to the needs of Negroes
have all set the stage for the rise of black militantism. And no
one can ignore militantism. But the race problem does not stand
alone in the problems that face communities today. There is
fragmentation occurring between the young and old, between
liberals and conservatives, between the religious and irreligious.
Consequently we witness a growing interest in vehicles of in-
tercommunication. True community is formed by communication. We have to be concerned about any means that serves

to weld individuals together in close inter-personal relationships. Interest is mounting in T-groups and group theory in general. Businesses are learning to operate more and more on a principle of delegation of authority, on subsidiarity and trust. In Catholicism the success of the *cursillo* movement even among non-Latin people trenchantly calls attention to modern man's hunger for unity and solidarity with his brothers. Even the official Church has responded to this need by spotlighting the notion of collegiality in the Second Vatican Council. But the fact of continuously progressing fragmentation despite all of this signifies perhaps that the archetype of community cannot be the completely effective panacea we are searching for. It works only with limited numbers of people. It does not heal the deep-seated rifts between segments of society at large. It serves only to solidify the intention of the various factions and unite them more fully in their opposition to others.

The continuous splintering of cultural elements in America today has rendered all of the old archetypal images more or less inept in the task of creating presence. There can be no one archetype that will affect all. When it experienced societal division Israel was tempted to say that Yahweh had abandoned his people. America today has succumbed to that temptation. The only theology that is distinctively American says that God is dead. His presence is no longer felt. But, as we have seen, theology often tells us more about man than it does about God. Orestean theologians may be really airing the guilt feelings they sense in American life today because hallowed values have been overthrown. Dead in our society are the religious hopes once cherished by our forefathers. And dead too are the images that inspired them.

It seems to be a well-established principle that an organism becomes more alive the better it is able to support divergent elements within itself. Maybe America is actually more vital now than it ever was in the past precisely because it can sustain and support radically different views and philosophies of life. Everyone knows that the principle of freedom founds the American way of life. And so, far from destroying the archetypal ideal of American nationalism, splintering may actually have enhanced it. People today more than ever feel an awesome presence when the flag is raised or the anthem is played. Hawks and doves, draft-card burners as well as the judges who send them to jail, hippies and members of military compounds alike protest their patriotism. If such a thing exists as a national archetype which makes Americans everywhere almost constantly aware of their philosophy of government, if wherever we go, in offices, homes, public conveyances, if repeatedly on radio and television, we hear conversations, discourses and tirades on politics, taxes, personalities in Washington, conduct of the war, efforts for peace, relations with the United Nations and other governments, then perhaps we have discovered the archetype that could also be used to inculcate in our people an awareness of the presence of God.

The difficulty is, of course, that unlike Israel of old, the medieval nations and some European countries today we have divorced religion and politics. In virtue of the principles of our government themselves, people cannot view in the same light the things of God and the things of Caesar. It may have been considered possible to do this in the early days of our development, but not today when the establishment clause in our constitution has been definitized by decisions of the Supreme Court. The word "God" is fast disappearing from public school texts as well as army manuals. The fact is that many different and radically opposed religions thrive in our country. And people want to find unanimity and unity in their religion, not divergence.

Then, too, the Catholic Church portrays itself today as still quite monolithic. It abhors as just too threatening pluralism even in theology, apart from its legitimate concern about division, splintering and divergence in faith. It sees its life destroyed, not enhanced, by any kind of pluralism. The death of God theology in America itself symptomatizes the Church's and any ecclesial community's radical opposition to diversification. If God is perceived to be the bond uniting men as brothers, once religious unity is destroyed God has to be considered dead.

Though they may not have formally thought about it, the search for a viable archetype of divine presence in our milieu may be playing a major role in driving priests out of the parishes and into specialized work. They find it much easier to minister to homogeneous groups of people who have a definite identity and consequently have already achieved unity through the operation of a more clearly cut archetypal image. For example, the sea still retains an aura of numinosity. We are reminded of Vahanian's treatment of *Moby Dick* in his *Wait without Idols*. A sailor has to be aware both of his complete dependence upon others and consequent solidarity with them as well as of the ominous transcendence of the sea reminding him constantly of forces that surpass the puny power of man. So many priests who are dissatisfied with the unrewarding Sisyphean toil of their parochial assignment seek a navy chaplaincy. The same observations might, of course, apply to the other services, for wherever life is imperiled, community among men is more easily established and an awareness of the transcendent is more readily inculcated. Many priests too once sought to work among the black community. Here too, seemingly, a more easily identifiable archetype was presumed to be operative. But recent developments among blacks have made it clear to them that no white man can really appreciate what it means to be black, that it is not possible for white priests to completely understand or be fully moved by black archetypes, and, consequently, applications for this kind of ministry have dropped off sharply.

Phenomenologically priests who have attempted to or actually made such moves are on the right track. At least in their bones they felt what grace implies. If a Christian community is to be established, if a really graced Church is to be called forth, people must have an abiding awareness of God's presence. And they understood that such an awareness is somehow connected with a people's self-image, with its principal archetypes. In practice they realized full well what we shall now propose for lack of a better name (and at the risk of appearing somewhat immodest) as Meyer's law. The influence of an extra-sensory empathic presence varies in direct proportion to the extent of association of the represented person with dominant archetypal images.

The search for such archetypes in our society at large is, of course, not precisely the task of the theologian. It must be an interdisciplinary quest. It requires the assistance of the sociologist, the psychologist and the historian as well. Perhaps if such assistance is not forthcoming, ministry will have to restrict itself to small groups. Even if such a search is carried out scientifically with the cooperation of qualified persons in the various fields mentioned, it may well disclose that our society is just too heterogeneous today for any simple dominant archetype to be found. Maybe the job just cannot be done for our people as a whole. If this is the case, then Church authorities may have to reconsider the specification and division of ministry along other lines than the strictly parochial and diocesan. Division of ministry along territorial lines was introduced very early in the history of the Church when the life of people was much less diversified and their self-images vastly less complex. Since these early days the issue has not been reconsidered. But in our day the basic dynamic of the Christian life itself may be totally neutralized unless it is.

In some some places the redistribution of ministry along lines other than geographical has already been inaugurated at least on an experimental basis. But this does not necessarily presage full-scale future adjustment. Bishops are notoriously slow to act. While the search for archetypes is being conducted, while the possibility of new types of priestly service is being considered, it still may be possible for individual pastors whether by native instinct or careful investigation to discover a dominant archetype among the various groups of people whom they have been assigned to serve. It is still a fact that homogeneous segments of our splintered society tend to band together in the inner city or the suburbs. By observing, judging and acting the concerned and alert pastor will be able to find out what makes them tick, what constitutes the principal value in their lives. He will see how they devote themselves to their work, their home, the care of their families, and community projects. He will discern their attitudes on key issues like use of authority, peace, progress, and education. He will then be in a position to conjecture at least about their self-image and the archetypal forms that focalize and render present their life objectives. But he must be highly motivated to undertake such a difficult and tedious task of community psychoanalysis. He must see that unless he succeeds in this work, unless he finds the right image, sensitive archetype, his people and very likely he himself will never experience the abiding presence of God. They will never live to the fullest the life of grace. They will never completely activate the power for authentic existence God's love has given them.

Few people, unless their attention is expressly directed to the fact, are conscious of the gravitational fields in which they live out their lives. Only when they see on television or in magazine pictures weightless astronauts floating around in spaceships do they become more aware of the earth's pull upon their own bodies. Even then they are not apt to be focally conscious of the same kind of force field emanating from the sun, moon, other planets and stars. Even those people who live in the heart of a large city do not think about the fact that they are caught up in a literal maelstrom of electromagnetic fields. Yet they are constantly exposed not only to the constant bombardment of radiation from the sun, ranging in frequency from infrared to cosmic rays, but also to the influence of energy fields of countless radio and television transmitting antennas. Even while watching television most persons do not attend to the fact that their own bodies are in the same electromagnetic field as their receiving aerials. Their tissue is incessantly assailed by more or less minute amounts of energy from Radio Moscow, the Voice of Christ from the Andes, Radio Free Europe and rock n' roll from the local teenie-bopper station.

If presence is, as we have said, a function of consciousness, we cannot consider it àdequately apart from its psychological implications. But if we want to address ourselves to the quasi-physical or metaphysical aspects of grace as God's loving presence, we might best view it under the analogy of an energy field in which all men are immersed. God's love is to be found everywhere. We are bathed in it. If we do not advert to it, if we do not recognize it, we have to blame the lack of a handy psychological vehicle which can convert our subjectivity to a continual awareness of it.

The question of experiential knowledge of God's presence has been treated also from the scholastic viewpoint by a few theologians in our time. We have already mentioned the work of Poulain and Mouroux. John F. Dedek has studied St. Thomas' doctrine on experimental knowledge in his doctoral dissertation entitled *Experimental Knowledge of the Indwelling Trinity: an Historical Study of the Doctrine of St. Thomas.* But the work of integrating questions about divine presence with scholastic psychological theory has more fully been conducted by Galtier, Gardeil and Garrigou-Lagrange.

Galtier attributes consciousness of God's indwelling in the soul of the just to the operation of a discursive process. The graced person is immediately aware by reflection on his own acts of faith, hope and love of a certain superhuman element they enfold. He senses a kind of numinal quality in the good acts he performs. He experiences contentment, joy and peace from the well-ordered and meaningful life he leads. From these phenomena he should be able to reason to the presence of God. The transcendental aspects of his experiences postulate a cause outside the human subject. God is the only adequate explanation for the person of faith. And since cause must be conjoined with effect, graced acts herald the presence of God. The just person is cognizant of a supernatural presence through his application of the principle of causality to account for those of his own actions which his faith tells him can be produced only by God.

Gardeil and Garrigou-Lagrange agree to the extent that they reject discursive knowledge in the explanation of the graced person's consciousness of God's presence. Experimental knowledge of its very nature has to be immediate, non-discursive. The sense of presence is not the result of any reasoning process. Experimental knowledge does not emanate from an inference to God's subjective presence, his presence as a co-producer of human supernatural acts; it must be directly produced from contact with an object. Objective presence alone creates experience. But in all supernatural acts one perceives an objective presence; and this perception is immediate, while one has to reason to a subjective presence. God has to be present in any supernatural act as its object. All supernatural acts insofar as they are supernatural have to be referred at least indirectly or implicitly to God. So he must be present in them in the intentional order. Garrigou-Lagrange presents this objective presence as one formally perceived by means of a concept. The conceptual image of God as present emanates especially from the act of filial love which is essentially directed to God as its object. When the Christian loves God, he is aware of the fact that he is God's adopted son. He conceptualizes God as his Father. In that very notion he apprehends in faith the reality of his relationship with God and thus contacts the objective divine presence. Gardeil, on the other hand, views the experience of the divine in acts directed to God as their object as being itself supra-intentional, as being without any medium or species. Experience is *per se* pre-conceptual. The object of the supernatural act is a given. It is not really distinguishable from the act itself. No special additional conceptualization is necessary. No explicit intentional directing of the act is required for contact with what is objectively already there. The mere conception of God implies presence. If the believer directs his mind toward God, by that very fact he has affirmed God's presence.

Theologians of every persuasion have always been interested in what has become a special concern of our times—consciousness of the presence of God. But we live in an era of personalism. It is not sufficient that in our contact with God's loving presence we experience him merely as a being, howsoever numinal his being might be. We desire to have a truly interpersonal relationship with him. Through Christian revelation we know that God is not a single person, but triune. How then are the distinct persons present in our experience of God?

St. Thomas (I, q. 43, a. 5, ad 2, 3) seems to suggest some proper personal action of the Trinity in the relationship of grace. He speaks of an assimilative action whereby the graced person is made a true image of God. This is precisely how through grace a man comes to be a partaker in the divine nature. But St. Thomas goes further. The graced person through the assimilative action of God bears a likeness not only of the divine nature, but also of the distinct persons themselves. Though all the actions of the Trinity *ad extra* have to be seen as emanating from the common divine nature, that nature reflects the fulness of the reality that it comprises. *Omne agens agit simile sibi.* And as a matter of fact the divine nature is possessed by a trinity of persons, each having his own distinctive quality in relation to the others. Following the line of St. Thomas, then, theologians have shown how the supernatural creativity of the graced person has reflected the special genius of the heavenly Father, how his wisdom images the Son and his love manifests the Spirit. Although a careful reading of the text of St. Thomas in the first part of the *Summa* which we summarized above might hint at something more, interpreters generally have taught that this assimilative activity of God in the soul of the just person is to be appropriated and not really attributed to the distinct persons of the Trinity. What they say seems true: they can base their arguments on other texts of the Angelic Doctor where he too appears to be referring to some kind of appropriation and not setting up any proper personal relationship between the graced man and the three persons. But the most recent writing on this subject evidences a tendency to break somewhat with this traditional interpretation. Undoubtedly under the influence of personalist philosophy theologians are now beginning to explore the possibilities of having a truly proper personal relationship, not just an appropriated one.

The greatest *actio ad extra* of the Trinity is the Incarnation. If we consider the Incarnation precisely as an action of God, it is to be attributed to the common operation of the three persons through the divine nature. But when we focus on the

formality of the Incarnation as a relationship, as the relationship of this particular human nature to the person of the Word,
there can be no question of mere appropriation. The human nature of Christ has to be fully, completely and exclusively attributed to the person of the Word. But the Incarnation is the
prototype and exemplar of the grace-relationship. Why then
speak of appropriation in respect to it? Rahner points out that
it is correct to speak of appropriation in regard to the operation
of the distinct persons of the Trinity in an action *ad extra* only
when one is viewing it under the aspect of efficient causality.
All efficient causality of God *ad extra* is a function common to
the divine persons. But if one considers the action from the
standpoint of formal or quasi-formal causality, there is no reason to deny the possibility of proper personal relationships.
Anything else would be totally inadequate.

To describe the relationship with the three persons established by grace in terms of appropriation would actually give
the lie to the absolutely supernatural and numinously divine
character of it. The numinal element in the grace-relationship,
like that in the hypostatic union, lies precisely in the fact that
it is a relationship person to person with God. To see it merely
as a relationship of natures, albeit individual natures, would
belittle its unique character. It is precisely because grace is a
personal relationship that it can be explained in a framework
other than that of scholastic philosophy—in terms of existentialism, which is a more satisfying world-view for people today. The fact that grace is given precisely to persons and not
to human nature as such or even to individual natures is emphasized by St. Thomas. He uses this fact as an argument when
he explains why human nature can still remain wounded by
original sin while persons are restored and exalted by grace.
What grace originally implied for man, immortality and im-
munity from concupiscence, has not been restored by the action
of Christ precisely because his grace is not given to nature as
such (as God's original dole was) but only to persons.

Theologians have always seen grace as the beginning of a
state of friendship with God that will ultimately flower into

the most intimate relationship possible for man with God, what they called the beatific vision. Grace and vision are in the same order; they are just different modalities of the same reality. Grace is the seed, vision the burgeoning plant. But the beatific vision would hardly seem to be the most intimate and immediate relationship with God imaginable if it were in no way personal, and each divine person were not playing his own proper part in it.

Galtier and other opponents of the view that a proper personal relationship with the Trinity can be achieved through grace reject the idea on the grounds that it infringes upon the uniqueness of the Incarnation. They say that the hypostatic union, in order to preserve its absolute singularity, has to be considered the only union of God with man based on personal contact. Rahner denies apodictically that the only type of personal relationship that God can have with man is of the hypostatic order. Nor would he admit that a personal relationship founded on grace would in any way detract from the uniqueness of the hypostatic union. After all, in the Incarnation we are not dealing with a human person at all, while in the case of grace we have a relationship person to person. Rahner thinks that the basic difficulty arises from too abstract a notion of what a person is. If in the beatific vision there is contact with the Father as Father, the Son as Son, and Spirit as Spirit—and there has to be if the beatific vision is all that it is cracked up to be—and this intimacy does not create a union in the hypostatic order, why should there be any difficulty about grace? Then too, Scripture describes the union of grace in personal terms. Christ did not say that if anyone loves him, God would abide with him; he said rather that he and the Father would make their abode with him.

The fact is that the most striking kind of presence that men can experience is contact with other persons. Personality lies at the very core of human life and interests. Men realize that they can perfect and fulfill themselves only in contact with other persons. Their own personality can be forged only in the crucible of interaction with other persons. If this is true in any human relationship, it must also be valid in human contact with God through grace.

There is, however, a special difficulty in speaking about a personal relationship with the Trinity to modern man. The problem does not lie in the fact that there are three persons in God. This mystery can be accepted through faith. The heart of the issue is in the language the terms used to describe these persons and the philosophical setting in which the theology of the Trinity was developed. Why, for instance, is the first person in the Trinity called Father instead of Mother? If his love of men is unconditional to the extent that God loves even sinners, it would correspond more to what psychologists like Fromm have termed mother-love. The growing breakdown of familial life in our society has made increasingly difficult the description of divine personality to children in terms of any kind of parental love, but especially of paternal love. If God has no sex, does it really make a significant difference if we call the first person Father or Mother? Perhaps there would be difficulties regarding the role of Mary in the Incarnation. But then God's part in this action is attributed to the Spirit anyway, and not precisely to the Father. Certainly we see why the first person had to be called Father in the time of Christ. In the patriarchal society of that time any other term would be unthinkable. But does the word "father" have the same connotation and conjure up the same feelings today?

If there is a problem about the first person, there is even more about the third. Can the Spirit even be conceptualized today as a person?

The Alexandrian gnostic philosophy in which Trinitarian doctrine has been elaborated cannot make sense to people today. If the emanations of the persons of God are patterned after the operations of the human intellect and will people will be at a loss to see how theology really helps them to assimilate the mystery of the Trinity. For personality means something quite different to them than the word "*prosopon*" did for the Platonists. Once again we will have to agree with Dewart when he says that there has been a definite underdevelopment of certain aspects of our theology. We need an investigation of the larval theology of the Trinity as much as we need a study of the meaning of grace for modern man. But it is not within the scope of the purpose of this book to research that issue.

A theology of divine presence is necessary for elucidation of the concept of grace we have presented. But it also serves another and perhaps much more important function. The Christian concept of the identity of the graced person with Christ is psychologically a most risky and dangerous one. Some people need to be identified with Christ to the extent that they forget who they are. They cannot stand being themselves. They welcome and relish the idea of identification with Christ. But it is not understood by these people in the way we have explained it. Their identification with Christ is not a project, a to-be-made. In their mind it is a *fait accompli*. Their neurosis will not allow them to accept the fact that the grace-transformation gives one the potential to become the sacrament of Christ in the world, a potential which must be actualized not only by their own power but with the continuous influence of God's grace, a potential which will never be fully actuated until the time of the *pleroma*. For them to be one with Christ does not mean to identify oneself with an ideal to be pursued, but to be in possession of the God-man's own numinosity. It is not enough to reflect Christ by being transformed as he was in God's love, by doing his 'thing' in the liturgy and accomplishing what it signifies in life; it is necessary to lose one's own self entirely in Christ. To be Christ means to be obliged to see that others obey God; it implies that one has real power over others: power to command and to compel. To be Christ is to be fully an instrument of the Spirit.

Such ideas distort grotesquely the significance of the grace-relationship. They enable people in the name of Christ to become murderers, avengers, scourges, inquisitors, fanatics. They help sick people to repress themselves and become obsessed with Christ. They replace the divine element in grace with a daimonic one.

For the ancient Greeks *daimon* was a non-rational, obsessive power. Through *daimon* a person was totally enslaved: all his being was caught up in the pursuit of a monomaniacal fantasy. *Daimon* was an archetype of creative and destructive human power; but of its very nature it had to be the dominant and overriding archetype, one that pervaded every nook and cranny, every facet of existence.

The relationship of grace can be preserved from the tyranny of the daimonic only by the reality principle that is introduced through a correct conception of the presence of God to the graced person. A theology of presence has to assure the transcendence as well as the immanence of love. And to prevent distortion, perhaps it must emphasize transcendence over immanence. God must be present to the man whom he truly loves as the one who is totally Other, standing over and against him. This idea of transcendent presence will prevent immanence from becoming daimonic. Identification will remain in the objective order; the subjectivity of the lovers will remain intact. As we said, the presence of God conceived in such a way will at least invite, if not demand, dialogue; and dialogue forestalls self-obsession.

Those who love God make him present. In his presence they are transformed and achieve in accordance with their mode of being in the world a measure of self-transcendence. But in that presence they also find confirmation of their own authentic selfhood. For in identifying themselves with Christ they come to know that man can attain genuine self-transcendence only by accepting his humanity.

From the perspective of the moon man has gotten a better view of the universe. Where there is no atmosphere to diffuse light the sky even in the lunar day is freckled with the radiance of billions of stars. Man has transcended himself beyond his wildest dreams in the moon landings. But this accomplishment is as nothing when compared with what lies before him. From the universe extending two billion light-years out into space and perhaps beyond man gets some glimpse of the vastness of the divine presence. A man on the moon cannot be prejudiced; his mind cannot be closed to any possibility.

The Bohr model of the atom as a kind of miniature solar system is outmoded today. But scientists really do not know what the atom looks like. Their researches lead them to believe that because the atom evidences certain definite energy states the Bohr idea might not be too far-fetched. But then man will ask: Could it be that our own solar system forms an atom of which the earth itself is just a planetary electron? Can man have a vision in which the Milky Way is just one living molecule, say, in the solar plexus of a giant man who lives on a giant earth the size of which staggers the imagination? And could that earth itself be itself a planetary electron in another even vaster system, and so on indefinitely in the macrocosm? And if this is possible, could it be that my own solar plexus contains a molecule which is a galaxy in which there is an atom on the planetary electron of which live millions of intelligent beings whose bodies are made up of other inhabited solar systems, and so on indefinitely into the microcosm?

Ultimately we have to say that God's presence is a deep mystery, and theology with the help of science can only touch it lightly.

CHAPTER IV

The Supernatural

Most people today cannot give any really accurate definition of grace. But almost invariably they will know one thing
about it. It is supernatural. But it is precisely the supernatural
today which turns many people off. They see it as something
automatic and almost magical, as something inhuman and primitive, as a distraction and delusion that robs men of the responsibilities and concern they ought to have for the things of
this life. They perceive it as the wedge that has riven the sacral
from the secular. And since they hope to witness the day when
the secularization-theology of our time will have achieved its
goal, and the religious aspects of man's life will no longer be
compartmentalized, they view the supernatural as the chief
threat to their ambitions and desires. The idea of the supernatural these people say, is always a deterrent to human progress. It encourages men to dream rather than to act. It instills
fear instead of inspiring courage. It confronts men with their
weakness and ineptitude. It points up the basic powerlessness

of man before nature. It was an idea that could easily be bought by the man who tediously eked out his life in the fields or ateliers of the past, but not by the man who has set foot on the moon.

Theologians, on the other hand, have always seen the essential relationship of the idea of the supernatural to that of the natural. They have recognized the fact that the supernatural cannot even be conceived or defined except in relation to the natural. They have tried to explain the theological axiom, "Grace builds on nature" by placing the roots of the supernatural in the natural, by viewing the supernatural, contrariwise to the popular conception, as a call, as a stimulus and a challenge to transcend with the help of God the limits of the natural. But in seeing the supernatural as something that can be initiated and brought into being only by God, though adapted to, building upon and requiring the cooperation of, the nature of man, they have come face to face with a basic problem they have never been able to solve. They have come to grips with the problem of man's incessant desire to transcend his humanity, but only in and through his humanity, on the one hand, and God's absolute dominion not only over his creation, but over human destiny as well on the other. The full response of larval theology to this problem will be seen only after we have discussed it in a later chapter in which we shall consider the nature of human freedom. Here we must restrict ourselves to the question of whether the idea of the supernatural as it has been applied traditionally in the area of grace is still viable or desirable in our time.

What is meant by the supernatural? As we have said, the supernatural can be defined only in terms of the natural. It presupposes a more or less fixed notion of the nature of man, at least to the extent that it sets limits to the possibilities of man's power to transcend himself by his own capabilities and capacities. The supernatural in general is that which totally and absolutely exceeds the powers, demands and natural needs of man and creation at large, though it is in itself possible of attainment through an exercise of divine power. Theologians customarily distinguish two existential modalities of the super-natural. That which is in itself supernatural *(quoad substantiam)* is anything that directly and positively vectors a man toward the special destiny that God has established for him, the bea-tific vision—that knowledge of God which is patterned upon the way in which God knows himself and the ecstatic state that re-sults from such a contemplation of divinity. This divine kind of knowledge infinitely exceeds man's capabilities. Yet it might be seen as possible for man because the human intellect, if viewed absolutely and passively, is unlimited in its power to know. In a secondary sense the term "supernatural" can be applied to those things which, absolutely speaking, a man could achieve by his natural power, but not here and now, or not in the way they are attained. Right now it is not possible for man to land on Saturn. His state of technological development has not yet reached a point to enable him to accomplish this feat. But in a hundred years he might well be able to do it. If then to-morrow morning's newspapers were to carry the headlines: "Man sets foot on Saturn!" and it is known that he did not himself have the natural means to make that landing, the feat would have to be considered supernatural *(quoad modum).*

The kind of grace we are talking about in this section (ha-bitual grace) implies the total commitment of man with God in a common destiny. Without it man could never under any circumstances attain to the beatific vision. So theologians would call it supernatural in the strict sense.

In late medieval times the theology of the supernatural de-veloped to such an extent that it provided a clear picture of how grace essentially differs from man's natural endowments. Two different but mutually related orders of being were pro-posed: that of the natural and that of the supernatural. The natural order corresponds to God's act of creation. The super-natural order was the result of God's decision to elevate man so he could enjoy the beatific vision. By creation man would have had a destiny that can be extrapolated from a considera-tion of his natural needs, tendencies and desires. His ethically good life in this world would demand a reward. He would have been rewarded by living forever in an Eden of total delight. All his noble yearnings, those that well up from his humanity as such, would be perfectly fulfilled. His baser tendencies would be adequately sublimated. He would have a perfect, though still strictly human and consequently discursive, knowledge of God. This would bring him total happiness and satisfaction. He would stand in a new, more intimate and delightful relationship with his fellow-man and all creation. Since he would have had nothing more in this state than the complete and perfect fulfillment of his humanity as such, he would have been able to attain it by his own native power with only the natural concursus of God.

But revelation indicates that God decreed from the beginning that man was to be elevated to a different state. With his creation man was given all that he might be expected to have had in his final state had his destiny been only natural. He was given immortality. He was freed from concupiscence. He had perfect discursive knowledge of God. He lived in harmony with nature. The fact that these gifts were given by God to man before he earned them proved them to be supernatural *quoad modum*. But man's elevation implied much more. He was given a new destiny. He was given the opportunity to participate in the divine life itself. He had the chance of attaining to a knowledge of God similar to God's own knowledge of himself, and a love of God as he loves himself. God invited man to share his own glory, joy and happiness. The seedling of this destiny was grace. It was truly a share in the divine life, but until man proved himself, the divine life in him would remain largely enfolded, undeveloped, unformalized, unexplicitated, potential and only minimally activated. This gift was supernatural *quoad substantiam*. It is absolutely impossible for man on his own to share the divine. A vision of God as he sees himself and the resultant total envelopment of man in ecstasy is completely beyond all natural human capacities and desserts, and fully exceeds all his hopes and expectations. Such a destiny could be established only by a special act of God setting this new goal for man's striving. But since God has to deal with man on man's own level, since he does not destroy his original creation or change it essentially in elevating it, presupposing elevation, it was necessary for God to give man a token or pledge of this new destiny and the means to achieve it. Grace is this pledge of man's new destiny and the means to achieve it.

Through this conception of the two orders the distinction between the natural and supernatural is easy to see. Purely as a creature, man is complete in himself and set on his own to pursue a natural destiny. Then, as it were, a divine decree intervenes and alters man's destiny. To avoid pure extrinsicism and to enable man to cooperate in the achievement of this new destiny in truly human fashion God bestows his gift of grace upon man. This gift is, of course, in no way owing to man. It results exclusively from a special act of divine love associating humanity in a more intimate way with God. There is nothing in man's nature corresponding to it except what theologians called the *potentia obedientialis,* that is, the radical expandability of human nature under the influence of God to receive the gift of a totally different order of being. This potency is absolutely passive: human nature is elastic enough to respond to God's elevating act, but man is totally impotent to activate this possibility by himself.

We have said that this conception of the supernatural rests on the fact that there is nothing positive in human nature corresponding to it. If man were left in the state of pure nature, would it have been possible then for him to conceive of the possibility of such an elevation? Theologians answered this question in the affirmative. After all, man's intellect is a capacity for the infinite. Someone may well have thought that, absolutely speaking, a vision of God might be possible for man. The thought might even have elicited a desire for such a state. But without revelation the thought would have had to be a mere conjecture without substantiation in fact. And the desire which followed from it would have had to have been provisional; it would have had to be a conditioned wish: If things were different, if God had created man in another way, I would want this vision which might then be possible of attainment;

but it is not actually to be had, so there is no use thinking about it. But of course, the theologians who proposed these ideas hesitated in contemplating a further difficulty. Can man really be completely happy with what is second-best? If he could at least think of something better within the realm of possibility, can he truly rest with what he already has, wonderful and glorious as that may be? They could only respond by saying that theoretical questions with no possibility of practical implementation cannot really disturb the man who fully possesses the good that he does enjoy.

This nice, neatly packaged doctrine of the natural and supernatural might well have perdured even in the age of the moonlandings. But there is always someone who asks a hard question. The Church itself proposed St. Thomas as the model for scholastic theology and philosophy. Was this as a matter of fact his teaching? When attempts were made early in this century by Maréchal and others to answer this question, the wall between the natural and supernatural broke down. The theory of the two separate orders was shattered, and its defenders rushed back to their drawing boards. For it was pointed out that in the doctrine of St. Thomas there is a positive reality in human nature corresponding to the supernatural!

In his *Contra Gentiles* (III, c. 57) St. Thomas asks whether the beatific vision is possible for man. If it so exceeds his nature, how is it possible? St. Thomas responds by saying that it must be possible, because there is in man a *natural* desire for it. Now by natural desire St. Thomas did not mean the elicited, provisional, conditioned desire which we have just considered. By the term "natural desire" he normally means a tendency of nature itself—a tendency prior to all consciousness and rooted in man by virtue of creation itself. Thomas' argument is that God could not be conceived as being a good and wise creator, if having authored human nature with this tendency or desire for the beatific vision, because of the metaphysical impossibility of that vision itself for man, he lacked the ability to fulfill it. Therefore the beatific vision must be possible for man.

At the end of the second world war Henri de Lubac, S.J.

published a masterful study of the supernatural. By this time theologians had adjusted themselves to live with the problem of the natural desire created by the views of St. Thomas. While the question of the natural desire destroyed the complete dichotomy that had been established between the natural and the supernatural, it was not seen to threaten the notion of the supernatural itself. But De Lubac reopened the issue by carrying the question much further. He seemed to ally himself with Du Bay (Baius) who had taught that it would be impossible for God to create an intelligent being who would not be destined for the beatific vision. Actually all that De Lubac maintained was that the notion of a humanity not created for the beatific vision was totally unreal and should be abandoned by theologians. He saw the order of pure nature against which ideas about the supernatural were to be worked out as the invention of Cajetan. (More recently Schillebeeckx attributed it to Bellarmine, remarking that De Lubac had erred.) But really the idea of pure nature is idle theological speculation. There is not and never was any such actuality. What De Lubac did through his attack on the concept of pure nature was to recall theologians in their discussions of the supernatural away from an essentialist viewpoint back to an existentialist position. We must pass over the reaction to De Lubac's blast expressed first by rejection of it in the encyclical *Humani generis,* and now more recently by fundamental agreement with it evidenced in the writings of Rahner, Urs von Balthasar and a host of others.

We have said that the great contribution of De Lubac in the original French version of his *Surnaturel* to the problem of the supernatural was to call theologians back to a view that is more existential. The use of the word "back" might seem strange, since we have been at pains to describe the older position in completely essentialist terms. What we are saying is that only the essentialists have been able to produce an absolutely clear and well-defined picture of the supernatural. But before essentialist philosophy became dominant precisely because of its clarity on this point, there was another tradition which as a matter of fact was more existential in its orientation. It is not unlikely that St. Thomas' own views on the matter gave rise to this tradition. And even during the time that the essentialist view was dominant, there were some few theologians whose mental acuity and courage permitted them to defend an existentialist position against the all but overwhelming opposition of the essentialists. One such theologian was Juan Martinez de Ripalda.

Ripalda (1594-1648) lived at a time when the Inquisition was in full spate, but he was never formally condemned by it. It seems amazing that he was not, because he proposed ideas that would seem even to us today as somewhat bizarre. Among these we might list the following:

1. If one prescinds from actual divine law, knowledge obtained from a contemplation of purely natural things could be called faith in the wide sense, and this faith would be sufficient for salvation provided that it was assisted by divine grace.

2. The formal object of faith in this wide sense is not a revealed doctrine, but God's own faithfulness, constancy of will and efficacy of power.

3. It is not impossible for a substance whose very essence would be supernatural to be created by God and consequently to actually exist. To such a being it would seem that supernatural grace would be due.

4. Supernatural grace is conferred for every good act; thus every naturally good act is automatically an elevated act.

5. Mary needed no grace; the divine maternity is itself formally sanctifying.

6. Of themselves, apart from any divine decree, supernatural grace and mortal sin are not incompatible and mutually exclusive.

Even a cursory reading of these propositions manifests that Ripalda was reacting strenuously against the essentialist views of his time. Prior to the Reformation there existed among Catholics two basic views about the supernatural: the nominalist or extrinsicist and the essentialist or intrinsicist. Nominalism held the supernatural to be merely the result of a divine decree. God founds his relations with man on law. If man was to have a supernatural end it was so established by divine command. This supernatural end was the natural heredity of God's own natural Son. So by decree God made it possible for men by fulfilling certain conditions to become his adopted sons. Those who complied with his directions were adopted by God. They were justified because God no longer considered their sins: his sons could not be his enemies. They were sanctified to the extent that the holiness of Christ himself was imputed to them in accordance with the agreement Christ had made when he undertook redemption. As Christ laid man's sinfulness upon himself as he hung on the cross, so men could take upon themselves his holiness when they committed themselves to his cause in the act of faith.

The intrinsicist view repudiated legalism of this sort. The supernatural is a reality in the order of actual being; it is not just a being in the intentional order. Supernatural realities were real accidents, nonetheless actual because they were imperceptible and unknowable except through faith. As accidents they inhere in the human soul and its faculties. Human substance, of course, was purely natural reality, adorned with an array of natural accidents like height, weight, sex, looks, personality, etc. In addition to these a person might acquire with God's help supernatural accidents like the infused virtue of faith or justice. Grace is essentially a mysterious accident inhering in the substance of the soul (the spiritual demi-substance which with the body makes up the human composite) and rendering a person holy, just, an adopted son of God, partaker of the divine nature, and capable of merit. This sanctifying grace was infused in the soul through the operation of the sacraments or in conjunction with an act of love of God. It could be increased in the soul not only by reception of the sacraments, but by prayer and other good works. It was possible to place good, and even supernatural, acts like the act of faith even before one received sanctifying grace. Such acts were assisted by actual grace, a transitory supernatural concursus which served to elevate them and direct them to man's supernatural end. The Thomistic school in virtue of its principle of specification of acts

4

by their formal object considered acts as supernatural and consequently graced if they tended toward an object connected with God's revelation. The supernatural could be known only from revelation. It is only from God's revealed word, for instance, that I can know he is triune. If I believe in the Trinity, my act is supernatural, because it tends toward an object that can be known only from supernatural revelation. The catchword of this school was the idea so dear to St. Paul, that faith comes from hearing the word. The question of the salvation of infidels who never heard the word of God was a special problem for this group of theologians, and they generally solved it by urging greater missionary activity.

With the condemnation of Lutheranism by the Council of Trent the nominalist position on the supernatural became at least totally unacceptable, if not actually heretical. The essentialist school prevailed. The few theologians like Ripalda who theorized outside of its pale turned at times to existentialist solutions which in the course of time were eventually to offer a basis for challenging the idea of the supernatural itself.

Ripalda was deeply moved by the biblical idea that God sincerely wills the salvation of all men, even those to whom the gospel has not been preached. The discovery of America and its Indian population caused theologians to wonder about the teaching of the Thomistic school: the problem was now real, not just theoretical. Ripalda solved it by proposing his idea of faith in the wide sense (*fides larga*) which he saw as sufficient for salvation. Grace need only touch the subjectivity of the act, not its object, for it to be supernatural. So he moved the supernatural out of the objective order where it had been imprisoned by Thomistic essentialists. It is possible, he said, to have a supernatural act of faith that tends only toward some naturally known aspect of the divinity, some purely natural object. Andreas de Vega (1498-1549) had already proposed this same idea in his theological works, but later in his life he rejected it. In the nineteenth century Konstantin Gutberlet was to espouse it again. But it was Ripalda who was to become famous for it because of the clarity and tenacity with which he proposed it.

Eventually Ripalda moved the issue outside of the area of faith, and extended his idea to all supernatural acts. It was possible, he taught, and indeed the fact of the matter, that all naturally good acts are supernatural. The supernaturality of an act does not at all emanate from its object or content, but solely from the fact that it is elicited with God's grace. And God's grace is always at hand to assist man in the pursuit of the good, albeit the purely natural good. So Ripalda moved the question of the supernatural out of the objective, essential order into the subjective or existential one. The supernatural is constituted by the presence of grace alone.

In his monumental treatise *De ente supernaturali* Ripalda went much further in promoting existentialism. With his concept of *fides larga* he had freed the supernatural from the essentialist stricture of having to be found in the objects of acts; in this work he frees it also from the requirement of always having to be a real accident. He taught that it is possible for God to create a being whose very substance itself would be intrinsically supernatural. And eventually in his life when he proposed the notion that the divine maternity of Mary was itself formally sanctifying, he surpassed himself by further freeing the concept of the supernatural from any essential connection with grace itself! In proposing the idea that there is no intrinsic opposition between sin and the supernatural order, a notion that Duns Scotus had adopted long before him, Ripalda espoused a theological view that might be considered too radical and revolutionary even for today.

The upshot of all of Ripalda's elucubrations was then simply to move the notion of the supernatural out of the essential and into the existential order. No preset philosophical rules governed the concept and operation of the supernatural; only God's revelation and man's experience. And what must be emphasized is that, though his doctrine was many times reviewed by the authorities and generally rejected by theologians, it was never condemned or censured.

For Ripalda, then, the supernatural is not at all a matter of natures, of metaphysics, of particular philosophical systems, but solely a question of facticity, of actuality, of existence rather than essence. The supernatural is a concrete given or fact in a situation, not precisely a definable or completely identifiable essential structure. It is a numinal or transcendental quality of existence itself. It can affect acts, objects of acts, accidents or substances, but it does so not in virtue of what they are, but only because they exist in a special relationship to God. The supernatural then is free to move in all areas of existent being since it is an existential and not an essentially constituted modality of being. But if this is the case, if Ripalda is right, then we can ask legitimately if there really is any such thing as the supernatural. Since the concept of the supernatural, as the very word itself indicates, can be arrived at only by reference to constituted essential nature, fixed and unchanging, would it have any real meaning at all if one were to entirely embrace an existential philosophy? Or would what theologians have called the supernatural be better described in terms of some concrete and actual existential value to be found in man's love relationship with God?

In our era scholasticism both in philosophy and theology is on the wane. Existentialism is in vogue. Some of our theologians like Karl Rahner have tried to be eclectic and capitalize on the best features of both systems. They have had to face the question if the concept of the supernatural would be a meaningful and valuable theological tool for our times. Rahner shows himself existential enough to reject with De Lubac the notion of pure nature. Since it does not as a matter of fact exist and never did, the state of pure nature has no theological significance as such. But Rahner is reluctant to give up the corresponding idea of the supernatural. As a consequence he is necessitated to insist still on retaining the notion of pure nature at least as an idea. For him this concept is a *Restbegriff,* a kind of catalyst which, though having in itself no theological significance, is needed as a mental construct, as a reference point, in establishing the notion of the supernatural. For without the idea of pure nature, the idea of the supernatural either disappears or becomes so foggy it is unidentifiable. Theoretically

Rahner holds on to the supernatural as something valuable for even our times. Perhaps he does so because he realizes we are in a transitional period in the history of theology, and it would be difficult to communicate with older groups of theologians who are used to thinking in terms of this concept. Certainly he realizes too that the reality signified by the term "supernatural" has to be retained and considered valid in any theological system. And since the word still is associated with or at least adumbrates that reality to many theologians and teachers Rahner may still find the term useful. Practically, however, Rahner is an existentialist. He sees his chief contribution to theology to be in the area of pastoral application. Surely he is not unaware of the difficulty people are having with the notion of the supernatural today. But perhaps rather than disturb them with unfamiliar existentialist terms in this vital area of their belief, he may want to retain the word "supernatural" and just give it a new meaning, a slight twist that will make it more existential in content. Two of Rahner's basic contributions to theology relating to the question of the supernatural seem so existential in their fundamental orientation as to be reminiscent of the ideas of Ripalda. These are his notion of the anonymous Christian and the supernatural existential.

For Rahner the anonymous Christian is a person who leads a good life, a life of at least implicit faith in and love of God and his neighbor without having formally accepted Christian doctrine, or perhaps even been exposed to it. Such a life can be graced and supernaturally disposed for the reality of the supernatural is not centered in the objective order. The objects of one's acts may be purely natural, and the act itself supernatural because it is elicited with the help of God's grace. So too the whole existence of such a person can be subjectively supernaturalized by the transforming presence of sanctifying grace if the person has in some way elicited an act of love of God above all things. Rahner's notion of faith lies very close to Ripalda's *fides larga*. Though Rahner may speak of the supernatural as if it were an essence, he highlights its ability to operate existentially. In a more recent article on the nature of

Christian marriage he appears to have espoused even more fully the existential notion of grace and the supernatural proposed by Ripalda. For like the seventeenth-century theologian he considers all naturally good acts, that is, acts which tend toward the natural or ethical good, as automatically graced and hence at least subjectively or existentially supernatural.

Rahner's tendency to accept the supernatural as an existential phenomenon is evidenced even more in his doctrine of the supernatural existential. The expression itself indicates his reluctance to drop the word "supernatural" as well as his preference for an existentialist explanation of it. In proposing his idea he is evidently trying to address himself to the basic problem created by the Thomistic notion of the natural desire for the beatific vision. How can the supernatural be conceived as in no way responding to natural exigencies if one admits that man's nature itself is vectored toward an absolutely supernatural goal? How can there be something positive in human nature relating to the supernatural if it is completely above nature and ordered to the natural only negatively insofar as the doctrine of *potentia obedientialis* permits? Through the use of a kind of existential analysis Rahner charts a clear course between Scylla and Charybdis. Other theologians who try to respond to this difficulty tend to identify the natural desire defended by St. Thomas with the *potentia obedientialis* itself. The natural desire is really nothing positive, but simply a non-obstacle to elevation. But if this is the way they understand the natural desire, they could be well accused of nominalism. For their view would make the supernatural order extrinsic to man and completely arbitrary. If human nature has nothing positive corresponding to elevation, its roots must be sought in a divine decree, in a fiat quite distinct from and in no way grounded in the reality of creation itself. So the argument of St. Thomas from the natural desire would be rendered invalid, for in the final analysis the beatific vision would in no positive way correspond to the reality of man's nature. The only way we could know that the beatific vision is possible for man would be through God's revelation and faith's response to it. So faith would be needed to establish not only the fact but also the possibility of vision. Human nature might be seen as a non-obstacle to vision, but a non-obstacle could hardly be seriously described in terms of a natural desire.

Other theologians say that a natural desire is unfrustratable on the part of God since in itself it is not an act of man, but of man's Creator, and a wise creator does not direct a rational nature toward an end it can never attain by itself. If there were a *natural* desire for it, vision would not pertain to the sphere of faith, but it would be a provable fact from philosophy. In trying to provide for the *possibility* of vision, St. Thomas proves too much: the existence of a natural desire since it would not be frustratable on the part of God would prove the *facticity* of the beatific vision as the actual end of man. And if vision is the basis of the supernatural order, the whole idea of the supernatural vanishes, for it can no longer be considered gratuitous, that is, a free act of God fully independent of his will to create. A natural desire demands at least the possibility of being fulfilled by natural means. Otherwise one could not envision the Creator as all-wise and all-good.

From these arguments then it would seem that to preserve traditional ideas about the supernatural we must either describe the natural desire in terms of the *potentia obedientialis* (and thus reject it as St. Thomas conceived it) or else repudiate it entirely. But if we do either, we will have to say that there is to be found nothing positive in human nature corresponding to vision and run the risk of falling into extrinsicism. If, however, the natural desire could be conceived as something more than a mere *potentia obedientialis* and still less than a demand requiring fulfillment on the part of God, a middle position would be attained. Rahner plots this middle course with his idea of the supernatural existential. In trying to describe what has been for many a very elusive concept for the sake of clarity we shall have to run the risk of oversimplification. Basically the supernatural existential is man's existential openness. Man's being is limited, restricted, confined because he has an essence, a nature. But man's existence is open to almost limitless possibilities. To use the terms of Sartre, man's *en soi* is fixed and definite; his *pour soi* is basic openness.

Analogies sometimes confuse more than they clarify, but perhaps one will help in this case. From the start though we have to understand that to employ it we have to retrench in some part from the order of existence to that of essence. Think of nature as a sealed balloon. The balloon has a definite color and an identifiable form. It has clearly distinguishable capabilities and limitations. It will not rise from the earth by itself. But, absolutely speaking, because the balloon is elastic and permeable, it is possible for someone to insert into it a very fine hypodermic needle. Through this needle helium gas can be pumped into the balloon. Inflated with this gas it will now be able to do something it could not do before: rise from the earth. By the application of extrinsic agents the balloon was given new powers. This was possible because the balloon's nature did not resist penetration from without. The balloon had a kind of *potentia obedientialis* to be inflated with helium. But now suppose we conceive of the balloon representing man's nature as having as a matter of fact, in other words existentially (for this is not of the essence of a balloon), a small opening shaped to fit a pump. If the essence of a balloon required such a fitting, we might conclude that the purpose of a balloon is to be inflated, and hence every balloon to be a balloon would have to be filled with gas. The mouthpiece would be a demand for inflation. But if this is the case with just one balloon as it actually exists, if other balloons can exist as balloons without such a fitting, we would have to conclude that the mouthpiece is an invitation but in no sense a demand to be filled. This special balloon would remain a balloon even if it is not filled, and could serve some other purpose. Holes may be seen as an invitation to be filled, but they do not have to be. No one could logically conclude from the fact that the balloon is open to inflation that it must be inflated if it is to remain a balloon, if it is not to lose the reason for its being. A similar, and perhaps more cogent, argument could be constructed in relation to the uterus. The uterus in nature exists as an invitation but not a demand for the bearing of offspring.

Rahner uses the term "openness" in the sense of an internal existential condition. He conceives of openness as neither a mere non-obstructing potentiality for fulfillment on the one hand nor a positive demand for fulfillment on the other. Openness is a positive existential reality. But as indicating a possibility and not a demand, it is a reality of the existential and not precisely of the deontological order. To a person who is inclined to philosophize in the scholastic manner openness can indicate the real and positive possibility of a destiny and an end which lies beyond the obvious one. But by no means does it prove the actual existence of such a destiny, much less delimit it.

It is the openness of his existence to the order of grace, to the supernatural that Rahner has called man's supernatural existential.

The idea of the supernatural existential, of course, provides in Rahner's theology the underpinning of his concept of the anonymous Christian. If the supernatural is in some way grounded in human nature itself, and is not to be found merely in a juridical order established by what might seem to be not only a perfectly free but actually somewhat arbitrary divine act and communicated to man exclusively by revelation, then it is possible for man to contact this facet of his existence through his nature itself. Man touches the supernatural in his own existence. To grasp it completely, obviously he needs revelation. But Rahner would not deny the possibility of a genuine subjectively supernatural faith arising from man's basic nature itself. Understood in this light the old scholastic aphorisms: *Facienti quod in se est Deus non denegat gratiam* and *Gratia supponit naturam* take on a more credible and significant meaning.

We have to seek the ultimate reason for the concept of the supernatural existential in Rahner's theology of the mystery of the Incarnation. As we have already seen he relates the existence of other men to that of the incarnate Word. Other men, he says, came to exist because of the existence of the Son of Man. The incarnate Word is at one and the same time concretely God's greatest revelation of himself and God's greatest grace to man. But the Word was manifested and Grace was given precisely in that Humanity which was the existential pattern for all humanity. Existentially it was on the basis of humanity that God instituted the supernatural, that he provided man with a new destiny, that of his own Son, and the means to achieve it, the life of that Son. In his very being the incarnate Word synthesized into one reality the natural and the supernatural. Because of the Incarnation and because of this alone there can really be no such thing as the purely natural. And maybe—and at first blush this might seem quite astounding and foreign to Rahner's thinking—because of the Incarnation Rahner should have concluded that there cannot be in reality any such thing as the supernatural.

Holding on to traditional words and ideas relating to the supernatural, Rahner has done the same thing for our time that Ripalda did for his. He moved from a strictly essentialist conception of the supernatural to a more existential one. But, as we said, he shows himself still basically devoted to scholasticism. He did not let go of essentialism entirely. His notion of the supernatural existential is really a compromise, albeit a good one. But the world today seems to need more than just a compromise. It is demanding relevance not only in concept but also in language. If larval theology means anything, it is trenchantly indicating that what is totally supernatural according to scholastic descriptions can be assimilated into ordinary daily life without radical diminution of significance or essential alteration of meaning. The world today finds the essential meaning of the supernatural most relevant, but the word and the way it has been described in the past totally insignificant.

As we have said, the full-blown concept of the supernatural, if it is to be adequately apprehended, demands a clear-cut notion of the natural as a counterfoil. In this we agree with Rahner. But is the notion of nature as proposed by the scholastics valid today? Is there any such reality as nature? Does man really

have a nature, a fixed, absolute, unchanging and immutable
delineation of his being apprehensible as such by the human
intellect?

Back in the late fifteenth and early sixteenth century a noted
humanist Pico della Mirandola had some doubts about the
scholastic philosophers' description of human nature. While he
was willing to acknowledge a fixed nature in other creatures he
rejected such an idea as applied to man. In his *Oration on the
Dignity of Man* he pictures God in confrontation with Adam.
God says in effect: "We have given you, Adam, no fixed seat of
being, no form that you can call your very own. We have
given you nothing that you can possess and be satisfied with
because it is your very own. You are only what you make yourself to be. You can be whatever you desire. The law of creation has given a fixed, limited nature to other beings. But you
are an image of Us. You have freedom. Accordingly your being
has no bounds. You have to fix the limits of your own being
for yourself. You are really a creator: the molder and maker of
your own self. You can make yourself into whatever shape you
prefer."

According to Pico, then, man's nature is totally protean. The
nature of man is to have no nature. Pico's ideas reflect very
much those of Cardinal Nicholas of Cusa which we considered
before. But they correspond very closely also with those of existentialist philosophers today. And while existentialism has perhaps said all that it can say to the modern world, it still remains
influential inasmuch as it has begotten offspring in other forms
of philosophical speculation which are now in the ascendancy.
These maturing philosophical systems themselves are forms of
larval theology and show forth the influence the notion of the
supernatural had had on their development. We take note particularly of personalism and process philosophy.

Like existentialism itself personalism is hardly a closely knit
and highly organized philosophical method. It is true to its own
protean principle. It represents more a reaction against former
ways of philosophizing in an almost excessively rational and
logical manner. It posits as the highest value and starting point

of all speculation the human person himself. All reality must be interpreted in the light of and ordered to the human person. A person as such is completely unique, irreplaceable, free and responsible. Personality is not an essence. The human person is not hemmed in, confined, restricted by immutable laws which make his actions predictable. Nor is personality fully definable. Basically it is completely open and modifiable. It can be grasped only in terms of the choices it has made. It is intelligible only because of the modes of existence it has freely set down for itself. Its highest and most significant act is that of love. The human person can totally commit whom and what he represents to other personal values outside of himself. Through such commitment a person achieves a measure of self-transcendence. When the values lying outside are other worldly ones, as we have seen, self-transcendence signifies a new mode of existence that has to be described in terms of older philosophies as supernatural.

Process philosophy as expounded by Whitehead and Teilhard de Chardin zeroes in on the mutable condition of personal existence. It apprehends the whole world, what in previous systems might have been described as the world of nature, as being essentially in motion. So it proves itself to be in greater accord with current physical theory as well as with today's ideas about history. Like personalism this philosophy does not divert itself from its purpose by insistence upon internal logic and order. Its bent is to be existential rather than self-contained; it pursues the factual, not primarily the ideological. Perhaps it is incorrect to speak of process philosophy as if it were a single system with one clear purpose. Rather it amalgamates a number of philosophical views or perspectives by providing the integrating element of change. It teaches that everything, some things more perceptibly than others, is constantly in motion, is consequently undergoing modification. In a world that is thoroughly processive, even apart from any consideration of the exercise of human freedom, one can predict that there will eventually emerge new and radically different forms of being. Motion begets change. And process means motion. To be sure, process goes on in a

somewhat foreseeable and orderly fashion, at least as it is apprehended by the human mind. It is thus possible for man to
conceive of and deal with the reality with which he comes into
contact. Man gives meaning and order to process. He judges
some change to be deleterious, other change as beneficial to the
ideals and purposes he imposes upon reality. As such the world
is neither immutably orderly nor hopelessly chaotic. Reality is
neither the shadow-world of Plato's ideas on the one hand, nor
just sound and fury signifying nothing on the other. The world
is essentially relational. Its relationships are not to be projected
or preconceived by logic, nor on the other hand totally explored
and exhausted by experience. But process philosophy must prefer experience to logic in addressing itself to the question of
reality. Otherwise it would contradict its basic premise of the
likelihood of the emergence of radically novel forms. And experience itself must be described in terms of a relational, processive, forever modifiable growth in knowledge and understanding.

Not only because of its stress upon experience rather than
logic, but also because of its closer correspondence with the
world-view emanating from the findings of today's physicists
and the general tendency of people today to break away from
the inertia of the past, process philosophy is becoming more and
more influential in modern life. Only in the world of man's ab-
stractions can there be a universe without change or movement.
Only where sense knowledge is relied upon too much can man
have a concept of reality as essentially immutable and only ac-
cidentally variable. Motion in the microcosm is much too rapid
for man to perceive it. That in the macrocosm, because of the
law of parallax, though really as rapid, seems too slow for man
to perceive it. The nature of light and color as related to vision
has long posed a difficult philosophical problem for those who
must defend the validity of their ideas on the basis of sense
knowledge. An even more difficult problem is raised when one
considers the length of time required for an impulse to traverse
nerve fibers from end organ of sense to cerebral cortex. Few
people watching a movie realize the fact that half of the time

they are in total darkness watching a blank screen. Television viewers are usually oblivious of the fact that at any given instant the scanning beam in the picture tube is illuminating only a few square millimeters of the screen. If manufacturers of kinescopes were to use a phosphor of less persistence than the P4 or P5 types, people would become painfully aware of the marvel of motion that television really is. Heisenberg's principle of indeterminacy manifests the impossibility of accurately measuring two parameters simultaneously in the microcosm. The most delicate instruments will not reach all reality. There is no conceivable way of even detecting bodies whose dimensions lie in the picomicron range since the rays that could ferret them out are of a much higher wavelength. Einstein's principle of relativity suggests that it is not always possible to detect motion itself.

Human senses are most limited in detecting motion. The philosopher who designs his concept of reality upon sense-data will, as Aristotle did, see the world as basically static. He will envision the substance of things as unchanging and motion itself as accidental. But such a philosopher could not seriously profess to be anything but a home-spun, popular savant. For the ordinary, work-a-day world of man's senses his system would be fully adequate. There forms do seem to be permanent and movement proportional. But he can make no serious claim to be representing things as they really are. He can have no pretensions of being scientific. For the world of thought today his system is totally outmoded and unreal. Reality is totally but imperceptibly in motion.

Only a psychologically sound person can truly espouse process philosophy. It poses an ultimate threat to security. Where one encounters resistance to the new, the novel, the unexpected, the untried, a process world-view is not viable. Process throws man back upon himself and reminds him of his responsibility to direct the course of the world's evolution. And if this is threatening what it implies is even more so. Process makes it clear to man that whatever he is, whatever he has achieved will pass. A colleague of Sigmund Freud, Otto Rank, sought the explanation of all psychological disease in what he called the birth-trauma. The individual first exists in the relative security and comfort of the uterus. Here all his needs are provided for. He is cut off from the threat of the changing environment outside his mother's body. At birth he is suddenly ejected into this frightening new world of change. He has now to fend for himself or to rely on the good will of others for what he needs even to survive. He feels totally helpless. Each time in life that he experiences a new development or seemingly radical change, each time he is required by circumstances to revise his way of living, to slough off old, comfortable, secure patterns: when he has to start going to school, at adolescence, when he marries, as he grows older and loses his capacities, in the dependence of senility, and when finally he dies, his mind hearkens back to the subconscious, repressed, but still overpowering, experience of his birth. He experiences the same insecurity and dread. A psychiatrist of our own time, Rollo May, looks to the other end of the process and views death as the basic trauma which engenders all psychic disease. Every change, even the relatively minor ones of daily life, foreshadows the final radical change of death. Every loss of past security is a premonition of the complete separation from every vestige of security that death is. Life for May is simply the process of growing used to dying.

Now we might think that the proper locus for the flowering of such ideas would be the Church. Here is a larval theology pregnant with meaning and possibility of development. The Christian himself, as we have explained, lives to die. His initiation rite represents a running ahead in time to anticipate his own death. His faith provides a basis for hope and strength in which he can face and endure such a process. Yet the Church, though committed to live and manifest in every age the paschal mystery of Christ, is afraid to die to old forms. It is the most conservative of all organizations. It cannot at all abide by novelty. Only a person who truly lives in hope can embrace process. It would seem that the Church as an instrument of hope for mankind would in no way be threatened by process philosophy. But it is. And so the Church seems not really to have any hope.

In practice it seems to deny the idea of the supernatural it seems so strenuously to defend in theory. The thought of a Church without hope is appalling indeed. That is why men like Pannenberg, Moltmann and even the communist philosopher Ernst Bloch have made such an impact upon theological thought in our time. They have reminded the Church of what it seems to have forgotten: its own basic message of hope, its own good news. At times the Church appears to disbelieve its own power to believe. It has no hope in itself. It often responds to the challenge of change not at all like a credal community of hope and love, but after the fashion of a worldly organization, a state, by seeking security in those methods which have worked in the past: by enacting new laws or setting up new punishments—by repressing change with a show of fear rather than encouraging it in hope. It often refuses to take the risk of trusting that the doctrine committed to it by Christ will be understood by men or will be able to inspire them. It holds fast to the doctrine of the Spirit, but puts more reliance in purely human devices. It feels comfortable only with the self-concept of statehood suggested to it by the territorial donations of Pepin and Charlemagne, grants which at the time had to be theologically justified by forging a supposedly much more ancient document known as the "Donation of Constantine." It feeds on its history more than on its eschatological doctrine. It violates its own principles. Toynbee has remarked that the whole course of world events today might well have been completely altered if the Roman Curia in the seventeenth century had acted upon its own doctrine. Red China might not have emerged, and India might have been the largest Catholic nation. The Church has always taught that salvation is for all men. It has always maintained that its doctrine is not eternally wedded to any one particular philosophical system or to the western way of life. Yet when pioneer missionaries like Matteo Ricci and Roberto de' Nobili tried to adapt the message of the gospel to the philosophy and life-style of the peoples of China and India in the seventeenth century, the gigantic strides they took in making converts were nullified by decrees of the

Congregation of Propaganda. All future missionaries to these countries were required to take an oath that they would not indulge in so-called "Oriental rites." It was only in 1939 that these decrees were revoked in regard to China. But by then it was too late. It is no wonder that a theologian like Charles Davis could write: "For me Christian commitment is inseparable from concern for truth and concern for people. I do not find either of these represented by the official Church." His words may reflect a modicum of truth.

The Council of Trent under the guidance of the Spirit solemnly defined against Luther the orthodox idea that human nature is basically good and not totally corrupted by sin. But the Council then seemed to give the lie to its own doctrine by multiplying laws, regulations and punishments and implementing the power of the Inquisition to enforce them. One might find it amazing that in some so-called purely naturalistic societies there seems to exist a greater element of trust, or at least a greater appreciation of the value of hope and trust in human life, than is apparent at times in the Church whose very existence springs from hope. A Soviet magazine insists that in some towns in Russia a full-blown honor system for shopping in the super-markets operates without notable incidents. There are no checkers or cash registers. The customer tallies up his own bill, leaves his cash, gives himself change and departs with his goods. The local movie theatres function on the same plan. On the big island of Hawaii one finds remnants of the ancient Pu'uhonua-o-Honaunau or city of refuge near the town of Kailua. In ancient times those who had committed some crime or violated the law of kapu were subject to death unless they were ritually purified in this city. Yet archeologists and anthropologists have come upon no evidence of any kind of testimonial, whether in writing, body marking, or any other form to indicate that the purification ritual had been performed by the culprit. Evidently when he returned to his village, his word alone was accepted by the authorities. An extreme and wholly vitiated idea of trust could, as William McDougall points out, be discovered among the natives of Fiji where a son had the solemn duty, after his parents had reached an age where life was becoming too difficult for them, to fondly embrace them and then dispatch them to a better world.

Unfortunately however, in the only truly other-worldly society, in the only really supernatural society, the Church, the sign that men have sought is very often lacking. It upholds the idea of the supernatural, but often denies what it means in practice. It preaches trust in God and hope in man as called by God to share his destiny, and excoriates Pelagianism. But it often lives as if it had no hope save in its own power.

The considerations we have been making undoubtedly have influenced the disaffection for the supernatural that we experience so widely among Christians today. But we have pictured the Church as it existed before the Second Vatican Council. It was a Church that needed reform and was reformed by the Holy Spirit. The Council itself pointed out the need for hope. It proved itself much more open than the Church even of the recent past to the idea of process. It envisioned its membership as a pilgrim people on the march. It called for change in structure and life. It proved its ability to live in the world of process.

Since the writings of Teilhard de Chardin were published before the Second Vatican Council, it is not at all surprising that Rome restricted their use by seminarians. Neither are we astonished by the fact that an attempt was made to suppress them before they were published. Teilhard is above all a process philosopher. No doubt one of the principal reasons for such repressive action was the downgrading of the supernatural which process philosophy seems to imply. Yet despite all the measures taken against them, the ideas of Teilhard became more and more popular, and have clearly influenced current theological views. The implications of Teilhardianism for the theology of the supernatural as concretized in the doctrines of the Incarnation and grace have been analyzed in a stimulating way by Eulalio R. Baltasar in his *Teilhard and the Supernatural*. From this study as well as from our own reflections upon traditional notions in the light of process philosophy we shall attempt to arrive at a new understanding of the meaning of the supernatural as it is applied to the field of grace.

Certainly we would err were we to imply that Teilhard de Chardin had completely cut himself loose from the trammels of scholastic philosophy. His terminology and basic orientation is quite often patently Aristotelian. But we can discern in his writings two definite trends which run directly counter to the Aristelico-Thomistic position. He tends first of all to rely much more on the data of revelation, anthropomorphic though these may be when describing the reality of God and his Christ, and secondly, he finds in the concept of salvation history as a process of man with God the basis for extrapolating material from the world of man to the world of nature, from noosphere to biosphere and lithosphere, from the actually to the potentially conscious.

For nineteen centuries theology has not once succeeded in tearing itself loose from the cocoon of Greek philosophy. One should not expect that it can be done now in one fell swoop. It took eleven centuries for theological thought to be divorced from Platonism. Then it fell under the spell of Aristotelianism. Perhaps no single thinker, not even Teilhard, can free it from the Stagirite's web. Mathematics has undergone a similar phenomenon. Riemannian geometry still bears traces of the Euclidian. Physics too is still haunted by the spectres of the past. Even though experiments tend to disprove any law of parity in matter, the idea of anti-matter which is still largely accepted gives ample testimony to the ever-present influence of Greek thought-constructs in a branch of knowledge seemingly far removed from ancient domination. One could not have expected Teilhard to make a complete break-through. But the significance of what he did do has not been lost to the modern world. He pushed philosophical ideology from a cosmotropic orientation to an anthropotropic one. Not that he downplayed the cosmos in any way; just the opposite: he enhanced its value by relating it more directly to man. He sensed the widespread tendency among scientists to view the cosmos as more important for man today than ever before in the past. If man emerged in some way from the cosmos, its importance for him is nonpareil. But the significance of Teilhard's contribution to philosophy and hence to theology lies in the fact that he perceived and taught so clearly that human values do not derive worth and meaning from the cosmic, but viceversa: the cosmos has meaning and worth only because of the mediation and intervention of man. So he reaffirmed in a more concrete and positive way the dictum of the ancient philosopher who said that man is the measure of all things.

If anyone should be aware of the phenomenon of process and the centrality of man in the world it should be the historian. Yet many historians see history itself as basically cyclic and by that fact betray a cosmic orientation. History follows the pattern of nature. The music of the spheres is echoed in the life of man. Teilhard de Chardin's approach to salvation history on the other hand evidences a definite linearity and highlights the unique and unrepeatable relationship of God to man in world development. Teilhard indeed is cognizant of the analogic element in history which casts it into a seemingly spiral development; he notes man's proclivity to order experience in terms of a *déjà-vu*-complex. He knows that interpreters of the Old Testament will see in it a kind of prophetic symbolism in relation to the New. And his world-view makes use of the parallelism he discerns by emphasizing two apices in the evolutionary process, the first culminating the Old Testament in the Christ-event and the second terminating the New Covenant at the end of time with the *anakephalaiosis,* or recapitulation of all creation in the mystic Christ. But the spirality of analogic insight does not inhibit the linearity of concrete development. Of itself evolution is open to both degeneration and progress. Insight reassures man that it is actually generally progressive.

But it is especially the Christian faith that introduces a note of optimism into the process of human history. In the long run process is bound to result in the betterment of mankind as well as that of the cosmos. One is reminded of Toynbee's rhythm of routs and rallies, three and one-half beats to the extinction of a civilization. But this rhythm is out of kilter with the one which Teilhard envisions for mankind at large. Apart from any individual civilization, there are only two arses, two upbeats for mankind as such. Toynbee's rout-rally, rout-rally, rout-rally, rout is transposed by Teilhard into rout-rally in the Christ who seeks to be all in all; rout-rally in the Christ who will be all in all. Humanity will not end in extinction, but in triumph with Christ. Teilhard's view of history is fundamentally an explicitation of St. Paul's which is all-encompassing in Christ and fully optimistic. Teilhard's distinctive contribution to the thought of the Apostle is his catching up all of creation in the final glorification of man precisely through the introduction of an evolutionary process ordered to and issuing ultimately in the production of man. Thus man himself stands as a recapitulation of the whole cosmos, and when he is recapitulated in Christ, Christ truly becomes all in all. So the whole of creation, originating in the Logos, receives its final exaltation through humanity also in the Logos.

Teilhard's world-view, then, is thoroughly Christian. By that very fact it is also a spiritual world-view, not a materialistic one. But Teilhard's emphasis upon the spiritual by no means excludes the material. He completely eschews the Manichean tendency apparent in the writings of so many theologians. His approach to spiritual reality follows the way of man's thought: it is precisely through the material. The very basis of his theory of evolution, of his notion of process, is to be found in the so-called laws of dialectical materialism.

The first law states that opposites tend to become united. In the lithosphere the positively charged body attracts and seeks union with the negatively charged one. In the biosphere one observes that organisms become more fully alive and adaptable as they are able to support within themselves contradictory elements. The protoplasm of the amoeba is able to engulf and ingest food particles. But the stomach of vertebrates is much better suited for this purpose. Yet its cells produce hydrochloric acid concentrated enough to dissolve living tissue. But in the healthy individual the stomach itself is not destroyed by its own acid.

The nematocysts of the sting ray do not poison it, but enable it to survive in an hostile environment by killing or disabling its natural enemies.

The second law proposes that in nature there occurs a transition from quantity to quality. It scores the ability of matter to modify itself and give rise to new forms precisely to preserve the old in new settings. Water heated up to the boiling point merely grows hotter. But at 100 degrees centigrade it changes its form. It becomes gaseous. Individuals in a species tend to multiply to the point where they can no longer be sustained by their environment. Then new biological species emerge. The antelope that ultimately developed into the camelopard or giraffe was fond of eating leaves off the low-lying branches of trees. When it multiplied to the point where it used up all the food available at lower levels, only the beasts with longer necks survived.

These first two laws of dialectical materialism found the key Teilhardian notion of complexification. All beings seek union. Only in union with others can individuals preserve their identity. But union eventually brings about modification and better adaptation. The principle of complexification is especially important at the self-conscious level. It reaffirms an idea that lies at the root of modern psychological research. Only in contact with others can one develop as a person. Only in contact with others can one really be aware of what it means to be a person. But it is precisely in recognizing one's personhood, in fostering and developing it, that one becomes uniquely distinct from others. The closer the relationship of one person with another or with others, the more each will grow in his own distinctive identity. As Buber has intimated, it is the Thou that establishes and defines the I. The possibility of distinctive modification in the I varies directly in proportion to the number of contacts with a Thou. But so does the solidification of the I as an I.

The third and final law of dialectical materialism is that which gives rise to the basic notion of process itself. It proposes that every negation of being will eventually itself be negated. Posed more positively, the law states that every old form will eventually be replaced by a newer one. This process will go on in every order and at every level of being. It will appear to be cyclic in relatively short periods of time and more linear in longer ones. The development implied in the law itself is *per se* neither progressive nor retrogressive. Thus in accordance with the law of negation we see the seed negated in the plant, the plant beginning to be negated in the fruit, and the fruit negated again in the new seed. In longer term application we note how the eohippus was negated in the pliohippus, the pliohippus negated in the plesippus, and so on.

Whether Teilhard de Chardin realized it or not, the philosophy of process which he elaborated in his evolutionary theory is diametrically opposed to the Hellenic thought-forms which have supported scholasticism. If the whole universe is in process then its course, direction and rate of movement are parameters constantly to be rediscovered. So any philosophy which pretends really to probe its finality, meaning and inter-relatedness cannot remain fixed and rigid forever; it must continually be reconstituted and recreated. Such a philosophy alone can make sense to the modern intellectual, for it alone can be integrated with current scientific data, and it alone can correspond with what is the most intrusive and startling manifestation of process itself in our time: the so-called knowledge explosion. So if theology is to be relevant to coming generations it will have to cease to be a logical game played with pieces like substance and accident, end and means, matter and form, natural and supernatural; pieces freighted with fixed and permanent values and allowed to move only in definite preconceived patterns on the chessboard of reality. Theology itself will have to become process.

The scholastic philosophy in the matrix of which the theological distinction between the natural and supernatural was developed, and in terms of which it made total sense, was, as we have said, fundamentally essentialistic. And this philosophy was generically Hellenic and specifically Aristotelian in origin.

The world of Aristotle was basically one of being and not of becoming. He wrestled with the same problem that had beset his fellow-Greek Heraclitus. But his notions represent a direct reaction against the conclusions of the pessimistic Ephesian. He could not accept a metaphysic of the one and the many that (like the law of dialectical materialism) reduced opposites to unity. For him a being that is entirely in flux is not completely knowable. It could not therefore be an object of philosophical research, since in his view scientific knowledge had to be absolutely and forever true and thus certain. The processes that he observed in nature could be made intelligible only through the establishment of fixed polarities, the so-called *termini a quo* and *ad quem.* Everything in the world must be seen as substantially complete and finished. Otherwise philosophizing would be impossible. If it is possible to have substantial change, this has to occur through an almost magical and instantaneous substitution of one essence or form for another. The only kind of free-flowing change this system can envisage is accidental. Otherwise what is would be undone, and reality would not be able to be conceptualized. With Parmenides Aristotle held that it is essence that gives being both identity and intelligibility. The problem of the one and the many is solved conceptually by acknowledging the plurality of individuals in reality, but binding them into one form by an exercise of the mind's ability to abstract their common essence. The individual precisely as such is not completely intelligible. It is essence and not individuality that gives being self-sufficiency. Individuality as such is viewed almost like a kind of accident that constitutes a specific essence as unique in a definite complex of accidental qualities. In accordance with the doctrine of the four causes each essence or nature has an end toward which it tends and contains within itself the means—or if it is conscious and responsible, at least the right to the means—which it needs to attain that goal. The end of the nature is discernible from its internal structure. If I examine the mechanism of a watch, I can see that its purpose is to tell time. Aristotle's accent is on mechanics and justice, for he conceived each individual as a kind of self-contained mechanism whose very form elucidates its meaning and goal. The end is attainable either through the inner forces, the built-in powers of the unit, or through what it can, if it is conscious, rightly and justly acquire from others. Man's na-

ture is seen as a complex of tendencies and desires which demand fulfillment in accordance with right reason. His virtues
are habitual ways of responding to his real needs. These have to
be completely in tune with his nature and to correspond with
what his reason tells him is good for it. Any defect or excess in
this response is a vice. It is thus unthinkable that there should
be in nature itself a tendency or demand for that which exceeds
its goal or the means it is able to marshal in pursuit of its goal,
for that would be a vice not of man himself but of man's Maker.

The Parmenidean notion of truth is evidenced both in the
Aristotelian and scholastic philosophical systems. Epistemology
runs parallel with metaphysics. Since being is considered an absolute, so also is truth. Truth is simply the conformity of the mind
to the reality of being. Most perfect conformity and consequently
the highest order of truth is attained when the mind focuses upon
the immutable essences of things. But when the system comes to
explain the truth of the knowledge of individuals it runs afoul of
the problem of the principle of individuation. Aristotle himself
proposed that matter was the principle of individuation. St.
Thomas seems to have agreed with him for he calls angels species, not individuals. But since matter pertains to the essence of
material being, other philosophers had some difficulties about
seeing it as the principle of individuation. Francesco Silvestri of
Ferrara teaches that quantified matter individuates. So he sees
individuality as emanating ultimately from an accident of matter,
quantity. Boethius centers individuality in a complex of accidents. Others like Durand, Aureoli and Ockham look to actual
existence as the individuating principle, while Suarez and Scotus,
in an apparent departure from Aristotle dismiss the problem by
saying that being is its own principle of individuation. From
these disputes it is clear that what is central to the system is essence and not individuality. Individuality has to be conceived as
a kind of adjunct of essence rendering it unique in the concrete.

And if there is a problem about knowledge of individuals in
the system, personality is a greater paradox. Personality is usually seen as the individuality of a rational being. It is that prop-

erty of the individual rational nature to which its being and actions are attributed. As in the case of individuality the system has difficulty in not viewing it just as a permanent and basic accident. Cajetan and the Thomists in general consider it to be a mode of subsistence while Scotus and his school hold it to be formally a negation of communication to others. The general scholastic tendency is to see it as an incommunicable essence that is substantial, complete, existing by itself and rational. Personal qualities like sex and grace have to be conceived of as accidents. In the final analysis grace has to be a totally unfathomable mystery. It can be conceptualized only as something absolutely supernatural since it orients a person toward an end that totally exceeds his nature. Otherwise the system would have to brand its excessiveness a vice, an evil imposed on nature by the Creator himself.

The semantics of the scholastic system allow only for univocal or literal and various kinds of analogous understanding of words in relation to concepts and the essences they represent. Statements like those of Tertullian who said that man is naturally Christian, or like those of Anselm and Augustine who taught that one has first to believe in order to understand obviously cannot be taken in a literal sense. They would contradict the main presuppositions of the system. What is purely accidental to man's nature, revelation and the grace of Christ, cannot either complete it in the order of substance or be prerequisite for its autonomous functioning in its own order.

Process philosophy, on the other hand, starts from the Heraclitan principle that all being is in flux. The world is primarily not one of absolute and complete being, but of becoming. What being there is results from process, is in process, and will eventually be modified by process. In appropriating this philosophy Teilhardianism must logically initiate its own proper *Weltanschauung* not from the world of absolutes, not from the world of essences and substances, but from experience which evidences constant change. Inasmuch as it is Christian in its orientation, that *Weltanschauung* must accept as an integral and all-pervading element of human experience God's revelation to man. Basically Teilhardianism has to be seen as a *fides quaerens intellec-tum*. Insofar as he is above experience and the reality of the universe which is the object of experience God is the only supernatural being. We might say that since the tendency among theologians today in speaking of grace is to understand the primary grace, the uncreated grace, that is, God present outside himself in a unique loving way, grace as identified in this wise with God is also itself *ipso facto* supernatural. Nor would there be any real problem about understanding the supernatural in this sense. But certainly there would still remain a difficulty about the secondary but nonetheless absolutely necessary aspect of grace, that is, man's transformation in God's loving presence, created grace.

In the Teilhardian view creation in its various levels is an extension of God's love outside of himself in different degrees. Creation is an act of love, a projection of love. As such it is essentially a process of union. What is outside of God through love is united with him. Of course, there is no question here of pantheism. Creation is not in any true sense identical with God as such. It is only in union with him. And in accordance with the law of complexification it is precisely in union that identity and distinction are established. Process as Teilhard sees it is a kind of becoming, a growth from within responding to and emanating from different intensities or types of divine love, and resulting in an ever-mounting complexification, or the establishment of unique and separate identities. Process therefore requires union. The seed needs the ground. The union of the seed with the ground is precisely the wherewithal of process. And if the whole universe is in process it, too, needs a ground. As Tillich has remarked, the ground of being is God. The more the seed is united with the ground, the greater is its ability to differentiate itself from the ground and expand its own being. The more beings in the universe are united with God, the more intimately they are associated with his loving act, the more distinct and perfect they will become and the better they will be able to reflect the act that gave them their being.

Now a process has a beginning and an end and an indefinite

number of stages in between. Teilhard designates the beginning
of the process of creation as Alpha and its end as Omega. Now
if process philosophy recognizes a beginning and an end and a
directed movement from the one toward the other, it is not totally
relational. It has some absolutes. But to remain true to the idea
of process it must hold that an absolute state of being is achiev-
able only at the end of the process. Here and here only is to be
found a completely finished and permanent product. Even in accordance with the principles of Aristotle a process that has a goal
and a beginning, a *terminus ad quem* and *a quo* is intelligible.
It is only from the Omega, however, that the process can be completely understood and denominated. If one is not a biologist and
examines a marine egg, he can designate it as the ovum of *rana
pipiens* and the resulting polliwog as that of *rana pipiens* only
after seeing the frog that marks the final stage of development.
It therefore is only the Church as custodian of God's prophetic
revelation that can provide the ultimate answer to the process
that one observes in the universe. Only through and because of
belief in God's word about the future can the present be apprehended as a structure of hope and not of despair. Only the self-
in-the-future, projected there through faith in the One who alone
sees the Omega, can attain the absolute and lay hold of the key
to the totally relational now.

If truth is conformity to reality, then it must present reality
as it is, as in process. To be conformed to what is, truth is necessarily contextual. But this does not mean that all truth is relative.
Absolute truth is attainable where absolute reality exists, at the
end of the process. The Omega is the only valid principle of intelligibility for the absolute and the process related to it. The
Church, then, as the safeguarder of revelation about the Omega
is certainly in possession of absolute truth. But truth about the
intermediate stages of the process cannot be, like the process itself, completely immutable. It can be completely unchanging not
in regard to content, but only in regard to direction, only in relation to the Omega. It is only the grasping of the reality of a particular stage in the process. It is the uncovering or unveiling of
the process as it runs its course. What the mind possesses in the

intermediate stages is certainly the truth, the reality unveiled as far as it has gone; but not the whole or complete truth, not a truth that is incapable of further development as reality develops. The relating of the absolute truth of the Omega to various stages in the process itself involves a process which requires adaptation and modification of formulas. Though the Church as caretaker of divine revelation possesses a truth that is absolute, the tailoring of its message to suit the times implies the possibility of a development of dogma.

The semantics of process allow for only a provisional statement about its intermediate stages. Totally literal statements can be made only about the Omega. So in the semantics of process the statement that this tadpole is a toad is to be taken as neither literal nor metaphorical. It is best described as symbolic. By this is meant that it partially reveals and partially conceals the total truth. Thus it corresponds perfectly with the concept whose symbol it is. It expresses perfectly the idea that later stages in a process derive their reality from earlier ones while earlier ones are directed to and get their meaning from later ones. Only a symbol can adequately set forth the real situation of the truth about an intermediate stage of a process as partly veiled, partly unveiled, partially realized, partially to-be-established, and thus come to grips with the relational aspects of process as applied to concrete reality. The appropriateness of terming the Church's credal expressions "symbols" is apparent from this consideration.

Current thought does not view the world of man as one of natures, substances, accidents and ends. It is a world of persons. Man's essence is not an absolute. Man like all reality is in process. He is partly finished, partly to-be-made. The basic dynamism of human process, like that of all process, is union. But in man union is not just the affinity of being for being. It is not just physical union. It is love. And while in the semantics of process all union can be said to be a symbol of love and thus essentially related to it, when the word "love" is applied to man it must signify primarily an interpersonal relationship. Natures do not properly love; only persons do. And as we have seen, love is based precisely on the subjectivity and the uniqueness of individuals.

It can in no sense be universal and objective. It can in no sense be an essence or abstraction. As being-toward-another, finding its identity only in union with others, the I is intrinsically ordered toward love. Its end and goal, if we can speak of one, is necessarily personal love. And thus the human person can in no sense be conceived of as a self-contained mechanism. The I is not self-sufficient because love requires another. But the I is not created in vain, for it can find its identity and sufficiency in union with a Thou. At every stage of the process there are others to stand over against the I and define it. But complete self-sufficiency for the I can be had, of course, only in union with the Thou-Omega.

The pivotal notion about man in ancient philosophy is, as we have seen, his nature which is considered to be largely self-sufficient; the pivotal idea about man in modern philosophy is his personhood which cannot even be apprehended except in relation to others. A nature-centered philosophy must concentrate on justice. Whatever is lacking to nature can and, in accordance with right reason, must be demanded in justice. A person-centered philosophy on the other hand concentrates on love. But it is of the very essence of love that it be freely given and freely received. Exigency and demand are words that belong to the semantics of justice, not of love; they are words sounded often in the world that places primary emphasis on natures and essences, not on persons. As we saw before, true love must be freed from all types of instrumentality. Otherwise it is vitiated; otherwise it is not really love and cannot provide the assurance and satisfaction that the loving person craves. So while a person can appeal for love, can in some wide sense demand love in return for love, he must realize that the response of the other to his request is in no sense really owing to him. If he somehow claims the love of another in justice or by any title other than his own offer of love, he cheapens and destroys his own love. He makes himself unworthy of love.

It is the nature of woman to be structured for man. Scholastic philosophy, as we said, has to consider sex as an accident even though it is so influential in the formation of personality itself. Otherwise scholasticism would be confronted with the anomaly of having to say that all women must have husbands or could demand a husband in justice. Women would sin against their very nature by not marrying. In Hebrew thought masculinity and femininity are personal attributes. They constitute what a man or woman is. Woman is made for man. That is what the book of Genesis indicates when it states that Eve was taken from Adam and a wife must cleave to her husband. But, alluding to this primordial revelation, St. Paul, as we have seen, says that the union between man and woman symbolizes a greater mystery, the union of man with God. As Eve came from Adam, man came from God. As Eve's body was structured for Adam, man is structured for God and for perfect union with him. As we stated, the covenant of grace in the Old Testament is proclaimed under the symbol of marriage. God is the masculine element. Traditionally it was the man who initiated and arranged the marriage contract. Israel is the feminine element. It was the woman who responded in fidelity and love to the man's overture. But despite all structuring, despite all the indications of nature, the marriage was not considered valid from the beginning unless it was undertaken by both parties in perfect and complete freedom. Structure was viewed only as a condition and in no sense an exigetive cause of the marital relationship.

Because Hellenic scholastic thought is so very different from that in which God's original revelation was made, that which was the very heart and the real value of human existence according to that revelation—union with God in a familial kind of love —was relegated to the category of accident. To counterbalance the seeming upturning or reversal of values it was necessary to propose a new order, the supernatural, the order of elevation to God's own level of operation, to stand over against the natural order, the order of creation. In this system Redemption and consequently the Incarnation at times came to be seen as a kind of divine afterthought evoked by God's total goodness and love to rectify the mess man made by his initial rejection of that which was only accidental to his nature, perfect union with God.

In a previous chapter we mentioned the problem of divine immanence and transcendence which haunted all theologies outside of Israel. Pagan philosophy does not envision any personal relationship such as that of marriage as being possible between the gods and mankind at large. True, at times in the popular myths, human beings were used by the gods to breed heroes. But even in the myths of the gods one does not encounter a relationship like that of Israel with Yahweh. The gods normally have goddesses as their marriage-partners. And as we explained, the goddesses, though fully divine, reflect earthly and human qualities more than the sky-gods, and so are able to be perfect mediators between heaven and earth. In them both the transcendence and immanence of the divine is preserved for cosmotropic theology.

Scholasticism fell heir to the cosmotropism of Hellenic pagan philosophy. Thus it had to wrestle with the problem of the immanence and transcendence of the divine. The perfect paradigm, of course, was Christ. But what about other men? How can God's love be immanent in them and God remain transcendent? Goddesses, of course, were too crude a solution; the accidental supernatural order was the answer. Had Christian theology not reflected the anti-Semitism of the cultures in which it developed, had it seen Christ as fulfilling the Old Law and not destroying or replacing it, theologians today might not have been faced with the problem of the supernatural. The holistic personalism of Hebrew thought never conjured up any opposition between divine immanence and transcendence, and so did not have to preserve either the one or the other by creating goddesses or inventing a supernatural order.

Because it is personalistically and not cosmically orientated, Teilhardianism like Jewish thought admits only one order: that of God's love. As a free act creation itself is a manifestation of divine love. But the love of God is differentiated by the object toward which it is directed. The kind of love that God offered to man would have to be seen as personal love for man's personality resulted from it. But as a matter of fact the type of personal love that God offered to man and structured him to receive was one of the highest order possible, a familial kind of love, a love that elevated man to God's own level of operation. It did not have to be that way, but as a matter of fact the kind of love that God manifested toward man was one that *pares aut invenit aut facit*, a love of true friendship. Man was given the possibility of loving God not merely as his creature, but in some astounding way as his equal, as his cooperator, as his spouse, as a member of the divine family. Now this has to be the most gratuitous and absolutely freest love conceivable. In no way—if we can speak of love in relation to nature—could it correspond to man's nature, no matter how it might be conceived, but to his personhood alone. And man's personhood today cannot be seen, as it might have been in the Hellenic philosophy of the past, merely as a function of his nature rendering it concrete in the individual. Man's personality has to be the uniqueness of his very being; it has to be that which constitutes him a man, a free rational creature, an image of God, and in some mysterious way makes it possible for him to respond to God's elevating call. In his personhood alone man is free like God. Natures cannot be free; they must act according to the laws of their inner mechanisms. In his personhood alone man is in a sense a creator like God. Natures do not create; they merely cause. In his personhood alone man can truly love like God. Natures do not really love; they merely react to love. And such a reaction can be called love only in the symbolic sense of process philosophy.

When St. Thomas asks the question whether one can say that grace is created for man, he responds by stating that one ought rather to say that man is created in grace. He was too much of an existentialist not to see the trap posed in the original question. For Teilhard, too, it is clear that in no sense can one say that grace was created for man. Just the opposite is true. Man was created for grace. First in God's intention is the total grace that is Christ, the Omega. Then come other men. We have already elaborated on Karl Rahner's expression of this idea. All other men came to exist, and not merely to have a capacity for an elevated existence, because the Son of Man exists. The Divine Logos in the fullest sense mediates creation itself. All creation exists because of man, not any man, but the Man. The Divine Logos in his humanity is the Omega that gives meaning to all being and defines the process of which God is the ground. That is why Teilhard terms the world-process "Christogenesis." But the Divine Logos is also the Alpha through which the process came into being. This is so clearly the Pauline message that it is amazing that it should so long have been largely neglected in theology. Grace is not tailored to creation, to nature. The Incarnate Word does not come to exist because of man. Such an idea turns the real order topsy-turvy. It can emanate only from a cosmically-centered view, only from a philosophy which in attempting to preserve the primacy of God in the universe actually puts him in second place, and makes his action a response to contingency and his love only an accident. If grace is seen as an adjunct to creation, the only way its supreme and sublime dignity can be preserved is by terming it "supernatural."

But in a universe where God and his self-image from within, the Divine Logos, and from without, the Incarnate Logos, occupy the first and central position, creation, the cosmos, has to be viewed as an adjunct of grace, of God's presence through love. Nature, that is, process is tailored to suit grace. Man comes to exist as he is because of the Incarnate Logos.

Unencumbered by Hellenic cosmotropic thought-forms, the ancient Israelite was able to look upon creation as the first in a long series of God's *saving* acts. It was a kind of crypto-Manicheeism that arose from later theology's dualistic view of the natural and supernatural orders that led theologians to downgrade the secular as not pertaining to salvation. The receptivity of the Christian world today to secularization-theology presages its ennui with the distinction between the natural and supernatural orders. More and more writers today are calling the attention of the Christian community to the fact that Jesus was at some pains to redefine the relationship between the sacral and the secular among the people of his time. The ancient Jews had really never made any distinction. But when the people of Israel came under the dominance of the Romans questions like that about the coin of tribute were bound to arise. Certainly the distinction was rampant in pagan society, even from the earliest days of recorded history. With an almost humorous pathos a Sumerian inscription, dating possibly from the second millenium before Christ, laments the inhumanity of religion: "My wife is at the outdoor shrine; my mother is at a religious rite down by the river. And here I sit starving." Theologians today are telling us that Christ came to end all of that. In Christianity the measure of one's religious fervor is his concern for his fellow-man. St. James indicated in Apostolic times that religion exercised in detachment from worldly concerns like care of widows and orphans is vain. The central act of Christian worship, the paschal mystery of Christ, had its origins not in the Holy City, but in the countryside outside its walls, not in the magnificence of the Temple, but in the garbage-dump called Golgotha. It was not carried out in the caparison of high ritualism, but in nakedness. Its priest was consecrated not by anointing with oil, but with humanity itself. After this act there could no longer be any such thing as holy places, holy times, holy objects. The world itself became a sanctuary, and writers like Maximus the Confessor were able to speak of a cosmic liturgy. Schillebeeckx has pointed out that the early Christians were accused of atheism by their pagan contemporaries because they had no altar, no temple, no sacred objects. He alludes to the rejoinder of many of the Fathers that the Christians' workshops were their temples, their benches altars and their tools instruments of worship.

So it is with Teilhard that the whole process of evolution is considered sacred because it has been inaugurated in and tends toward Christ. Just as there can be no such thing as the purely natural after Christ, there cannot be anything wholly secular. The world is really Christ's world.

It was, then, the nature of Christ, God's grace *par excellence*, that determined the structuring of man, not viceversa. God does not bestow grace and what it leads to, the beatific vision, because man is intrinsically structured to receive it. Rather he equips man with an intrinsic ordination in his personality to grace and the beatific vision because of Christ, because of grace, because of his love present in this primordial manifestation of himself outside of himself. So in this perspective there can never be any question about the complete gratuity of grace. It is gratuitous by a two-fold title, that of creation itself, which is the absolutely free act of God, and that of love of friendship, which, as we have said, has of its very essence to be completely free.

In conclusion then we must ask the question whether the larval theology of today which we have expounded demands our abandoning entirely the term "supernatural" and relegating the concept it expresses to the darkened corridors of a theological museum. If we are tempted peremptorily to respond in the affirmative, we must remind ourselves that the concept does have, apart from all philosophical considerations, a valid and permanent theological content. This cannot be done away with. It must be sedulously safeguarded in any new formulation of thought. Grace must be seen, first, as an absolutely gratuitous undertaking of God, and, secondly, as his very special act in relation to man, calling him to be what he could not have been in any other order of creation. But in a person-oriented, existentialist process philosophy such as we have employed these two notions are automatically preserved and insured. For if God's love for man transforms him and makes him an image of the Incarnate Logos, a sharer in God's own life of love, it must be seen as something very special. This type of love has to be markedly distinct from that which God in some other order (non-real and only imagined) would owe man as his Creator. And if this type of personal love is, as it has to be, the most perfect love conceivable, then it has to be totally gratuitous, for as we have explained it is of the very essence of perfect love that it be freely bestowed and freely received.

If with these cautions we can lay aside the idea of the supernatural, the theology of grace will become much more intelligible and much more vital in today's world.

CHAPTER V

Justification

Among the effects of grace mentioned by the Council of Trent are numbered justification and the possibility of merit. The idea of sanctity is closely allied to the question of justification. The state of justification is basically one of formal sanctity. But there is marked confusion if not actual disdain manifested in modern attitudes toward these notions which are so intimately connected with the concept of grace. All of these ideas bear the definite connotation of a kind of legalism, perhaps even a tinge of Phariseeism, in the mind of many people today. Many experience a kind of ambivalence even in regard to sanctity. They want to be Christians, but not saints. This is true not only because of a kind of inferiority complex which some think is really humility or fundamental honesty, but also because of a definite misunderstanding of just what sanctity is. The word seems to connote weakness, lack of manliness, total submissiveness and suppression of aggressiveness. That is why men in more countries than the Latin ones feel exercises of piety are for women. *Machismo* casts out sanctity. Those aspects of the lives of the saints which have been signalized by spiritual writers of the past tend to reinforce this persuasion with the result that the very notion of sanctity has left a large part of the Christian populace quite apathetic in regard to this primary and most important element in the Christian life itself. The word "virtue" which radically signifies manliness and strength has created exactly the opposite impression in the minds and feelings of many. It seems absolutely necessary, then, to re-examine these basic concepts connected with the life of grace not only by tracing historically their original denotation in the language of theological and other writers of the past, but also by relating them to larval faith positions in the present.

Justification is defined by many as simply the application of Christ's redeeming act, performed objectively once for all, to the individual. Man is well aware of the fact that he is a sinner. He has personally violated the law by involving himself in evil actions. In the Roman world in particular great stress was laid on the idea of law. The Romans were perhaps the world's greatest law-makers. While the Greeks devoted themselves to philosophy and gave the peoples they conquered a memorable ideological and cultural heritage, the great Roman contribution to civilization is universally recognized to be a wise and extremely effective legal system. So we see that the idea of conversion from a life of lawbreaking, of sin, to a life of justice, of living in accordance with the law of God, is strongly emphasized in Western theology, especially in the works of Augustine, whose outstanding service to the development of Western theology was to recapitulate in a form most palatable for the Western mind the doctrine of the earlier Fathers of the Church. In the Eastern Fathers this idea is certainly in evidence, but occupies a secondary and much less important place. In their descriptions of the baptismal liturgy, for instance, the Western Fathers highlight as the effects of the rite the forgiveness of sin, absolution from an illegal status and, positively, participation in the life of Christ, the holy and just One. In the East, on the other hand, stress is laid almost exclusively on divinization. Through baptism one becomes a participant in God's own life. Such a situation obviously excludes sinfulness, but the main preoccupation of these writers is with the more positive aspects of this condition. While the Latins seem at times to be almost Pelagian in their insistence upon the personal exertion required to bring about a conversion, a change of life-style, the Orientals seem to be almost Lutheran in their devotion to the idea of the coming of the Spirit and the indwelling of the Trinity in the soul of the baptized. The idea of grace that we have presented thus far draws heavily from the doctrine of the Eastern Fathers, because the modern world is evidencing much less interest in legalism and much less concern about sin. But these ideas have to be squared off with the traditional view of Western theology.

Later theologians drew much of their doctrine from the works of St. Augustine and consequently have given it a definite legalistic cast. As we have already seen, Scotus maintained that grace and sin are not in metaphysical opposition. Grace excludes sinfulness because divine law has so ordered. St. Thomas, on the other hand, compares grace and sin to heat and coldness. The one metaphysically excludes the other. Though his doctrine on the question of justification leans toward legalism, he manifests a deeper awareness of the position of the Eastern Fathers (obtained most likely from parts of St. Augustine's writings in which it is at least adumbrated). While an in-depth study of St. Thomas' theory of justification would prove most interesting, it would not be consonant with the purpose of this book, since it is based fully on a philosophical perspective that has been largely rejected today. Analyses of the doctrine of the Angelic Doctor are presented in Maurizio Flick's *L'Attimo della giustificazione secondo S. Tommaso* and my *The Thomistic Concept of Justifying Contrition.*

The position of the Council of Trent on justification was almost totally precipitated by Protestant doctrine. Formulated initially by Martin Luther, the Protestant view declares that man is in reality forever a sinner. In justification he is not actually changed internally at all, but the hideousness of his sinful condition is hidden, as it were, by the cloak of Christ's own justice. Man can never undo the consequences of the fall. Redemption and reconciliation must always be seen as exclusively God's work. In no sense can it be an achievement of man himself. This is the clear message of the gospel. Man is able to do nothing but throw himself upon the mercy and loving good will of God. This he does in the act of fiducial faith. Good works will and must follow as the fruit of justification through God's grace, but because of them man can never have any merit that he can call his own for withal he remains a sinner in his inmost core. He is *simul justus et peccator*: at one and the same time both just and sinful. The justice he has is really the justice of Christ; all he has on his own is his sinfulness. No person or organization can mediate to the sinner the justice of Christ. It can be secured only through the highly personal act of self-humiliation required to place oneself entirely with full confidence in the hands of God through faith. The only act possible for man the sinner in the face of God is total self-abasement and acknowledgment of one's sinful condition. The gospel message promises that such an act will provide for the sinner, because of God's mercy, of course, and not because of the worth of the act itself, the wedding garment of Christ's own justice to hide his inner unworthiness.

Luther's doctrine had and still exerts a definite appeal precisely because of its genuine human quality. It arose because of Luther's own psychological difficulties with the principles of Catholic asceticism. He could rid himself of feelings of guilt and sinfulness only by acknowledging them, facing up to them. Doctrine, sacraments, spiritual exercises and counsel: all proved inefficacious in helping him. He had to believe that God demanded total self-abandonment. He trusted that God himself permitted these *Anfectungen* and would use them to good purpose.

While Luther's way was largely intuitional, Calvin, though accepting the basic idea of his predecessor in Protestantism about faith, tended to be more logical and systematic. For him faith itself was the result of the inner witness of the Spirit. That witness assured the believer of salvation. Revivalism much later would make this witness of the Spirit the most important factor in the conversion-process, in the decision for Christ. Calvin considered good works to be both necessary and possible. They gave further.testimony to the operation of the Spirit, evidenced the perdurance of justification, and betokened predestination.

Later Protestants tended to eschew a concept of faith which would primarily be involved with the dialectic of sin and justice. In this they followed Calvin more than Luther. For Spener faith was an encapsulated experience of the Christian life itself: the act of faith opened the individual to the outpouring of the Spirit and inaugurated an experience that was to be all-pervading and enduring. Zinzendorf viewed faith more as a mystical experience. The original insight of Luther about the importance of faith as an experience remained paramount, but the more positive aspects of justification as an encounter with the Spirit prevailed until neo-Orthodoxy under Barth redirected Protestant thought once again to the question of sin and justice.

The response of the Council of Trent to the Protestant challenge is difficult to summarize, but the central notion it proposes is that in justification sins are really and truly remitted. It definitely rejects the doctrine of mere non-imputation of sin, and moves the issue out of the sphere of pure legalism. In addition the Council teaches that justification brings about a real change, an internal and objective modification in the soul of the sinner. He is actually totally renewed by grace and the other supernatural gifts that come with it. A third key notion stressed in the teaching of the Council is that man is totally free in his acceptance or rejection of these supernatural gifts, and that faith which is not perfected by charity is not sufficient to justify. Over and above these basic doctrines the Council proposed many others less directly but nonetheless closely connected with the question of justification. Among these we might mention the Council's views on the operation of the sacraments, the role of the Church, the value of good works, and so forth. It is interesting to note that one of the leading theologians at the Council, when addressing the crucial problem of whether the just man was so constituted by a justice that he could really call his own or through an imputation of Christ's justice, favored a compromise with the Lutherans. He tried to conciliate them by advocating that the graced man was to be considered just by reason of a twofold title.

First of all, Christ's own justice was imputed to him. Through it he became fully and completely holy in the eyes of God. But in addition to this and because of it he had a justice that was truly his, one that at least partially resulted from the good works that he performed. Though this second justice was essentially imperfect in itself, it was, to be sure, one that had to be considered real and valuable. Needless to say, the Council did not accept this opinion in the decrees it advanced for promulgation.

One element in the doctrine about justification that is common to both Catholic and Protestant positions is that it is primarily the work of God. Justification does not result principally from any merely human efforts no matter how good and noble they might be. It is fully and exclusively the result of the operation of grace. On the other hand, the main area of difference lies in the fact that Protestant theology does not recognize any kind of objective change in the sinner, while Catholics insist that the justified person is actually internally transformed. Even in this point, however, there are some elements of agreement. Protestants seem to imply that the psychological change, the attitudinal change in the sinner resulting from his act of faith, is sufficient to produce in him the true likeness of the God-man that Catholics consider to be the very essence of the transformation they require. Then too, Catholics do not insist that the objective change they require is necessarily all-pervasive and totally constitutional. In a sense they too admit that the justified person is *simul justus et peccator*. Sanctity does not suffuse every facet of man's nature. It remains still under the influence of sin. Even the just man is subject to the tyranny of concupiscence. Though grace is remedial it leaves man free. And so it is possible for even the just man to fall.

In relation to the just man's susceptibility to sin St. Augustine proposed an idea that has been largely accepted in Catholic theology. He taught that in justification concupiscence *transit reatu, manet actu,* that is, though all guilt associated with man's infirm and sin-oriented nature is fully removed, his nature itself is not changed, and consequently he remains still a victim to the attraction of sin. St. Thomas too, as we have already mentioned, addresses himself to this question. Through his redemptive act Christ did not restore human nature as such, but only offered to individual persons the possibility of recouping the essential gift lavished upon man in his original creation in justice. In the present order when a man is justified his personhood primarily, and only indirectly through it his nature, is disposed favorably toward God. Basically his nature remains what it is, and since a man is not in complete control of his nature even through grace (unless that grace be an extraordinary one such as was given to the Blessed Virgin) man is still left with a radical proneness toward sin. If nature itself had been restored by Christ, not only would concupiscence have been destroyed, but man would enjoy immortality and the other preternatural gifts of the original state of justice. St. Thomas concludes that it is possible to fall from grace precisely because personality is essentially variable in man, and one can lose that disposition which through grace renders it acceptable to God.

There is no doubt that the question of justification has loomed so large in recent Catholic theology because of the emphasis placed upon it by the Council of Trent. And the Church would not have been so much concerned about it were it not for the fact that Protestant theology made so much of it. Yet Luther was faced with fundamentally the same dilemma in this connection as we are today with regard to the problem of the supernatural. Basically he had to attempt to reconcile intrinsicist and extrinsicist philosophy. Apart from his personal psychological difficulties, his mental disposition was principally a conservative one. Trained as he was in Nominalism, Luther could not help but favor an extrinsicist solution of the difficulty. He reacted against the new theology of his time, the so-called *devotio moderna* that was spreading through the Netherlands and giving rise to new schools of asceticism in the Church. Its chief theological positions were foreshadowed in the writings of the great "Father of German Mysticism," Meister Eckhart. Eckhart's works were at first proscribed because they appeared to reflect a kind of pantheism in the stress they placed upon the divinization of the human person through grace. But they were eventually to be vindicated when,

after the time of Luther, Denis Petau inaugurated his masterful
study of the teaching of the Eastern Fathers. But even before
the time of Petau, Eastern theological concepts were beginning
to filter into the Western Church. Up until that time the quasi-
legal or juridical effects of justification so dear to the Latins were
dominant. They were especially supported in the Nominalist
schools where the intentional order, the order of ideas and legal
entities, was apprehended as taking precedence over the ontological. When through the *devotio moderna* ideas similar to those
of Origen, Cyril of Alexandria and Maximus the Confessor began to be promulgated many theologians were shocked. The followers of Amalric of Bena and Joachim of Flora had launched an
analogous doctrine in the twelfth and thirteenth centuries and
were condemned. Up until the time of Petau authentic texts of
the Eastern Fathers were not fully and thoroughly studied. Consequently their real notions about divinization could not be appreciated and understood in their total context. Expressions of
this doctrine that characterized the *devotio moderna* were largely
borrowed from the pseudo-Dionysian writings. Here as in the
case of Amalric and Joachim the doctrines of the Eastern Fathers
were distorted and confused. Dionysian spirituality smacked of
gnosticism, pantheism and magic. It was redolent with expressions that skirted the heretical. It was not surprising then that
Luther reacted so violently against the New Theology and moved
to a position about justification so extremely opposed to the new
ideas that it too was bound to become heretical. The Council of
Trent gravitated around a middle position, retaining and emphasizing a legal and juridical notion of justification, but affirming
also its ontological aspects.

Since Luther claimed to have based his notions about justification on the doctrine of St. Paul, the Apostle's teaching was
bound to play a key role in the dialectic between Protestants
and Catholics. Paul treats of justification especially in the epis-
tle to the Romans, but there are important references to the topic
also in his letters to the Corinthians, Galatians, Ephesians and
Philippians as well as in his pastoral epistles. He speaks both of
the justice of God and of the justice of man. In reference to the

latter use, we call attention to the fact that he labels Christians as "children of justice" and encourages them to pursue the way of righteousness. He sees as links between the justice of God and the justice of man both faith and the law. He points up the futility of a justice emanating solely from the law. God's revelation has always inculcated faith as an absolutely necessary ingredient. In Romans and Galatians he argues that the justification that Christ preached was firmly rooted in Old Testament ideas. It opposed only the teaching of the Pharisees, according to which the fulfillment of the prescriptions of the law was the exclusive means of justification. In the famous fifth chapter of Romans a distinction is at least implied between the moment of justification and a lifelong dedication to the pursuit of justice. For the act of justification all that is required is faith. (Catholic theologians interpret this as *fides formata,* that is, faith informed by charity.) Without faith the works of the law are useless. But for the preservation of the state of justice and sanctity that results from this act good works also are needed. Abraham was justified even before he fulfilled the prescription of the divine law requiring circumcision precisely because he had faith. But to remain faithful he had to submit to the command of God and circumcise himself.

At first glance the doctrine of St. James seems to be diametrically opposed to that of Paul. That is why it upset Luther so much. James insists that for justification both faith and good works are necessary. And he seems to be referring to the moment of justification itself. Before one can be justified he must have accomplished some good work. But it may have been that St. James wanted only to correct certain misapprehensions of Paul's doctrine both on the nature of faith and the imminence of the parousia that were rampant in his time. Many had concluded from Paul's statement that all things were permitted to him that one who simply believed and was baptized had no further obligations. They had, in other words, failed to observe the distinction that Paul made between the moment of justification and the life of justice. If the parousia was at hand, the important thing was the present moment, not a future life in this world that was not to be. And they failed to comprehend that the faith that Paul was speaking of was an informed faith, that is, a faith suffused with love for God and one's fellow-man. They failed to understand the context in which Paul was speaking. He was addressing himself in particular to the Jewish community at Rome which had been obviously indoctrinated with the principles of Phariseeism. In his letter Paul excoriated these and reminded his readers that the law was fulfilled in Christ.

Pharisaical doctrine was at loggerheads with the orthodox traditions of Judaism itself. The Old Testament books clearly indicate how Israel became just: only because God took hold of his people and made them generally faithful to his covenant was Israel able to lay claim to any sanctity. According to the Pharisees fidelity to the prescriptions and traditions of the law constituted a person just. The fidelity they demanded was primarily related to the law itself, and only indirectly to God the author of the law. By faithful observance of the law it became possible for Israel to take hold of God. So the doctrine of the Pharisees exactly reversed the idea expressed in revelation. It took the initiative away from God and gave it to the observer of the law. Any religion which makes law paramount runs the risk of falling into Pelagianism. And this is exactly what Phariseeism had done. God was moved from the central position; tradition, which was mostly tedious rabbinical reflection on the revealed law, took his place.

Paul was at pains to show his readers that Christ in no wise modified the authentic notions of the Old Covenant. Christ did not come to abolish the law. Not one yod or diacritical mark was to be changed in God's original revelation to his people. The vagaries of the Pharisees had, however, substituted law for God. Observance of the law was the test of faith. One must concentrate on good works, on fulfilling the law, if faith was to be assured. By alluding to the story of Abraham, Paul showed his readers how erroneous a notion of the relationship between faith and the law the Pharisees had. He sets forth genuine faith as the acceptance of God's word, as a direct commitment to God in his person and not just in the law; and such a commitment, he says, is what justifies a person, not observance of the law. He implies, of course, that faith, once restored to its central position, will assure observance of the law. Because Abraham believed God's word, he obeyed God's command and circumcised himself. But the right order of things so clearly manifested in the Old Testament was reversed by the Pharisees and had to be restored by Christ. Faith as the work of God in man must occupy the central place in the reckoning of what makes a person just; and the accomplishment of the works of the law must be considered subsidiary to it.

So also in the other books of the New Testament the word *dikaiosyne* is used to signify something more than the justice of the Pharisees. Justice according to them is mere legalism; but for Christians it is an internal quality that is rooted in faith and love, not just external compliance with the law. As in the case of St. Paul, here too the term is employed in the fully personalistic and theotropic sense of the Old Testament and stands in stark contrast to the mechanistic and anthropotropic attitude inculcated by Pharisaical aberration.

True, as it is used in the Old Testament the root *sdq* is strictly a legal term. It signifies the justness and correctness of a juridical decision. In an applied sense the word was used when a person was declared innocent of having committed some crime. To render a decision of innocence when a person was apprehended as actually guilty was grossly unjust according to Old Testament usage of the word "justice"; so God does not justify, but punishes the sinner. There is only one instance (Is. 53, 11) where the word is used in the way it so often is in the New Testament —to signify the action by which one who is actually guilty of sin is rendered innocent. Here it is stated that the Servant of the Lord, when he comes, will justify many people. The scarlet of their sin will be converted into the whiteness of innocence. The action of the suffering Servant is no mere legal decision: if it were it would be untrue and unjust. Rather, through his Servant Yahweh will convert an objective and factual state of guilt into an equally objective and true condition of innocence. Then and then only a just decision of innocence can be rendered.

There is adequate evidence then in Scripture to conclude that the idea of justice as used both by Jews and Christians implies much more than a mere relationship to the law. In the New Testament especially the highly personal implications of the state of justice for man are scored. The New Testament too adumbrates an idea which, later on, we find to be so fascinating for the Fathers. A person's justice before God exists as the result of a divine act through which he is given a new mode of existence in which he can reflect the divine attribute itself.

If today the word "justice" conjures up thoughts of legalism, if it is hard for the modern mind to grasp the notion that grace as love is really freedom from the law simply because it is conceptually linked with justice, this is due to the historical and theological development of the idea of justice in the Western Church. What originally was only connoted by the term "justice" has now become its chief element. Not that this is an unusual phenomenon in the development of languages; to be sure, historical conditioning of words can often bring about a complete reversal of meaning. Few people, for instance, realize that the word "girl" originally meant boy.

The English word "justice" is derived from the Latin *jus* which everyone who knows the language will say means law or right. But the Latin word is actually a homonym. It means law all right; but it can also mean broth, soup or sauce. Both meanings must be traced to an original form of the word (from which the word *jugum* "yoke" is also derived) which signified something joined or brought together. This Latin root is akin to the Sanskrit *yu* which means to join or bring together. Now according to philologists both the Celtic-Greco-Italic (whence Latin) and the Iranian-Indic (whence Sanskrit) language-stems have a common origin in the ancient Aryan. Here the pertinent word *ja* or *ju* means to boil. In one of its applications the word may well have referred to a kind of alchemy with religious implications. One might think of the medieval witches' brew in which certain ingredients endowed with magical power were boiled to release the forces by which this power was bound to material elements. It was then after being loosened by boiling to be reused in binding men's wills and lives to shape for them a new destiny. Even in our highly sophisticated society in the cauldron of a cyclotron or linear accelerator the miracle-man of our day, the atomic physicist, seeks to release the binding force of atomic particles to produce astounding energies which can indeed shape the destiny of mankind for weal or woe.

Though it is what we think of immediately when we hear the word *jus*, "law" is only a derived or secondary meaning, as the term is applied in the intentional order. What is primarily signified is something much more objective and real: force or power.

If this is true, we can immediately understand how the word *juju* is related to the concepts we are considering. The power of a god or of supernatural forces in general stands in stark contrast to the weakness of man. Before such power man must react with awe, fear and trembling. The nuclear-fusion bomb is today a juju that has affected every stratum of life from world politics to home-planning.

In our society the word *jus* understood as law signifies the weakest of all bonds, legal power. But originally it implied the strongest of all bonds, that of abject and helpless fear in the face of an irresistible and ineffable power. We can easily see then how it might also in ancient times have denoted a binding force that can once in a while be stronger than fear itself. We can see its relation to love.

The Romans called their chief deity Jupiter (*Jupater*), the father of power. The Greeks called theirs Zeus. But if we analyze the Greek word "Zeus" we will be struck with the parallelism of thought in Latin and Hellenic society. For the word "Zeus," scholars think, comes from the Greek verb *zeō* which also means to unite, or more radically, to boil.

It is interesting to note how the word *Zeus* is declined. For construct states a derivative of the word *dis* meaning "double" is employed. Thus the genitive of *Zeus* is *Dios* the dative *Dii*, etc. One is tempted to conclude that while standing in the absolute state, the nominative, the word for the Greek father of the gods had the connotation of power and authority, and inspired in his votaries a corresponding feeling of awe and respect. But in the construct states, in grammatical relationships that would involve him verbally more intimately with human situations, a word that might indicate that he is really the double, the image, of man is pressed into service. Thus he might be considered more approachable and less awe-inspiring.

There is in the concept of power another element that is hinted at in the ancient terms that were used in relation to it. If magical, divine power is really to bind men, to hold them spell-bound in fear and awe, it must be clearly perceived by them. It must be open and evident. Otherwise it is useless. It itself is bound. That is why words which in the most primitive usage signify boiling come eventually to mean power. When, for instance, meat was boiled to nourish the sick, its healing, life-giving power was loosed from its cruder elements and concentrated in the broth. It was, as it were, the distillation of the powers of the cosmos itself that formed many ancient peoples' concept of the gods. Juju was concentrated and evident power boiled out of cosmic stuff.

In English "righteousness" is a synonym for justice. The old English word "riht" meant straight and undeviating. Most people are right-handed. The right hand is the chief source of power, of human strength. The right hand is strong, straight and sure. It goes without deviation to its mark. It is perfectly controllable. The *left* hand is literally that. It is what remains of human power, what is left over after consideration of the power of the right hand. The old English word "lyft" eventually came to signify something weak, almost worthless. Now if people did not deviate from the normal, from the general rule, one would expect them to be right-handed. The source of their power would be apparent to everyone. Everyone would know how to deal with them, how to react should they choose to display their power. Thus the word "right" came also to indicate a source of power that was open, predictable, and able to be dealt with by others. Eventually it began to imply frankness and honesty itself. On the other hand, a person who is unpredictable, sly, devious, full of tricks and surprises, a person who hides the source of his power with the presumption that he wants to use it malevolently is called sinister. The word "sinister" comes from the Latin *sinistra* meaning the left hand. The left-handed person departs from the norm. One really does not know how to deal with him. His reaction is always surprising because it is not the expected one. He can easily gain the advantage over one who is looking for the usual, normal, ordinary response. His is a non-conforming, secret power that can easily be used to deceive, that can easily be geared for evil.

We can see now how the word "justice" eventually came to be applied to law. Law is a power that overrides the power of individuals and makes them conform its use to standard, pre-dictable, clear and undeviating modes of operation. The automobile has tremendous power. It can destroy life and property. But the existence of a traffic code reduces the threat it poses. The law assures me that an auto will stop at a red light so I can walk in safety in front of it. Legal norms provide universally understood and accepted modes for the use of power. Because of them I am reassured. I know how to deal with a tremendous potentially threatening power like that of the automobile. I can predict how the power of a vehicle will be used in different circumstances. From the law I generally know what I must fear and what I must dare. I know what rights I have. I know what power I and others have.

If the word "justice" is applied chiefly in the legal sphere today, we ought to trace the original significance of the word "legal." Obviously, it too is derived from a Latin term meaning "to bind." It also has to do with the binding and loosing of power. It also is involved with the norms set up for the right and correct, the evident and undeviating use of that power.

We can see now how faith is tied up with justice. It is really an essential element of justice. For faith is a reliance on the right use of power. A power that is open and frank, a power that is truly just, inspires faith. Faith gives the individual in confrontation with power an assurance of personal safety. And faith engenders in the individual, in response to and in conformity with the example of a superior power, the desire to establish a norm for the right and just use of his own.

While all ancient peoples saw their gods as just, only the Israelites could apply that term most appropriately to their God. Consequently only they in imitation of him and under his direction could employ that term in its fullest sense of themselves. The gods of the gentiles were hidden gods. Their power was in the cosmos; it had to be boiled out by magic and ritual. But even then it was capricious and mysterious. But the God of Israel was different. His people always knew this. But especially at the time they were nomads in the desert did they apprehend their God as a just and righteous one. He was El 'alyōn, the power exalted above all the earth. He was 'Elî, the power who was situated even above Sinai, in a position for all to clearly see and comprehend. But he was also Yahweh, the one who moved with his nomadic worshippers, whose power was constantly felt. His wonders were always manifested to his people. He was a God whose power was in no way hidden. From his position above all he could direct his followers wandering aimlessly, it seemed, through the vast wastes of the desert. But his leadership of his people was assured because he was just. If only the people had faith in him, if only they trusted his power, they would follow the right path.

Quite different was the movement of Yahweh from that of the gods of the agrarian peoples. These were gods whose seat was fixed; they were clan gods, village gods. The only movement they knew was cyclic. It followed the turn of the seasons. It was a divine oestrous cycle, pursuing a never-ending pattern of birth, fertility, fruitfulness and death. Yahweh, on the other hand, moved on a linear course. From his position on high he was not only aware of all the peoples of the world, but he could clearly see the goal he set for his own and point out the direct, the straight, the right way to it. Yahweh was a God of purpose and direction. He was a God whose action was predictable, not because it followed a regular cycle, but because it was frank, honest and open; it was right and just. The course Yahweh would take was announced to his people, and because Yahweh was just his people knew that he would be faithful to his promises.

Because Yahweh was a just God, he was also seen by his people to be a holy God. He was *qādôś*. He was unalloyed, unweakened, total, full, solid, whole. He was the only one who was secure in the possession of his being. He alone because of his pure, unadulterated power was not affected by the vicissitudes of life. Because his power was absolute, Yahweh was holy. Before his holiness, his people could only stand in fear, respect and awe. They stood like the Seraphim proclaiming his holiness. They stood before him as before a king who has absolute power over life and death, who is able to effect his will in the fullest way possible upon his subjects. And they wished to be like him. They wanted to share his holiness. They wanted to participate in his strength, health and security.

As we have said, for people today holiness does not mean the same thing it meant for the people of Israel. Like "justice" the word "holiness" has undergone an historical evolution which has reversed its original meaning. Many today associate holiness with weakness, insecurity, neurotic anxiety, natural unwholesomeness: the holy person is the one who has to rely on God; he is not able to stand on his own two feet. Yet the English word "holy" in its original denotation was a very good translation of the Hebrew *qādôś*. For it comes from the Anglo-Saxon word *halig* which meant healthy, strong, wholesome. Transfer of meaning probably occurred when Greek and Latin translations reflected a derived sense of the Hebrew word instead of its root meaning. The word *qādôś* of course, was also applied ritualistically to refer to health-giving food, blessings, etc. Thus it was charged with a definite religious tone. To convey the notion of religious holiness instead of soundness or health, the Greek word *'agiotēs* was used in translation, whereas *'ygieia* would have been more appropriate. The Latin followed by employing *sanctitas* in place of *salus*. In Latin Church usage *salus* came to be reserved for references to the final goal of the process of sanctification where total and absolute security was achieved in the pursuit of personal wholesomeness and power. Thus the notion of the incompleteness and relative weakness of any state of spiritual health in this world came to the fore. In their desire to score pride and false security in the life of grace spiritual writers put too much emphasis on the essentially weak condition of the human being in this world and his constant need of divine help. So they tended in their descriptions of the lives of the saints to lavish attention upon the miraculous and supernatural with the result that their subjects were often deprived of their true humanity. Purely human strength and power were more likely than not to be downgraded with the result that the saints often appeared as almost inhuman, vapid and seemingly neurotic individuals whose sanctity was hardly something to be emulated. An attempt to counteract this tendency was evidenced in the efforts, for instance, of St. Francis who extolled the humanity of Christ, and of Luther who, according to Helmut Gogarten, held that in the question of justification one should forget about God and rely solely on the humanity of Christ.

We could institute a similar linguistic analysis of the notion of merit. Today it also is seen in the light of a prevalent religious legalism. Very often spiritual writers and theologians themselves attempt to set up a kind of calculus of merit. The more virtues one amasses, the holier he becomes, and the holier one is, the more he can merit. Such authors are often oblivious of the derivation of the word "merit," from the Greek *meros* which means "part." The original significance of the word "merit," too, hearkens back to the idea of divinization. Through love the graced individual comes to share in the divine life. Hence his actions become in some limited way theandric. As he shares in the divine life his actions, too, become in some symbolic sense divine actions. His charity is really a manifestation of God's own love. That is why, for instance, the love of the Christian community lavished upon the infant when he is baptized is really the sacrament, the symbol, of divine love. In some true sense it is God's own love, and so it can be a pledge and guarantor of divine grace and protection. Merit is defined as that quality of an act which makes it deserving of a reward. But in the Christian system this has to be love. And love is indeed its own reward. The fuller explicitation of this love when it is consummated in a death that images that of the God-man is not to be seen as something essentially different from the less perfect state of union that love of God initially implies, but only as a further development and better appreciation of it. For the Christian, merit is intelligible only in terms of love. He knows full well that he can have no merit of his own apart from the working of God's love in him. In this context merit has to be referred to the good will of the divine lover in trying to provide for his beloved all that their love suggests. Merit itself then is simply an expression of love which as such tends further to stimulate, unfold and augment love. It is the part, the share one has in God's all-consuming love.

Traditionally theology has stressed the therapeutic value of the justification-event in a person's life. When he is justified, an individual is converted from a life of sin, from a state of radical sickness, to salvation, to a condition of spiritual health. He is cured of evil and enabled to dedicate himself wholeheartedly to the pursuit of the good. And this cure is effected through the openness and power that love brings to him. He is cured by becoming just. Carl Rogers has set down three conditions which must be met if one is to have a genuinely psychotherapeutic relationship with another. His first requirement is congruence. There can be no masks or defenses to hide the true selves of those involved in such a relationship. There can be no fronts or façades. Both parties to the relationship must strive to maintain an attitude that is completely open so that each may see the full strength of the other. In the justification-process the power of God, his justice, is made evident to the sinner through faith. By opening himself to acknowledge his own sinfulness and repenting of the evil that marked his past life the person called to grace manifests both his own appreciation of God's justice, as well as his desire to be like God in this regard. So there is achieved between God and the sinner a state of congruence that is based on justice and will promote a truly therapeutic relationship.

The second element that Rogers considers essential to the climate of therapy is an unconditional positive regard. This means that each partner in the relationship must look upon the

others with complete concern and benevolence. This look must
be focused upon the good that is in the other. In other words,
each must truly accept and love the others as they are. And this
love cannot be a conditioned one. It cannot be made dependent
upon the fulfillment of any requirement on the part of the
persons involved. It must take each exactly as he is, but, of
course, with the hope of transforming all in the new relationship
into better and healthier individuals by curing any disease that
might affect or impede the full cooperation of the parties. It
must be, in other words, love of the highest order, perfect bene-
volent love. After congruence is established between God and
the sinner in the process of justification, the dynamic of love
can go into full-blown operation. As we have explained in the
chapter on grace, this love takes the sinner as he is, but in its
very grasp it transforms him, frees him and gives him a share
in the divinity itself, a new power to act that is so resplendent,
so numinous, so ineffable that it can be seen only as a reflection
of divine justice itself, but a power that truly belongs to the one
who was and still in a sense is a sinner, a power he can claim
only through God's loving largesse as his very own. Through
God's positive regard the justified person can see himself as *simul
justus et peccator.*

The third condition required for the fostering of a truly
therapeutic relationship according to Rogers is empathic understanding among the participants. Once the foundation of love
is laid it is possible for the involved persons to see themselves
as deeply involved with one another. Each is a part of the
other in a dyad, and they have set up between themselves a
project in which each has a part, in which each plays an essential role. In this relationship it is necessary that each be completely sensitive to the other, that each have an understanding
of the feelings of the other, that each respond to the other as
he would want him to, and that each complement the other in
the relationship they have established. In the process of justification, of course, as we have already explained, the Incarnation
itself is the basis for empathy. The relationship between God
and the justified person is patterned upon the Incarnation. It is

the Incarnation that makes such a relationship possible and real. The Incarnation brings it out of the merely intentional order, the order of thought and will-action, and makes it existential. Because of the Incarnation justification is not mere nominalism, not just a question of legality or formalism, but a fact.

The very words, then, which tradition has employed in describing the process of justification—justice, holiness, merit—contain larvally in their original denotation a theological significance which is in no sense inconsonant with today's expectations. The concept of justice associated with grace by no means weakens, but, as we have explained, rather re-enforces and buttresses our description of grace precisely as love. For it is only as the clearly evident and overwhelming power of love that justice itself can be fully understood. This conception places in correct perspective the relationship of grace to the law and thus solves a problem that has long perplexed theologians: how grace can be considered as freedom from the law and at the same time bind the graced person to perform the works of the law. Grace must, as Scripture indicates, free a person from the law. It must loosen one from the lower, earth-bound, death-dealing (as St. Thomas would have it) binding force of law. It must center power where it ought to be, in God. As love it has to bind a person directly to God; it must impart a share in his own power, his own justice. A person in love knows how to deal with, how to please his beloved, and this comes from love itself, not from any universal law or book of etiquette. Only the person who is truly in love can be absolutely sure even of himself. Only he can know that he is absolutely right. Only he can be fully undeviating and single-minded. Grace is the love that boils out the binding force, the power that is in the law and reconstitutes it in a higher, more evident and more cogent order, its own, that of love itself. Love sets a totally new norm over and above that of the law. For only the beloved can really know how he must deal with the person who loves him.

Justification then means love. It is the person in love alone who really has power beyond his own. Only he has an openness that is unparalleled and yet always correct. Only he in his love constitutes for himself a norm that is all-embracing and absolutely undeviating. He alone is absolutely predictable as to how he will use the power that is his by virtue of love. He alone is just.

Finally we must say that whenever the idea of the supernatural is attenuated, as it may seem to have been in our ideas from what we said in the last chapter, one runs the risk of being accused of espousing pure humanism and thus of having abandoned Christianity itself. Of course, as Barth says, if theology becomes completely humanistic, if God is not made to stand over and against man as his Creator and Lord, then the value of the Incarnation itself is lost, and the supreme dignity of man flowing from it is also gone. Humanism in religion would destroy the very thing it wants to establish. By centering our theology of process in the Incarnation we really have not made it humanistic, but fully Christian. But if there is any doubt still about a value having been lost, the very idea of justification which we have presented should be reassuring. For we have insisted that only God can forgive sin. Only God has that much power, that much justice. If the believing person feels that his sins are forgiven, that fact has to be seen as the perfectly free and extraordinary exercise of the power of God; it has to be seen as the totally undeserved and special work of God's love which as a matter of fact in the final analysis is his real power. And if the justified person's own justice is actually a share in the numinal power of God, it is in no way commensurate with his own unaided human capacities and abilities. So it would have to be said that no matter how far man can advance in improving himself and his condition in the world, no matter how perfect he can become by himself, he could never even begin to attain the level of the divine. He could never justify himself. He could never become the ultimate norm according to which one might judge what is just or unjust.

Of course, this is not to deny that man has some definite power for good, some justice that he can truly call his own. This is not to say, as Protestantism often did, that man of himself is totally corrupt and that he corrupts whatever he touches.

What it avers is that man by himself cannot attain to a share in divine justice. Just how his own ability to do good, his autochthonous justice, is related to God's grace will be the principal topic of the next and following chapters of this book. We can in conclusion recapitulate this one by proposing the five principles about justification that Charles Moeller contends are held by all truly Christian confessions. First, it must be admitted that only God can impart the divine: only God can give God. Secondly, man's very essence is to be free; in justification he must freely cooperate with God in order to become graced. Thirdly, justification is not some kind of metaphorical expression; it is a reality: it changes the sinner and makes him holy. Fourthly, grace and justification are strictly personal commodities. But fifthly, justification is not merely a personal event; it affects the whole of creation.

CHAPTER VI

Actual Grace

In our treatment of the process of justification we insisted that it is primarily the work of God. But, following the lead of the Council of Trent, we also stressed the necessity of human cooperation. Justification is primarily but not exclusively the work of God. Man has a part in it. And the state of justice that results from man's cooperation with God's offer of love is a common mode of existence which he shares with God. In it both God and he play a part. It is God's own justice as well as his own that he possesses. Though fundamentally this condition of common possession is a deep mystery of faith that we cannot fully understand, we can get some grasp of it by comparing it with the paradigm of human love which we discussed in the chapter on grace. It is a condition that both Scripture and the mystics have described as a marriage between God and man. In marriage it is easy to see that the common way of life is achieved through the free contribution of each partner not only of his full love but also of all his possessions in regard to the

other. The partners in marriage really change their whole mode
of existence in the world. The permanent state of truly common
existence that results from total commitment is itself a sign and
sacrament of total self-giving, of perfect love. This is easy
enough to see even when the analogy is applied to the graced
person's relationship with God. But is this analogy valid also in
the case of the preliminaries to marriage? What is the condition
of the love of the prospective partners before they have made
a full commitment? How does the love of courtship differ from
that of marriage? Does love play a role in what we have called
the seduction process? The theologian must ask these questions
about the preliminaries of the graced state. How does the process of being graced start? Who initiates it, God or man? What
exact role does God play, what role does man have in the
process?

To make it easier to answer these questions, since the late
Middle Ages theologians have distinguished two different kinds
of grace. The first, habitual grace, they considered to be a permanent personal quality corresponding to full commitment, to
the enduring relationship of love between God and man which
is so much like marriage. The second, actual grace, they envisioned as the transient attraction of God's love affecting principally man's condition before his full commitment, during the
state which might correspond in human love to flirtation, seduction and engagement. Modern theologians rightly see habitual
grace as central, as the *propter quod unumquodque tale et illud
magis* of all grace. It has to be the root from which actual grace
springs. That is why we have chosen to deal with it first, though
others reverse the process. But the ancient Fathers and theologians, seemingly like Scripture itself, were much more concerned with what we would call actual grace. When they used
the term "grace" without qualification seemingly it invariably
meant what later theology was to recognize as actual grace. This
is not to say that they were not at all interested in the condition
that medieval theology was to dub "the state of grace." But
they did not often use the word "grace" to describe it. Much
in the vein of the Dutch catechism of our own time they viewed

it simply as the Christian life itself. They were more apt to call it "life" than "grace." For the Doctor of Grace himself, St. Augustine, the big problem about grace was whether a man could begin to live the Christian life without it. To that question he, in general unanimity with the other Fathers, responded with a resounding "No," saying that God's grace, God's special help was absolutely necessary to bring a person to the condition of being a Christian, of being saved. The further question then of just what a good man could accomplish without that help was also posed. Much later theology was to ask the more sophisticated question of whether even the justified person, the person who possessed habitual grace, also stood in need of the help of actual grace. The issue of actual grace opens up more fully and more squarely the problem of just what part man can play, and what must be attributed exclusively to God and the operation of his love, in the process of human salvation.

Before we address ourselves to more specific issues we must first inquire why actual grace was considered to be of such paramount importance in patristic times and consequently in the tradition of the Church about grace. We must understand by the term "actual grace" what the early writers meant: God's help given to man to draw him toward the state of divinization, of justification and eventual salvation. The chief acts preceding justification for which actual grace was deemed necessary were (1) some initial pious interest in the data of revelation, (2) attraction to faith, (3) the act of faith, (4) hope in God, (5) sorrow for sin because of fear of divine punishment, or because of the ingratitude sin manifests toward the Creator who has been so good to his creatures. In short, any good act performed from a motive of faith, but not as yet influenced by charity, required the assistance of actual grace, as did also those acts directly leading to the act of faith itself.

The interest of the earliest Fathers of the Church in actual grace quite obviously stems from the great emphasis it receives in the New Testament. The gospel of St. John (1, 9) seems to be referring to something more than the mere power of human reason when it speaks of a light enlightening every man that

comes into the world. The early Christians viewed Christ as a
new Orpheus charming the world with the dulcet tones of his
doctrine. John makes an even clearer and more definite reference to the fact that the heavenly Father must himself draw
to faith anyone who is to believe in that doctrine, and that a
person has to be docile to the beckoning of God if he is to reap
the benefits of faith in Christ (6, 44-45). Finally, it points up
the absolute impotence of the human individual in the matter of
his own salvation when it puts into the mouth of Christ the
words: "Without me you can do nothing" (15, 5). In the Acts
of the Apostles (16, 14) there is a striking allusion to the operation of God in leading a person to faith in the statement that
the Lord opened the heart of Lydia to understand the real implications of Paul's speech. The writings of Paul himself constantly
reflect or imply the operation of actual grace. Several times it is
described as illumination or enlightenment (Eph. 1, 18; II Cor.
4, 6 for example). Through it one receives the spirit of wisdom
(Eph. 1, 17). Paul's own efforts in regard to the Christian message are viewed as the planting of a seed; development and
growth are attributed to the direct action of God himself (I Cor.
3, 6). These few examples of the many which could be given
illustrate why the Church from earliest times was so much concerned with the elaboration of a theology of actual grace.

But later on, in the time of St. Augustine, there can be no
doubt that this concern and interest was greatly heightened because of the ideas of Pelagius and his followers. Unfortunately
we have very few of the original writings of this heresiarch.
Much of what we know about his doctrine is excerpted from
the arguments of his adversaries against him. Recently Robert
F. Evans has published a new appraisal of his life and ideas.

Pelagius was born in Britain around the year 354. He seems
not to have been a priest when he came to Rome about 380,
but nonetheless he became a spiritual adviser to many prominent
persons, both ecclesiastical and lay. Because his ideas seemed
so clear and so logical, because they responded so well to a deep
human instinct, he exerted a great influence upon these people
and won their sympathy for his cause. Very early in the four

hundreds he went to Africa with his *fidus Achates,* Coelestius. Eventually he reached Palestine, but later returned to Rome. After his ideas were officially challenged he literally vanished into thin air, and there is no record of what happened to him personally.

Theologians have singled out the basic error of Pelagius about grace. He denied its internal nature. They say that for him grace is simply the external helps God offers to man in the pursuit of salvation. Precisely as external these helps merely facilitate what the will, absolutely speaking, can accomplish by its own internal resources. Pelagius' view about grace is rooted in his ideas about original sin. He thought it absurd to think that the perfect freedom of the human individual can be intrinsically affected by the sin of another. There can be no such thing as original sin as it was traditionally conceived. The so-called results of original sin are mere modalities of the human condition as such. Thus, for instance, death is not to be considered as a punishment for sin, but merely as the natural lot of mankind, as for animals. All humans who die in infancy unquestionably go to heaven since they have in no way offended God; they are totally incapable of doing so. (Later on, as we shall see, this doctrine was modified). While even in those times heretical doctrine as such was to make relatively little impact upon the theological world, and Pelagius may well have escaped notice entirely were it not for the practical implications of this particular idea of his, any doctrine which affects the cherished and time-honored customs of Christians was bound to be limelighted. When some of his followers began to discontinue the practice of baptizing infants, Pelagius, despite the fact that there were no newspapers, radio or TV, became notorious. He was forced to set up a rationale for his doctrine. Redemption was described by his followers much after the fashion of the gnostics of earlier days as being important not because of what it ontologically effected *per se,* but only because of the good example and comfort it afforded. Prayer for others was considered as useless, as being of no avail even in saving souls, since a man can be saved only through the proper direction of his own will. Pelagius also denied that there could be such a thing as predestination. For him God was a mere spectator in the drama of human salvation.

In 411 the bishop of Carthage summoned Coelestius to face a Council to answer charges against his and his mentor's opinion about infant baptism and original sin. It is interesting to note how elusive a character Pelagius himself was. While he was a thinker and was able to inspire a great theological movement, he largely left the promulgation of his ideas up to his more enthusiastic lieutenants. Apparently he himself was so low-keyed, so self-effacing, so quiet and retiring that the original charges against the movement he had inaugurated were not directed against him, but against his friend Coelestius. When Augustine heard that Pelagius intended to visit Palestine he sent his disciple Orosius to the Holy Land to warn St. Jerome of the heresy. A council of bishops in Jerusalem in 415 considered charges against Pelagius, but its findings were not conclusive. Finally Bishop John of Jerusalem referred the question to Rome. The Synods of Diospolis and Carthage had also by this time reviewed the doctrine of the Pelagian party. But Pope Zosimus seemed convinced of its basic orthodoxy. The Pelagians had apparently successfully defended their views at Diospolis, with the result that that Synod dropped its original charges against them. Pope Zosimus then simply warned Pelagius not to agitate any further. But though Pelagius himself seemed inclined to pursue the quiet and peaceful life, some of his devotees were much more rabid. They kept pushing until finally riots and other civil disturbances broke out in Rome. The Emperor Honorius was constrained to expel Pelagius from the City in 418. Meanwhile the Sixteenth Council of Carthage had concluded its deliberations about the alleged heresy. It specifically condemned a number of ideas attributed to Pelagius, excommunicated him and forwarded its findings to Pope Zosimus. The Pope eventually ratified the anathemata pronounced by the Council against the heresiarch. At this point Pelagius disappeared, but his doctrine continued to be propagated especially by Julian, the Bishop of Eclanum, against whom Augustine inveighed.

The body of doctrines that eventually came to be known as

Pelagian was perhaps not in all its aspects the direct result of the heresiarch's thinking. While the core principles were undoubtedly his, these were modified and adapted by others like Coelestius, Leporius and Julian of Eclanum. The following notions came in the course of time to be recognized as the principal teachings of Pelagianism:

1. There is no such thing as original sin in the sense of one which internally affects the descendants of Adam and renders them liable to eternal condemnation unless it is remitted through baptism.

2. There is no such thing as the supernatural. Whatever man needs to attain the end God has established for him is owing to him in strict justice.

3. Man through his own natural powers is able to avoid all personal sin and achieve a state of justice which will be rewarded in heaven.

4. If one speaks of grace, the greatest gift of God to man, the grace nonpareil is man's own free will. In his creation man was endowed with free will, and through the correct use of it he can work out his own salvation.

5. The law of God by which man knows clearly what he must do to be saved, the Scriptures, and the example of Christ and the saints can also be considered as graces. These are, of course, only external aids to man in working out his salvation. They were and are not absolutely necessary, but they make it easier for man to accomplish what is needed to attain the goal God has set for him.

6. The tradition of the Church requiring the baptism of infants is correct, for without baptism infants cannot get into the kingdom of heaven about which the Scriptures speak. One can reach the kingdom only by becoming an adopted son or daughter of God. Baptism is the covenant of this adoption. But a distinction has to be recognized between heaven as a kingdom and heaven as eternal life or the everlasting vision of God. Infants dying without baptism can attain eternal life, that is, the vision of God, but

they do not do so as members of the kingdom. Hence they do not enjoy the full glory that accrues to Christians in heaven.

7. The remission of sin is one of the effects of God's grace. But this grace of forgiveness is not supernatural and internal; it is purely natural and external.

8. One may, as the Scriptures do, speak of some graces as an internal illumination. But such graces are in no sense supernatural, or the result of any special action of God. Everyone has an ability to appreciate the significance of God's revelation. Like existence itself and free will, this has to be seen ultimately as a gift of God, and so it can be called a grace. But it does not manifest any special or extra-ordinary divine concern or providence.

9. If God does at times give an individual some special help, if he does at times intervene to bestow supernatural grace, he cannot do it arbitrarily. Such grace has to be meted out in accordance with a person's merits.

These specific teachings of the Pelagians might well be seen as emanating from a basic philosophical orientation that has as its chief objective the avoidance of three key difficulties indigenous to the traditional approach to the relationship between man and God in the question of human salvation:

1. If supernatural grace is needed for and effects a person's salvation, then the great marvel of God in creating man, the free human will, is rendered useless or at least minimized in relation to the very goal (and the only possible goal) of human life itself.

2. God cannot demand the impossible of man; therefore man must be able with his own merely human power to observe the law and fulfill any requirements that God has set down for the attainment of the end and purpose of life.

3. God would have to be considered an acceptor of persons—he would not be really just in providing equal opportunity for all and giving each man what is due to him—if

without any recognition of merits, he would give grace to one person and deny it to another.

Obviously then the fundamental error of Pelagianism is that in considering the relationship of God to man, in examining the part that each has to play, in the process of salvation, to preserve and maintain the rights and dignity of man, God's own are denied or given second place.

Pelagianism is not just an historical contingency that we could pass over lightly in elaborating a theology of grace for our time. Of all the heresies that have existed in the Church it is the one that is most alive and influential today. In some larval form it is reflected in the chief philosophies of the current day. In considering the question of the supernatural in the light of process philosophy we had to take great pains to avoid it. While existentialism is so attractive and provides so much that is beneficial in explaining to a modern audience traditional theological truths, in its totality—as it is expounded fully by its originators—it has to be rejected because logically it leads to atheism or agnosticism. This is true because radically it is Pelagian. It extols man's power of freedom to the point of eliminating God. In his work *The Flies* Sartre points up this fact in Orestes' taunt to Zeus. God erred in creating man free. He really freed man from himself. If man has a free will he no longer needs God. God can no longer be his Lord and Master. Man's free will and not God must be the sole power in which he places his full reliance. The reason that Sartre is an atheist is that basically he cannot reconcile the complete dominion and absolute power that a God must have with the facticity of human freedom. For him to posit one automatically eliminates the other.

There is hardly a person today who has heard a homily or sermon even remotely touching upon the question of grace that is completely clear and free of every taint of Pelagianism. Because of their fear of the complicated distinctions and precision of thought required to avoid this insidious and all-pervasive heresy many preachers sedulously avoid the whole issue of grace as such, or satisfy themselves with vague generalities.

Pelagianism is the most subtle and naturally human of all the heresies. If this book seems at times confusing to the reader, if the restrictive language and highly modified precision of thought it employs prove a barrier to easy comprehension, that is true because any such endeavor is constantly haunted by the spectre of Pelagianism. It is extremely difficult to propose an anthropotropic theology of grace, one which preserves the essential dignity and centeredness of man, without denying the prerogatives of God. This can be done only by constantly keeping in mind the basic reference point given by Scripture itself: man is the shadow, the very image of God.

If Pelagianism is viable even today, one might well suspect that it was in every age of Christian history. It did not die as a result of its condemnation. It looms large in every era, metamorphosized in an ever-flowing series of kindred heresies.

Shortly after the damnation of this doctrine by the Sixteenth Council of Carthage, like a hydra, it produced a new head. Theologians at Marseilles in southern France proposed new principles which eventually were condemned at a Council held at Orange and formed the basis of the recrudescence of the original doctrine known as Semi-Pelagianism. This compromise position can be summarized as follows:

1. Grace is necessary for good works, but not for the beginnings of faith, that is, for the desire and will to believe. This man achieves on his own.

2. In relation to good works grace is needed to attract men to the good and for the final execution of the decision to do good. It is not needed, however, for the actual willing of the good. The will can will on its own.

3. If a man perseveres in doing good, this is not to be seen as the result of any special gift or grace.

4. Baptism is necessary for salvation. The kingdom of heaven is precisely the beatific vision. But as a matter of fact infants die with or without baptism according as God foresees that they would or would not have produced good

works had they lived. He sees to it that those who would
have led good lives die with baptism while those who
would have done evil die without baptism.

The hydra regenerated another head in the later heresy of
Baianism. Du Bay taught that:

1. Man because of his great dignity could not possibly
have been created without a direct orientation toward the
beatific vision. All the so-called supernatural gifts with which
the Creator endowed him are actually and radically owed
to him to enable his free will to operate in present circumstances.
2. All good acts presuppose faith. All acts of infidels and
sinners are sins. Without grace a person can do nothing
but sin.

The second principle of Du Bay represents an attempt to
avoid the accusation of Pelagianism. But he tries to escape the
embrace of Pelagius by falling into the arms of Luther. This
principle conceived in reaction to Pelagianism inspired the later
ideas of the Jansenists.

Jansenism avoided entirely the vacillating position of Baianism between Pelagianism and its extreme opposite. It can be said
to stem from the ancient heresy only inasmuch as it represents
a kind of horrified recoil from it with a resultant landing in the
ambit of a diametrically opposed error, exaggerated Augustinianism:

1. Man is not really free from internal compulsion. For
free will and its exercise it suffices to have freedom from
external coercion.
2. The will is internally compelled by delectation. If a
person is caught between the delectation that comes from
doing good, the delectation of grace, and the delight that
comes from a sinful act, it will be the stronger delectation
that will always win consent.

3. Consequently, without grace man can only sin. With compelling grace man cannot do evil.

So in the view of the Jansenists man is made a kind of puppet of God. His true freedom is negated, and he is forced to react to delectation like a pleasure-programmed computer. Quesnel, a later writer inspired by Jansenism, totally agrees with the mainline opinion with the exception that he views grace as nothing else than God himself who irresistably impels those he calls to salvation to perform good works.

Of course the basic question which Pelagius and those he influenced attempted to answer, the question about the relationship of the human and the divine in the working out of man's salvation, is one that involves in the final analysis a perplexing mystery, one as deep and unfathomable as the mystery of the Incarnation itself. Indeed, because this relationship is patterned on the Incarnation it is so mysterious. But for that very same reason it has to be the central question in the theology of man. That is why so many have assayed to provide some kind of explanation of it. The gradually mounting consciousness of the importance of this mystery in theology has led the Church periodically to lay down certain directives through its conciliar teaching as a response to the aberrations of those who have exaggerated one side of the question or the other. Theologians have systematized these guidelines and their own conclusions from them into a kind of enchiridion indicating just what man can and cannot do without various kinds of grace. It will be helpful to enucleate the chief elements of this teaching.

Theologians consider first of all the situation of those who are not yet justified, who have not as yet committed themselves fully to the love of God. They consider first of all under this heading the case of the person who is not justified because he is not yet a believer. They vindicate for him the ability to avoid sin at least in certain instances, for they say that it is theologically certain that not all acts of unbelievers are sins. They then look at the more general case of any person who is not graced, who is therefore a sinner, be he believer or unbeliever. They say that it is a doctrine defined by the Council of Trent that not all acts of those not in the state of sanctifying grace are sins. They hold the positions we have considered thus far to be conclusions from or at least implicitly contained in the data of revelation. The book of Josue (2, 1) praises the action of Rahab the harlot, and Exodus (1, 15) extols as good the practice of the Egyptian midwives. In his letter to the Romans (2, 14) St. Paul explicitly refers to the fact that the Gentiles, the pagans, naturally accomplish what is commanded in the law.

In the second place the manuals consider this same point from a more positive perspective. They state that without grace it is possible for man in his present condition to place acts which are substantially good. Obviously since they are considering only the case of the person who does not have habitual grace this statement does not say much more than the previous ones, since if it is possible for sinners to avoid sin in every act, and every responsible act has to be either good or sinful, then it is necessarily possible for the sinner to do some good. Most manuals, however, move the question a little further. Is it possible for a person to accomplish some good without grace when one considers that good not merely substantially, that is, essentially, but existentially, that is, with reference to the fact that in this order the good is directed toward man's supernatural end? Here they run into some difficulty. They have to say that every act that positively orders a person toward the beatific vision is graced. But if they can admit the existence in this order of a good act, as for instance one of an infidel, that is not consciously directed and thus not really directed to man's supernatural end, they can vindicate its goodness apart from grace. But the Augustinian school of theology has traditionally held that some kind of grace is necessary for every good act. Ripalda and Rahner, as we have seen, also imply something of the sort in their teaching. The final question the manuals ask is whether that good which can be accomplished substantially (that is, if we prescind from whether the good is attained in a salutary fashion or not) without grace can ever be the affective love of God above all things. Most respond with St. Thomas (and us) and say no, for such an act would in reality be an act of charity, and for it grace is absolutely necessary.

The third issue considered by the manualists with reference to the person who is not yet justified is whether he can without grace for a considerable length of time continue to observe the natural law. The question is posed in reference to the mere observance of the law, there being again no doubt that grace would be required for a salutary compliance with the law. The answer is unanimous that a person could not. He needs grace to avoid sinning over a long period of time. Some theologians are of the opinion that this doctrine is defined in the canons of the Councils of Carthage and Orange where it is indicated that a man must pray if he is to obtain help needed to keep the commandments. The Councils, however, seem to be concerned with the observance of the law in a salutary manner, not with mere observance as such. So most of the manualists call the proposition they defend theologically certain, but not a matter of faith. In establishing biblical documentation for their thesis they rely heavily upon the statements of St. Paul in the seventh chapter of his letter to the Romans. Theologically the reason for the proposition is the traditional doctrine on original sin. Man has fallen into an inferior condition because of this sin. His very nature has been affected by it. Though basically that nature still remains good, and capable of accomplishing some good, its ability to see and to be attracted to the *bonum honestum* in preference to the *bonum apparens*, which often is more immediate and more delectable, has been considerably impaired by sin. Thus while theologians vindicate the complete ability and freedom of a man without grace to choose the good in an individual case, and even over a relatively short series of choices, they say in the long run the odds against his doing good are too great for him to overcome. He needs divine assistance. The impossibility he experiences is one of the moral, not of the physical, order, but it is absolute, that is, without exception. Yet theologians have to say that the law itself does not become void because of this moral impossibility. Normally absolute moral impossibility to comply with its precepts would excuse one from the law. But in this case, in each single confrontation with the law a person does have the ability to act in accordance with it. The impossibility emanates from the lack of power to persevere for a long time, not from loss of freedom in each individual decision. More power is needed for a sustained effort over a long time than a man can marshal by himself.

A second series of three questions is posed about the condition of the person who has been justified. It would seem at first glance that he would need nothing further. He already possesses grace. God's life is in him. He has been divinized. Yet he, too, is still under the influence of original sin. In the course of his life he will be sorely tempted, unless God exercises a very special providence in his regard. Is habitual grace all that he needs to overcome these difficulties, or does he require something in addition? Scholastic theologians call habitual grace "habitual" because it is a perduring quality. It is endowed with a kind of supernatural inertia by reason of which it tends of itself to remain dominant in the life of the justified person. But in the traditional view it is under constant onslaught by the world, the flesh and the devil. And the Council of Trent has clearly taught that it can be lost.

First of all, theologians state that the justified need over and above the habitual grace they already possess an additional help in order to be able to persevere in it for a long time. They view this proposition as theologically certain from the teaching of the sixth chapter of the Acts of the Council of Trent. They allude to Scripture's portrayal of the Christian life as a spiritual combat (I Tim. 6, 12) for which a whole array of armament is needed (Eph. 6, 11-12) as well as to Christ's injunction even to his loved ones constantly to pray (e.g. Matt. 6, 13; 26, 41).

Secondly they teach that actual perseverance in grace until death is a very great and special gift of God. They see this doctrine as very closely associated with matters of faith from the insistence upon it apparent in the Acts of the Council of Trent. In lining up Scriptural proofs for their position they refer to David's prayer that Yahweh preserve forever the good intentions of the people (I Par. 29, 18), Christ's prayer for Peter and the warnings he issued that a time would come when the faith even of Christians would grow cold. Theologically they say that perseverance in grace until death involves something outside of the order of grace itself. It involves a fact: death in the state of grace. This is accomplished not by grace itself but by providence, by the exercise of God's special care seeing to it that the graced individual die in the graced condition.

Thirdly, the manuals teach that the just person without a very special and extraordinary help from God cannot avoid all venial sin. They view this as a proposition defined by the Council of Trent if it refers to a whole lifetime, and as theologically certain if it is restricted to a long period of time in one's life. They point to the petition in the Lord's prayer asking for forgiveness of daily faults as well as to the statement of St. James that we all fail in many things (3, 2) and that of St. John that if we say that we are not sinners we are liars (I Jo. 1, 8). Theologically here again there is question of a special providence rather than of something pertaining to the order of grace itself.

The more careful theologians in considering what besides grace is necessary to the just man employ the word "gift," rather than the word "grace." We have seen that in all the cases they consider there is question of a special providence involving facts, which *per se* lie outside of the order of grace itself. While the exercise of this providence can be called a "grace" in the widest sense, it is not necessarily an *internal* grace in the sense in which theologians define it.

If we ask the question whether actual grace is necessary for even the justified person, we find theologians divided in their response. There are some who will say that it is not, because habitual grace as the *propter quod unumquodque tale et illud magis* of grace is able of itself to accomplish whatever actual grace can. *Quod valet magis,* they say, *valet minus.* They employ Ockham's razor. There is no need for actual grace in the case of the justified. But, on the other hand, the greater number of manualists, for purely scholastic reasons, require actual grace even in the justified person. They say that a habit can be reduced to act in a specific case not just by the positing of an object with which it is concerned, but only by movement which draws it toward the object and stimulates its act. Thus a man confronted with choices about his supernatural destiny can bring his graced condition to bear upon the issue only through some illumination of his mind and stimulation of his will by actual grace. Since this requirement, however, is only a postulate of a particular brand of scholastic philosophy emanating from one view of the nature of a habit, it does not involve doctrine, and can therefore be rejected. Needless to say, we would reject it today.

A further question could be posed about the need specifically of *actual* grace in the case even of a person who is not yet justified. This is not to ask if grace is necessary even to accomplish any good over a long period of time. We have seen that it is, and this is a matter of doctrine. A *fortiori* some kind of grace is necessary for any action that is salutary, that is, which leads a person in some positive way toward the goal that God has actually set for him in this order of creation. The question revolves solely about this point: is that grace *actual* grace? We have said that the ancient theologians did not make any distinction between actual and habitual grace. The grace they seemed to be talking about was some kind of transitory divine movement evidenced in salutary acts of the as yet unjustified person. So in the light of the later developed scholastic theory of grace we would describe it as an actual grace. But it might be surprising to note that St. Thomas himself, whose writings appeared rather late in the history of the development of the theology of grace and were definitely scholastic in orientation, did not require an actual grace in such a case. He seemed to admit only one kind of grace. This would have to be described in later terms as habitual grace. He viewed this grace as both a movement and a state. The later distinction between actual and habitual grace was undoubtedly based upon this two-fold modality. St. Thomas saw the acts preceding justification and preparing for it, as well as justification itself, proceeding from this grace. He employed the Aristotelian notion of mutual causality to show how this was possible. The acts which precede justification are at one and the same time both a cause of and the effect of sanctifying grace. For Thomas temporal priority was not a major consideration, but only priority of causality. For him as for Aristotle in different orders of causality one and the same being or act can be both cause and effect of another being or act. There would be a contradiction only if one were the cause and effect of the other in the same order of causality.

Now formal and material causes constitute one distinct order of causality and are complementary to each other in it. Efficient and final causes constitute quite another order and complement each other in it. The first is the order of intrinsic and the second that of extrinsic causality. If we consider the intrinsic causes in the case of justification, grace and the infused virtues are the formal cause. Faith, sorrow for sin, and the other necessary dispositions of soul are the material cause. In this order of causality, then, the dispositions of the soul are quite obviously prior to grace, since the soul must be properly disposed before the form can be received. If we consider the extrinsic causes of justification, on the other hand, justification and what it leads to are the final cause, and grace and the infused virtues are the efficient cause. In this order of causality, though the end is prior in intention, it is brought into being by the operation of the efficient cause. So the dispositions of the soul required for justification have to be brought into being by the operation of grace and the infused virtues; thus in this order of causality grace and the infused virtues are prior to the dispositions. So in this system sanctifying grace itself can be seen as the efficient cause of the acts that precede justification while those acts are the material cause of the presence of grace as a form. Nor does this doctrine lead in any way to the semi-Pelagian heresy. Only a formal cause requires a disposition. (That is why actual grace was invented by those who did not understand or accept mutual causality; to provide a supernatural transient cause to effect the dispositions for the form these theologians called habitual grace). Dispositions of the soul are prior to grace only if the latter is considered as a form. So they are not simply prior to grace, but only under one aspect. But when grace is considered as an efficient cause, the dispositions are the effect of it, and so dependent upon it for existence. Now philosophers tell us that the extrinsic causes are simply prior to the intrinsic ones. You have to have a purpose and an agent before you can have any matter and form. So ultimately in the system of St. Thomas grace holds complete sway, and is simply prior to all the dispositions readying the soul for justification. Quite obviously then the grace about which St. Thomas is speaking is habitual grace, not actual grace. But later theologians had great difficulties with the theory of mutual causality. To make the dispositions preceding justification the effect of justifying grace itself seemed contradictory to them. So rather than consider, as St. Thomas did, one and the same grace as both a form and a movement, they proposed two graces: habitual grace corresponding to the formal element in St. Thomas' view, and actual grace to the efficient one. This solved all their difficulties.

For obvious reasons we have not fully elucidated here the doctrine of St. Thomas about sanctifying grace and justification. The only point that we are trying to make is that St. Thomas considered the salutary acts produced prior to justification to be the result of habitual grace under the aspect of *motio Dei* or efficient cause, and not the effect of another kind of grace, actual grace. Those who would require a fuller explanation and documentation of this assertion can consult my book: *The Thomistic Concept of Justifying Contrition.*

The modern world would certainly be less confused if without dragging with us a complicated philosophical system we could return to the doctrine of St. Thomas and say there is only one kind of grace. Perhaps this could be done without any great difficulty just by thinking of grace as love rather than form and movement. For it would seem that there is only one kind of love of God, which can be viewed both as a transitory drawing force and a permanent condition affecting the persons transformed by its influence. In the human paradigm certainly

it is one and the same offer of love that both attracts and dis-
poses a prospective partner and brings him to respond in kind
to the total commitment of the other.

In spinning out their theories about actual grace the later
theologians evidence their agreement with Pelagius that there
can be such a thing as an external actual grace. They admit
that sermons, helpful spiritual reading, proper execution of the
liturgy and many other salutary experiences and events of life
can be called graces. They emphasize that Pelagius was wrong
simply because he taught that the *only* grace that can be admitted is external grace. Since their works are largely congeries of
material aimed at the refutation of error, however, and are
not primarily directed, as it would often seem, at the inculcation
of positive doctrine, they tend to minimize the importance of
external grace. The manualists often concoct their definitions of
actual grace in such a way that they fit perfectly only the notion
of internal actual grace. But since thinkers today prefer to describe humanity in terms of self-conscious corporeity, it would
be best not to follow the lead of these older theologians. Grace
as God's loving presence has to be manifested first to the cor-
poreal being in external contingencies and events. The truth of
the old adage *nihil in intellectu nisi prius in sensu* cannot be
lost in current theology. But the fact that grace must be first
encountered externally under ordinary circumstances does not
deny that its influence has also to be felt internally. Unless
God's love is perceived in and is able to move the innermost
faculties of a man's heart, it will be totally ineffective and cannot be called a grace in the sense in which theologians have
understood it. Without denying the supreme importance of the
interior operation of God's love, we say that external grace has
to be emphasized today simply because it was so neglected in
the recent past. People otherwise might never advert to the fact
that God's loving presence is to be found today in the Church,
in the liturgy, in the testimony given by the lives of good people,
in every facet of our contact with Christ's world, with the process of Christogenesis. As was explained, unless each Christian
understands and accepts God's trust in him to do the "thing" of

Christ not merely in the liturgy but in his daily life, to be Christ, to be a manifestation of God's loving presence, the message of the Gospel is thwarted and grace is denied. Teachers today cannot let the dread of Pelagianism allow them to neglect any further the importance of the doctrine of external grace in the life of the Church. Overemphasis on the internal aspects of grace will really tend, as it has in the past, to take Christ out of Christianity. Because he was and is a visible reality, he will no longer be seen as the grace *par excellence*.

The manualists generally describe actual grace as an internal and transitory illustration of the intellect or inspiration of the will by God which has as its purpose the directing of a person's actions toward the final goal God has set for him and/or the curing of the wounds left in nature by sin. The nature of the human intellect demands that God's action upon it be direct and immediate. Some authors hold that grace's action on the will is also direct and immediate, while others think that a mediate influence is sufficient. This latter group points out that the will is blind. It must follow the guidance of the intellect. Therefore God influences the whole act of a person internally if he merely illumines the intellect according to his purpose.

It is interesting at this point to note the development of the doctrine of St. Thomas on the nature of grace from his earliest to his latest writings. In the *Scriptum super sententiis* he uses the term "grace" to refer to the external circumstances of the Christian life as such. If one did not know better, he might accuse the Angelic Doctor of being tainted with Pelagianism. But, of course, as St. Thomas sees it the Christian life exists as both a divine movement attracting others to embrace it, and an internal form or norm which manifests itself exteriorly. In his *De veritate* Thomas seems to refer to grace as a kind of internal instinct whereby one is able to carry out in life what Christianity implies. In the *Contra gentiles* he further specifies that internal instinct by relating it to the natural desire for the beatific vision. In the *Summa* he describes grace more fully as both the cause (movement) and effect (state) of God's justifying act which directs a person toward the beatific vision.

Later theology has also addressed itself to the key problem which the doctrine of Pelagius raised. Just what is to be attributed to the operation of God and what is to be considered the part of man in the graced act? Here again opinion is divided. The Thomistic school in general defines actual grace materially, that is, from the standpoint of its material cause, as the supernaturally effected illumination of the human intellect and inspiration of the will. Viewed materially actual grace is nothing else than the human vital acts of understanding and election. But formally actual grace is a movement of God, an exercise of divine power which has as its result the excitation, follow-through and perfect achievement of such an indeliberate vital act as will be able to direct man in choosing the good. In this conception the indeliberate vital act (inspiration or illumination) is produced directly by a divine movement which alone in the proper sense (formally) can be called the actual grace. In the process first we encounter God's movement directed toward a man. This is, properly speaking, the actual grace. Next we find in the human subject an indeliberate vital act which has been effected by the divine motion. Materially this can be called the actual grace. Finally there is the election or deliberate act which is made under the influence of the indeliberate act aroused by the divine motion.

The Suarezian school, on the other hand, states that the indeliberate vital human acts themselves formally constitute the actual grace. Actual grace formally is an illustration or inspiration. These operations cannot, as it were, originate as divine motions *in vacuo* but only in the human subject as his formal vital acts. As graces these indeliberate acts are produced simultaneously by both God and man. God is, of course, the primary cause of them, man the secondary. But both attain the act equally immediately. God's movement concretely is the concept that is described as illumination. But man's act too is precisely that concept proceeding from his vital processes. This theory avoids conceiving grace as a premotion. There is no previous act of God, but only a simultaneous concurrence of God and man in the same act. But the divine concursus is in this instance of the supernatural order, since it directs man's act to a higher end than it could attain by only its natural essence. God and man are co-causes in the operation, God supplying in the concrete effect the supernatural element, and man the natural.

The Thomistic school in general sees the intentionality of an act, its direction, its being vectored toward a definite goal, as a function of the object of the act. If God is to influence the direction of an act and realign it to pursue a higher goal than it is naturally capable of reaching, his action must somehow attain to the object of that act by means of a movement that is radically and causally prior to the human operation itself. When the human faculty attains the object already so transformed as it were by divine action, it actually reaches something supernatural, and so the act of man itself becomes entitatively supernatural.

The Suarezian view, on the other hand, does not so much concern itself with the object of the act, but with its subjective entity. As proceeding from a natural human faculty with only a natural divine concursus, an act would be entitatively natural. But if the divine concursus is a supernatural one, it renders the human act itself entitatively supernatural. What makes the divine concursus supernatural rather than natural is not precisely the object of the act, but rather the end toward which it is directed by God. The vectoring of the act on the part of God and not its object determines in this view whether the act will be merely natural or supernatural. The vectoring of an act toward charity and what it leads to, the beatific vision, is precisely what constitutes in the ultimate analysis the actual grace.

Here of course with Ripalda and Rahner we tend to agree with the Suarezian rather than with the Thomistic theory. Grace has always to be seen as love or a relationship to love. Even though a human act may not itself be an act of love because its object is not directly the beloved to be loved, the vectoring of the act considered as a conscious modification of the subjectivity of the actor toward an eventual condition or state of perfect love is sufficient to place the act itself in the order of love, and so of grace. Through this vectoring the act is transformed by love into a kind of love-act, a to-be-made act of love. The act itself then becomes a demand in the order of love for love. It pushes the individual toward the full commitment of himself in love to the one who has been perceived as having first loved him.

After these long reflections on the traditional doctrine about actual grace, we must now ask if, in the conception of grace as love which as we have said current larval theology demands, there is any room for a distinction between actual and habitual grace. Do we really have to posit an actual grace, or, with St. Thomas, can we transfer the functions attributed to it in the past to habitual grace, to love itself? Can we today dispense with the idea of actual grace?

If we refer to grace as we have defined it in the primary and fullest sense as the loving presence of God, then obviously there is no need to make a distinction. God is present in a loving manner to all, sinner and just alike. And his love reaches all, some in their very personhood, others only in their actions.

But if we understand grace in the secondary sense as the transformation of human reality in God's loving presence, it might be still useful, but by no means necessary, to sustain the distinction. For God's love transforms the very personhood, the very being, of the one who responds to it in full commitment of himself. This transformation is *per se* permanent and affects the whole life of the person so influenced by divine love. On the other hand, God's love transforms directly only the individual acts of the person who does not fully commit himself to it, not his personhood as such. Such a transformation by its nature is transitory, although it must leave in its wake some kind of disposition toward total commitment. The acts of a person in some way leave their mark upon him; they influence at least in a minimal way his self-concept. All that this says is that God's love affects different people in different ways. Because of the great divergence of response between the person who fully loves God in return and the one who is only partially struck by God's ineffable love, we might feel that some distinction ought to be made. We might think that the term "actual grace" is appropriate to express the way divine love affects those who have not permanently committed themselves to it. But if by the word "actual" we mean transitory or related entirely to acts, then this expression is deceptive. For it is the very same love of God that affects the person who is fully transformed in it and the one who reacts only partially to it. And this love in itself is permanently directed toward both kinds of persons; it is in no sense transitory. The difference, as we have said, is entirely in the effect that it has upon the persons who become aware of it. But even the one who has fully responded to it and been transformed in it is not constantly aware of it. It is true that since his very being has been affected by it, all his actions will also be transformed by it even though he is not expressly conscious of his condition when he acts. But this is an automatic ontological situation, and not a fully personal one. As far as his perfectly conscious and strictly personal relationship to God's love is concerned, it too must be seen as transitory, since a person in this world has to be engaged with many other things that he does not always view in the perspective of divine love.

Then, too, the response to divine love of the person who has not as yet fully committed himself may be relatively permanent and not just transitory. God's love may affect in a real and stable way the very being and life of such a person, not to the extent that he loves God in return, but inasmuch as he lives a life in some way, e.g. through faith and hope, related to God. Theologians have always allowed for the fact that an unjustified person may be graced by the supernatural habits of faith and hope. These were considered true habits, permanent and abiding faculties, not just transitory acts. And they are supernatural habits, sustained in being only by the supernatural action of God.

These reflections would lead us to conclude that the different modalities of transformation that God's love produces in the person who responds to it in kind on the one hand and the person who is only partially affected by it on the other should definitely be clearly distinguished. But when grace is seen as God's love in a personalistic and existential framework the terms "actual" and "habitual" grace are not appropriate. The core of the difference between the two cases is, as we have said, not in the love itself, but in man's response to it. And this response cannot always be well-categorized as actual or habitual. It is better described as full or partial. To designate it relative to the paradigm of human love perhaps the expressions "grace of espousal" and "grace of union" would be better. At least they would avoid the implication with scholastic philosophy and the confusing connotations that the traditional terms inculcate.

We have said that the traditional doctrine about actual grace has been elaborated as a reaction to the fundamental problem about God's love and original sin. Pelagius could deny the existence of actual grace because for him there was no such thing as original sin. But since his time God's love and sin have been viewed as two polarities between the influence of which man is suspended. He cannot escape being affected by either. Both relate to his freedom and native abilities. Both limit his action and the sphere of his influence.

The explanation of original sin proposed by theologians of the recent past was clear and reflected the doctrinal position taken by the Council of Trent. The supernatural gifts with which the first man was endowed by the Creator were possessed by him in trust, in the sense that if he lost them for himself, they would be lost for all his posterity. As a matter of fact Adam lost these gifts. He violated the divine command and thus sinned (*peccatum originale originans*). This was his own proper sin perpetrated by his own free act. After God once elevated man to the supernatural state, there was no longer any possibility for the purely natural. When Adam lost for his posterity the state of original justice, since the only alternatives were supernatural justice or sinfulness, men had to be born into the world in a state of sin (*peccatum originale originatum*). Just as Adam's posterity, had he not sinned, would have been born into the world in a state of justice which could be lost only by their own personal sin, so since Adam did sin, his descendants entered the world in a state of sinfulness, one from which they could not escape by themselves, but only through the grace of God since this alone could bring them to a state of supernatural justice. This condition of sinfulness was transmitted by generation from the stock of Adam. It had to be viewed as a prepersonal modification of every man, that is, a state which affected him even before he achieved self-awareness and was capable of personal sin. A person who died in this sinful state was condemned. Only baptism could save him, and bring him to the beatific vision. Original sin in the descendant of Adam is a true and real sin; it implies a state of voluntary aversion from God and enmity toward him. As a real sin, it had to be real and voluntary. Its voluntary character, however, emanated not from the personal will of the party affected, but from Adam's will. But in the individual this sin is not merely Adam's; it is also his very own, for which he can be justly punished because of the original covenant arrangement between man and his Creator. The individual was affected by his sinful condition not to the extent that his faculties were destroyed or completely impaired, but only insofar as they were weakened, somewhat debilitated, with the result that he was left liable and prone to further sin. Though his powers remained essentially intact, they were made subject to the domination of sin.

Many of these theologians assert that the essence of original sin is to be sought precisely in the lack of sanctifying grace that accompanies conception and birth. A man born without grace in the present order has to be in the state of sin, because he is as a matter of fact averted from his final end to which he can be directed only by grace.

More recent theologians have had great difficulties with this view of original sin, not because of its principal doctrinal implications, but because of its historical views. It was conceived on the presupposition that there was only one progenitor of the human race who was made responsible for all his progeny. It hinges upon a literal interpretation of the book of Genesis in its story of the creation of man. Yet for centuries theology has admitted that the rest of the creation story need not be taken literally. It is not an account that purports to be strictly historical and scientific; in its details it is only a myth illustrating the necessity of belief in creation, but based upon the then current views of how creation might have happened. Today's ideas about the evolution of man do not provide for monogenism. How then can the religious truth of the doctrine of original sin be reconciled with modern scientific data?

Popular among present-day theologians is the view of original sin as *Weltsünde*. Man lives in a poisoned atmosphere. His environment has been thoroughly impregnated with evil. Wherever he turns he finds sin. He cannot escape from it or its influence. Man's whole history has been characterized by sinful action. Original sin is the sinfulness of the race as such. The world has become a sinful place, for wherever it is touched by man and not perceived to have been redeemed by Christ, it has become an instrument of sin. A man without faith or love can see the world only in this guise.

So in this theory the question about *peccatum originale originans* becomes irrelevant. It makes no difference who committed the first sin, an individual or a clan. The pertinent fact is that this sin affected the whole world and the history of mankind in it.

But what about the infant, who because of his lack of personal awareness does not have a responsible contact with this sinful world? Does he have to be baptized? Devotees of the theory of *Weltsünde* respond with a unanimous yes. Individuals are prepersonally conditioned by the situation into which they are born. When an individual is thrust into the ghetto of sin that the world is, he has to be personally affected by it. He must form his own personality and develop his powers in relation to his environment. He can do no other. If what he encounters from the dawning of his consciousness is sin, he cannot help but be influenced by it. Because from the day he is conceived he is prepersonally conditioned to sin, *Weltsünde* is his sin. It is in him because it is in his mother and father, his brothers and sisters, and his whole environment. He must breathe, but the very air he takes into his lungs is poisoned by

sin. Everything with which he will come into contact is potentially sinful. Unless the Church spreads over him the protective
shield of its own faith and love he will certainly be condemned.
He has in effect already sinned, for without grace he cannot go
for a long time without sinning. Without God's grace he cannot
help but sin. The prepersonal conditioning to sin is for the infant his original sin. It is truly a sin in him. It is free because
it is due to the abuse of freedom by his progenitors. It is his
own because it is part of his mode of being in the world. It is
worthy of condemnation because it implies a lack of grace
through which alone a person in the present order can be directed toward union with God. The grace originally guaranteed
to man was from the dawn of his existence lost through sin,
but restored by Christ in the course of time.

This view of original sin provides a good backdrop against
which we can consider grace as the manifestation of God's love,
a love which in the case of adults usually does not produce an
immediate full response because of problems of faith. God's
grace, as we have said, is in the world. The whole world has
really been transformed by it. But it exists there in an ambivalent condition. It has been clouded over by the sinfulness of
men. Contemplating reality man can receive two signals from
it. He can hear the strong voice of God's love. But he is also
made aware of the strident and sometimes more alluring siren
cry of sin. Here is where his free will comes into play.

As was indicated before, humanity is literally bathed in the
fields of all sorts of forces. A man is at least indirectly conscious
of some of these, like gravity which he must constantly take
into account. Of others he is not even peripherally aware. He
rarely if ever adverts to the earth's magnetic field, the gravitational and magnetic fields of the sun and moon, the solar wind
and the literal maelstrom of man-made electromagnetic fields.
These then can have little influence upon his personal life as
such, though the effects they produce may be the source of his
income or the object of his interests. He is brought to a recognition of these fields only by reasoning from the results they
produce.

God's love and sin may readily be viewed as fields of force, as opposing polarities influencing man and drawing him in one direction or the other. From the time of the rise of his consciousness he is brought into contact with the effects of these two fields. His free will is poised between submission to the one or to the other. But whereas sin, like gravity, because of the ubiquity of its effects is the more intrusive of these fields and more easily captures the flitting consciousness, the field of God's love is the more dynamic and better fitted to the modality of man's being itself. For the business of a human being is to exist. As Sartre says, man is not what he is, but what he is not. When he reflects a person finds that he must confirm his own human existence by becoming what he is not, not by succumbing to what he is. And this he can accomplish only by the power of love. He wills constantly to be other to himself. He is initially a sinner. He sees opportunities for further sin everywhere in the world. But sin will only make him more himself. It makes him more conscious of his basic weakness and guilt. It makes him realize that though he tends to escape from himself by deifying himself, his culture, his society, his institutions, his accomplishments, this self-imposed deification is vain and idolatrous. It only makes him more what he is, a sinner. He can be really divinized only by God. And God has divinized him in Christ. And as in the case of Christ the instrument of divinization was God's love, so it must be in the case of every man.

Thus, though the field of sin phenomenologically is the stronger, existentially it is not. For in the depths of his personhood man is touched by love and by love alone. And while love must evoke a response from a person precisely, as we have said, by leaving him what he is and meeting him where he is—and so has to be distinguished according to the condition in which a person finds himself—it is this very fact that is its strength, and not its weakness. For sin must immediately transform. Unlike love, to paraphrase St. Paul, sin is impatient, ruthless; sin feels envy; it is proud, insolent, selfish; it takes pleasure only in its own aggrandizement and rejoices in the defeat of truth, for it has no faith, no hope or endurance. Sin cannot leave a person what he is, and it cannot make him what he is not.

Though the larval theology of grace indigenous in our culture may call for a different view from that hitherto presented under the heading of "actual grace," it really addresses itself to the same basic problem: the dialectic of sin and love, and the human will caught in the midst. Though our concept of what is meant by actual grace may change, the fundamental doctrine relating to this dialectic—just what a man can and cannot do without the assistance of grace—will not. These points must be maintained in any theology of grace. And while, following them, we have limned some kind of sketch of the relationship that exists between God's love and sin in regard to the human will, we have not as yet addressed ourselves to the most basic problem of all, the difficulty which plagued Sartre and many other modern thinkers. We have explained why God's love is stronger than sin, but if man is free, is he not stronger than God? How can human freedom be reconciled with divine supremacy? How can God be in the driver's seat of the universe if man is free and called to do his "thing"? What in the final analysis is the relationship between God and man in this act of love we call grace? What is the relationship between grace and human freedom? Does freedom rob grace of its efficacy? Does grace make the human person unfree? We shall have to consider these questions more fully in the next chapters.

CHAPTER VII

FReedom

The problem of reconciling human freedom with divine freedom is one of the most difficult in all theology. It has never been really solved in the past. Undoubtedly there is mystery involved in it, and a perfect solution will never be found. If a man is free in the sense that he can do anything possible, the divine mastery over salvation seems to be threatened. On the other hand, if man is made to be just a kind of divine puppet, he is robbed of his supreme dignity, of that aspect of his being in which he most resembles God himself. His love accordingly is attenuated in value. For as we have seen, unless love is perfectly free, it is cheapened. In the following pages we shall study this key theological problem, and with the help of the insights of current psychology and philosophy try to offer a new view of human freedom, one which we think can more readily be reconciled with the dogma of the perfect dominion of God in the economy of grace.

The first thing that strikes one about human freedom is that it is not absolute. It is essentially limited. I am not free seriously to will what I can in no sense accomplish. The exercise of my freedom is restricted to those ends which can be attained by means which are or will be within my control. Human freedom is contingent upon means. At present I am not free to will to be suddenly transported to the center of the sun. Even if spaceships could be built to withstand the surface heat and gravitational force, there is no possible way of building one that could endure the temperature of about 26,000,000 degrees centigrade and the pressure of one trillion pounds p.s.i. at the core of this celestial body. I could be free in this matter only by the assurance of the exercise of divine power. If God revealed his willingness to work a miracle, then I would be free to accept or reject his offer.

We have seen that the end which God established for man is one attainable only by divine means. The fact that God has revealed his willingness to supply the means to achieve this end under certain conditions makes the pursuit of this end an object of human freedom. The means that God supplies is grace, his own love. Grace then radically is freedom: the power, the ability to act.

We have also seen that grace can be viewed as freedom in a second sense. It is restored human freedom. When a person surrenders himself to God in love, he alienates his freedom. But through the sharing of his own love with that of God in the project of Christogenesis, a man is given a new ability, a new power to act in an area in which he could not act before; he is given a new freedom. His original human freedom which he surrendered in love is now returned to him transformed, enlarged, augmented to the extent that he can now achieve goals not originally possible for him. Through love his original freedom is not really lost but only involved with that of another. The result of this involvement is a common freedom shared by lovers which not only confirms the existence of the freedom of each in the first instance, but bestows upon them wider powers of action in the second.

Grace can, as we have explained, be considered freedom in

still a third sense. It is freedom from law. The person who acts
out of a motive of love, to be sure, accomplishes what the law
commands. But he does not do so in virtue of the law, but
ultimately because of his love, because of grace. Through grace
he is liberated from the force of law. A new bond ties him to
the lawmaker. And this bond, as we saw, is much more power-
ful, more perfect, more rewarding than that of law. It is of a
totally different order. It is the unshackled bond of grace.

Human freedom, then, is not just a matter for the philosophers and psychologists. It is a primary theological issue. That
is why the Councils of the Church and the magisterium at large
presumed to make pronouncements about freedom and to defend it against the aberrations of Baianism, Jansenism and
Quesnelianism. It is a prerogative of man that is recognized,
advocated and extolled in Scripture and the writings of the
Fathers. But it is a human characteristic that is enhanced and
made perfect by God's grace. Far from being a deterrent to the
exercise of free will, God's grace is seen to ensure and exalt it.

The gospel of St. John proposes the Holy Spirit, the Spirit
of love, as also the Spirit of freedom that can exercise its influence where it wills (3, 8). St. Paul makes an even more direct
reference to the connection between the Holy Spirit and freedom when he writes: "Where the Lord's Spirit is, there is freedom" (II Cor. 3, 17). He indicates that Christians are called
to live in perfect freedom (Gal. 5, 13). He describes grace precisely in terms of freedom from the law and the judgment of
those who live by it (I Cor. 10, 29-31). St. James calls the
attention of the Church to the new law of perfect freedom
(1, 25; 2, 12).

The Fathers of the Church pondering the text of Genesis
emphasize the fact that man was originally created in the image
of God. They say that it is especially in man's spiritual nature
that this likeness to God is to be found. Some pinpoint it more
closely by stating simply that man in the final analysis is the
image of God because he is free. Thus Cyril of Alexandria says
that man was created free so that he could really be like God
and have dominion over all the earth. Ephrem reacts in a simi-

lar fashion. Tertullian writes that in no other facet of humanity
does he find a closer resemblance of man to God than in the
exercise of freedom. In the second creation of man through
grace, in his elevation to the divine order, man's freedom and
will really become identified with God's own. In surrendering
his will to God so that his freedom might be identified with
God's, man is liberated from all his sins and imperfections.
So he is made even more Godlike. The original natural likeness
of man to God which the Greek version of Genesis renders as
eikōn, a likeness which is reflected radically in human freedom,
is greatly enhanced through a person's election to identify himself with the project of God's own exercise of freedom. This
absorption, as it were, of man's original liberty in God's is due
to a person's free action under the influence of God's Spirit.
It makes possible an even more perfect resemblance of man
to God which can properly be called divinization. Its dynamic
nature is indicated by the use in the Greek of a more active
word, *'omoiōsis.* So Clement of Alexandria can say: "The divine
will itself is injected into human souls." Basing themselves on
this tradition, modern theologians like Baumgartner can teach
in full truth: "Freedom is a fundamental trait of God in man
resulting from man's imaging God [in his nature] and perfected
when man achieves a resemblance to God [in grace]."

But the starting point of a relevant theology of grace for
tomorrow cannot be only the ideas of the past. It has also to
include the human situation today. And there is nothing more
central to human existence today than the question of freedom.
The civil rights movement, the rebellion against authority, the
hippie drop-out from society—all evidence the paramount concern of people today in maintaining their individual identity
and freedom in a society whose principal thrust seems to be
toward categorizing, stereotyping and homogenizing simply because the current knowledge and population explosions are too
much for it. But today more than ever man resists being put
into a box. He wants to make sure that people know that his
being cannot be captured by a few punches on an IBM card
or a few ferrite particles in the memory bank of a computer.

This is what he is telling the world by his constant protests. He counts. His freedom is something. Today more than ever freedom is the highest value of mankind.

Modern psychology and existentialist philosophy have responded to this current need by highlighting human freedom and placing it at the very core of human existence. These disciplines have been at great pains in exploring the true essence of human liberty. And they have had at their disposal in this investigation devices and means that were not even dreamed of in eras past. These have enabled us today to get a clearer concept of the real nature of human freedom than was ever possible before.

The traditional scholastic definition of freedom was that concocted by Luis Molina. A man is free if, when everything is ready and in order for action, he can act or not act, choose one alternative or the other, without any determination from within or compulsion from without. Of course, for its own age this was a remarkably fine definition of freedom. Its fundamental truth and viability is still vindicated today. Its main faults are that it does not say enough, and that it emanates from a world-view which is no longer widely accepted today. It comes from a world in which nature and not persons was central. It comes from a world dominated by absolutes, by the Aristotelian laws of mechanics and justice. That world viewed personality just as a kind of reference point on which to hang accidents like qualities and actions. It is true in the course of time advocates of scholasticism were forced by the contingencies of psychological research to focus more attention on personality. They began to describe it in more relational terms. The manuals of theology current twenty-five years ago might define personality as a property by which a concrete spiritual being belongs to itself in total immediacy and stands in relation to others. Or perhaps it will be described phenomenologically as the characteristic by which the distinctness of a spiritual being is grasped by others; or more succinctly as one's self-orientation in respect to others. But it is largely outside of scholastic circles that a fuller and more satisfying appraisal of personality is encountered. Only the personalists view it as the totality of man's subjectivity, the fulness of his concrete humanity, from which all things that are uniquely and distinctively his proceed. And only they see most clearly that it is a man's freedom that founds his personality.

A modern philosopher like Martin Buber poses questions about personality that everyone eventually must ask himself. Why precisely am I I and not someone else? Where does my ego come from? It is like others, like my parents', and yet essentially so different. Every person is absolutely original, unique and unrepeatable. Every person is essentially underived and underivable. Every person is basically untouched and untouchable. Yet every I can be defined and understood only in terms of a Thou. And if we were to ask what Thou perfectly corresponds to the essential uniqueness, underivability and untouchableness of the human I we would undoubtedly have to seek the answer in transcendental reality, in that Thou which is totally other, in that Thou which is unaffected by the contingency of being. Even with all the resources it has philosophy has not been able to produce a completely satisfying definition of personality. It leaves personality what it must remain, a mystery, a metaphysical riddle. It remands to the phenomenologist the task of describing what it cannot fully comprehend.

Phenomenologically a person can be described as the sum total of all his choices. He is uniquely what he has made himself be through the exercise of his freedom. If his psyche is integrated, if he is not psychotic or neurotic, his positive elections of projects for himself or at least his non-resistance to the life-situations in which he has found himself have determined how a person will be apprehended by others. Philosophers like Sartre see the very being of a person, as we mentioned before, as a to-be-made through the investment of his existence in freely chosen projects. This idea, of course, is pivotal in the existentialist definition of man's being as such. Personhood is the to-be-made of being. As such it is never complete, never finished, never in total possession. It is always in process. What there is of it has been made by election, by one's choice of how he shall invest himself, by an appropriation of intentions. It has been influenced by the patterns according to which he has chosen to operate. It may reflect a tendency to prefer one or other or any combination of the characteristic psychic styles of reaction: identification, introjection, projection, reaction-formation, regression, rationalization, repression, dissociation, sublimation. Its residue is the over-all organization and integration of all the structures of his being: his aptitudes, his attitudes, and his characteristic modes of behavior. It is the sum total of all the traits that might distinguish him as agreeable, dominating, anxious, depressed, hypomanic, temperamental, cerebral, ambiverted, etc. In short, empirically personality is the individual himself as he is apprehended by others.

As Schelling says a person becomes identified with what he thinks and chooses. If he identifies himself with an object that he has absolutized, he will be apprehended by others as having fallen prey to dogmatism. But if he permits objects only to delimit his own absolutized subjectivity, if he produces a self-image in accordance with his own dignity as a reflection of the absolute being, he will become a devotee of criticism. The philosophy he selects will determine what kind of man he is. But if he acts in accordance with what he perceives himself to be, he acts freely, even though the objects he chooses are necessarily determined.

If the first fault of Molina's definition was that it was object- and not person-centered, the second is that it is inadequate because it does not sufficiently distinguish freedom from spontaneity. Hume pointed out very clearly that a spontaneous action, a completely indetermined one, would be one to which neither praise nor blame, punishment nor reward, could be attached because it would not be connected with anything permanent in the nature of the person producing it. The free act has to be an act not just of a nature, but of a person. Otherwise it is not a responsible act. The older moralists recognized this fact about freedom when they distinguished between an *actus humanus* and an *actus hominis*. The first is a responsible act; it emanates from a person. The second is a spontaneous act; it proceeds only from a nature. If a person is truly the cause of an act, then something of himself must appear in it. His personhood must be reflected in it. It must be uniquely his act, attributable only to him. So the free act precisely in order to be free must be determined! This is the paradox of freedom that escaped Molina. The free act has to be determined by the agent's self-image. It has to express his personality and not just his human nature. Otherwise it is not free.

To be sure, as direction toward any number of possible goals, freedom must initially imply a certain detachment from any one of them. But as emanating from a formed and distinctive personality the free act cannot be completely indetermined. As the most characteristic act of the ego the exercise of freedom is wholly subjective, and totally defined by what the I perceives itself to be at the moment of choice. As a responsible act the exercise of freedom must reflect the personal ego-synthesis of the agent. If it involves love, the total disposition of one's very being in regard to another, it must be viewed as the full expression of the inner depths of the I. It must be the most completely responsible act. So freedom cannot really imply a total indifference in the face of alternatives, for such a posture would be essentially irresponsible.

To be responsible a person must choose only what he perceives is in accord with his own self-image. He must choose the good that is best suited to himself as he apprehends himself at the moment of election. If he does not, he will not feel responsible for his choice. And if he does not sense his responsibility, he knows that he has not acted freely. Still he also knows that he could have acted in another way. This too is essential if he is to feel that his act is a free one. The alternative of which he is aware, the possibility of having done otherwise, has, however, to be conceived of in terms of a different disposition. Had he seen himself in a different light, he might have willed differently. What is absolutely necessary for a responsible act is that it be rooted in a person's self-concept. But, as we have indicated, the self must always remain basically a mystery. It must forever be fundamentally untouchable precisely as self, and so capable phenomenologically of apprehending itself under a variety of aspects. It is a forever to-be-made, and so capable in accordance with its basic reaction patterns to render itself to the consciousness in a great number of projected guises. The essential determinism of the free act results from the fact that every choice has to correspond to one of these self-images entertained by the agent before the election takes place.

It is true that one modern psychologist, Eric Fromm, defines freedom as the spontaneous activity of the total, integrated personality. But it is clear that by spontaneity he means creative action flowing from the ego in such a way that a person can sense that the act is his. Other psychologists distinguish more clearly between spontaneity and freedom. Spontaneity implies automatic, inexplicable, and consequently irresponsible action. An animal may spontaneously devour one bowl of food rather than another even though both are identical in every way. A human in the same situation may act in the same way. But there is also a possibility that his choice may be made with reference to some self-concept—he may, for instance, be inclined always to prefer what is on the left to what is on the right—and so responsibly.

Freedom then cannot mean the absence of all internal determinism, for it demands that the free act proceed in accordance with the self-image of the agent. But it must also allow for some kind of determining influence on the part of the external object or project with which it is concerned. The freest person, paradoxically enough, is the one who is completely enthralled by the object he has chosen. Heaven has always been proposed by theologians as a state of absolute and perfect freedom. Indeed if a person were not really free in heaven he would cease to be human. Yet it is not possible for a person in heaven, theologians say, to choose to be elsewhere. Since the object of his will is the good, it is not possible for what is perceived as the total good of the individual in accordance with his self-image to be rejected. A person has most freely to dedicate himself to the pursuit of such a good with his total energy. Analogous situations can be had on earth, when, for instance, children are held in complete thraldom by a movie or concert. They experience themselves as both having most freely dedicated themselves to this entertainment, and still not being able to relinquish it for a moment.

If freedom, as it does, involves determination both on the part of the ego-synthesis of the subject and on the part of the congruence of the object for the agent under its aspect of being good, it should be possible infallibly to predict a free choice, or to foresee how much influence must be brought to bear on either the subject or object to alter a choice. But to do this, one would have completely to comprehend both the self-image of the agent at the time of contact with the object as well as the object's possibilities of being apprehended as good for the agent before the choice is made. As we have said, obviously a person is not always completely aware of his own self-image; he is never in full possession of it. Even with the help of depth-psychology it is not always possible for him to delineate it in a satisfactory way. Analysis can bring out some of its hidden facets, but never bare it completely. Myriad contingencies and circumstances are involved in the concealment or revelation of various aspects of good in the object to the mind of the agent. So quite often the agent himself cannot foresee or predict his future choices; much less then can the observer, close as he may be to the subject. Only God, whose understanding of both the ego of the agent and the contingent attractions of the object is absolutely perfect and exhaustive, can predict with infallibility the free choices of men.

Some recent philosophers contend that at least imperfectly it is possible to grasp the unique, concrete, individual personhood of an agent from his acts, and from knowing him in this way to get some idea of how he will react when faced with a choice. Typical is the idea of Schelling who depicts the intelligible character of the individual as being due to an original self-positing of the ego through a choice or option made in definite and determined circumstances. It is no secret that one gets to know a person through his actions. But the reverse is also true. One is capable of really understanding the actions of another only when he gets to know him as a person. Perhaps the law has always recognized this fact in admitting the testimony of character witnesses. A man's actions as emanating from his ego are, as we said, also predictable if one knows perfectly who he is; but they are by that very token absolutely free because through them the subject has been able to express who he is.

If Molina neglected entirely the determinist element in the free act, our own scientific world tends to exaggerate it. The principles of psychological determinism have influenced the development of various psychotherapeutic techniques. In every textbook of psychology one can read the most frequently employed quotation from Freud: "The deep-seated belief in psychic freedom of choice is indeed unscientific and must be abandoned in favor of determinism which is the major factor in mental life." It would be very easy to forget that the great pioneer in psychic research also said: "Psychoanalysis has as its purpose not the removal of the possibility of morbid reactions, but the strengthening of the freedom of the patient's ego to choose one way or another."

Schelling reflects the balanced attitude of more recent philosophers when he states that necessity and freedom are mutually immanent in one and the same act. These elements appear as divergent modalities only when human actions are considered from different perspectives. He uses the example of Judas' betrayal of Christ. That action of his was necessary and inevitable in the light of the two personalities and the circumstances involved. Yet Judas acted willingly and with complete freedom because through this action he manifested his own distinctive inner affirmation of himself. His action was fully conformed to his own personal ego-synthesis, and so perfectly free.

A more up-to-date model might be found in the recent movie, "Cool-hand Luke." Reviewers have stirred up a great controversy about this film. Some critics have seen in it only an account of life in a southern prison camp. Others claim to have detected a much deeper symbolism. They view it as a current larval theological rendition of the story of the New Testament.

Its central character is a modern Christ. At the beginning of
the film Luke is drunk. Christ was accused by his enemies of
being a drunkard. Luke is arrested for cutting off the heads
of parking meters with a large pipe-wrench. The parking meters
could well be symbols of Mammon, the money-idols which
society worships, and which Christ came to destroy. When
Luke arrives at the prison camp, a microcosm in which the
reality of the world is reflected, he is harangued by its director,
the Captain, a kind of God-the-Father figure. The Captain tells
the new convicts that if they obey the rules of the camp their
relationship with him will be a very pleasant one, but if they
get into trouble they will find him "one mean son-o'-bitch." The
Captain then goes back to his usual occupation of sipping mint
juleps on the cool veranda of his comfortable house, while he
observes what is going on in the camp. Luke is introduced to
the regulations of the camp by the "barn-boss": no spitting on
the floor; no smoking in bed, etc. Usual punishment for minor
infractions is a night in the box, a confining wooden shed with
no furnishings; for more serious violations like attempted escape
the prisoner not only spent some time in the box, but also was
fitted with leg-irons. From the beginning of the picture the
viewer senses that Luke is very different from the other prisoners. He is not going to play the game. He is a man of great
personal strength. He has an aura of the miraculous about him.
He will not be stereotyped. He is a truly free spirit, not just
an essence conforming to expectations. There is a hint of the
miraculous in the card game that Luke plays with other more
hardened and seemingly more worldly-wise inmates. He manages to win the pot by bluffing, and so is dubbed "cool-hand"
Luke. He wins further respect by holding his own in a fist-
fight with the largest and toughest prisoner in the camp, a
Peter figure named "Dragline" (an appropriate name for one
who symbolizes a fisherman). Because of his personal strength
and courage Luke manages to convert Dragline from the role
of being his principal challenger to that of his best friend and
loyal supporter. The process of conversion is a clear-cut example of what Sigmund Freud's daughter Anna called identifi-

cation with the target of aggression. Later when Luke on a dare states that he can eat fifty hard-boiled eggs in an hour, the camp is polarized into groups of believers and non-believers, and Dragline becomes Luke's promoter, taking on all who bet that Luke really could not do what he said he could. Even after the miracle is performed there are some inmates who will not believe it. One states that he cannot accept the fact because "No man can eat fifty eggs in an hour." Here again the viewer is brought into contact with the typical stereotyping reaction of the prisoners. They think in terms of essences, of preconceived judgments and normal expectations. They play the role of prisoners well because even their thought-patterns are rigid and restrictive. They are totally unfree. They are themselves just essences, just roles, not real men. Even during the dragged-out scene of the egg-miracle the viewer knew that Luke would succeed—not just because it was a movie and Luke was its hero, but because they had already come to know something about Luke and his self-image. Though a prisoner, Luke was really free. Necessity (assurance of success in the egg-eating performance) and freedom (Luke did not really have to, but he ate the eggs because of who he was: a real person and not just an essence) are immanent in one and the same act.

In the picture Mary Magdalene does not wash the feet of Christ. Rather she is portrayed as a sexy car-washer who attracts the attention of the prisoners as they were working on a highway outside of the camp. Other prisoners react to her in typical, stereotyped male fashion. Only Luke retains his cool, his freedom, even in this temptation.

When Luke's mother dies he is put into the box. It is routine procedure in the camp to confine prisoners during the days of wake and burial of a close relative, because every inmate is expected to attempt escape at this time.

The camp guards to all appearances are the freest people in the film. They come and go as they please, and do what they want to the prisoners. Yet really they, too, are just essences. Their essence is to guard. They constantly see themselves only in this role: this is their being. They sense the radical freedom of Luke and envy him. They feel that though he remains in the camp, he has really escaped from them. This situation irritates them, and they regularly take reprisals against Luke. Except for Luke they would feel perfectly comfortable in the camp. It is the quintessence of rules and expectations; it is the epitome of essence, and as mere unfree essences themselves they fit well into it. Were it not for Luke everything would be all right in the camp. There would be no deviation from the normal, from the expected.

While prisoners work on the roads they are guarded by a crew under the direction of the "walking boss." The walking boss is essence personified. He is in no sense a real person. The directors of the movie emphasize this fact by having him constantly wear reflector-type sunglasses so that no one ever gets to see his face, but only an image of themselves in his eye-pieces. He does not speak a word in the whole picture. He does nothing positive at all. The only thing he can do is walk and kill. He carries a cane and a rifle, walking with the one and killing with the other. He will shoot a bird or turtle for the prisoners' lunch on the road. He will kill any prisoner who tries to escape. He is simply a killer, a death-dealing essence. He may be viewed by the theater patrons as a symbol of the devil. They might recall that Satan appeared in Genesis to Adam and Eve in the form of a snake. One day as they are working alongside the road the prisoners come upon a snake. Luke stuns it, and the walking boss shoots it. But as it dangles in death in Luke's hand it looks remarkably like the walking boss' cane. And Luke calls attention to the fact that on this occasion the walking boss had appeared on the road without his cane. Or the walking boss may be considered as a perfect personification of the law, which, as we have seen, St. Thomas calls *per se mortifera*.

Luke is expected to do the unexpected. He eggs on the other prisoners to greater speed in accomplishing their work. The whole system is upset by an early finish. A certain amount of time is automatically allotted for work. It is not expected that a reluctant worker like a prisoner will be energetic on the job.

When expectations fail because of Luke the guards can only react by doing nothing. Their world of essence does not tell them what they should do in such a case.

Several times in the course of the film Luke succeeds in escaping for a time. He is shackled. Yet the greater the restrictive measures taken against him, the freer he seems to become. The Captain speaks of a lack of communication, but the viewers sense that Luke and the others live in two different worlds. After one of his escape attempts Luke is taunted by the guards. He is forced to dig a grave by one, and then told by another to get his dirt off the terrain. He fills up the hole only to have the first guard return angry because his order was not carried out. Luke is forced to dig again, and when he completes the job he falls exhausted into the grave. He looks up to see the Captain standing at the foot of the grave. After exacting from Luke a promise of obedience, the Captain calls him forth with the words: "Son, come out of there."

Temporal sequence was not a major consideration for the writers and redactors of the gospels; some of the events in Christ's life are out of order chronologically. The directors of the movie invert certain of the episodes too. The Last Supper scene occurs after the Resurrection. Still exhausted by his labor and ill-treatment, Luke is helped by his prisoner friends to the camp dining room. Here again rules prevail. In his condition he was not able to take much food. But the camp regulations required that if a prisoner did not eat all of the food put on his plate he would spend a night in the box. To do so would obviously kill Luke in his extremely weakened condition. So when the spiteful prisoner doling out rice piled it high on Luke's dish his friends expressed their concern for him. They saved Luke's life by filing past him and taking for themselves a portion of the rice on his plate. Alert viewers sensed here a better explanation of the Eucharist than one usually hears in homilies and sermons. Preachers generally speak of the Sacrament as life-giving food all right; but they belabor the idea that it gives Christ's life to the communicant. In the Eucharist the faithful get grace, the life of Christ. This is certainly true; but is it

necessary to appeal so often to the self-centeredness of people
who by their participation in the common meal signify their
desire to be unselfish? The picture gives a better perspective.
By eating his food the communicants give Christ life. Through
the Eucharist they pledge themselves to reflect his life in their
own. By communion with him they identify themselves with
him, as we have already indicated. So they make him live in
themselves, and recognize again their duty to manifest him in
their actions.

The final escape that Luke attempts ends in tragedy. Dragline tries to persuade him not to try to go to the city, but when
argument fails, decides to follow him. With guards in pursuit
Luke seeks refuge in an empty church. Here he expresses his
feeling of being abandoned by God. When the guards catch up
with him, Luke provokes the Captain by quoting his own words
to him as an excuse for again attempting to escape after prom-
ising not to. The relationship between those who are just essences and those who are free persons must always be characterized by total lack of communication. Luke is then shot by
the walking boss, and, instead of being rushed to a hospital
which is nearer, is returned to the prison infirmary. He never
makes it; he dies on the way. As the cars are moving away
from the scene of the shooting, Dragline makes bold to attack
the walking boss. His sun-shades are dropped in the scuffle and
crushed under the wheels of a moving vehicle. Evil is unmasked
through Luke's death; Luke's followers are spurred to coura-
geous deeds by their faith in him and love for him and what he
stands for. The death-dealing nothingness of essence is exposed,
and the prisoners are given an incentive to become true persons
like Luke.

The movie closes with a kind of ascension scene. As the
camera pans up and away from a group of prisoners working
on the road the audience hears Dragline, now shackled himself,
recounting to them the story of Luke. He too now is free.

Luke can be considered a Christ figure only if one perceives
what many people, because of past emphasis on his obedience
and devotion to the law, cannot believe about Christ. Jesus is

really the perfect ideal of freedom. Through the paschal mystery he escaped from just being an essence. In his person at one and the same time he escapes from being just God or just man. As man he is the alienation of the Godhead, and as God he is the freest of all persons. He came, as he said, to fulfill the law: the norms, expectations and stereotypes that men had set up for themselves. But he fulfilled it by converting it once again into the law of love, *agapē*, concern and respect for individuals as persons, not as essences, stereotypes or roles. He restored the pristine sense of the law as it issued forth from God.

Just as Christ's, Luke's death is the achievement of a state of total freedom. In death Luke becomes most perfectly what he was in life, an individual person. Essences cannot die; only individuals die. But in death they attain to the goal of freedom, perfect personhood. And even after death personhood exercises its influence. The story of Luke lives on, enabling even those who are prisoners to introject the freedom that is Luke's.

The idea of freedom inculcated by the film, "Cool-hand Luke," matches closely that advocated by the existentialist philosophers of our time. It is escape from being an essence. Sartre rejects the notion of Spinoza that men are not really free, but only think they are. He teaches that consciousness has always to be free because it is not enough. Man is free because he is actually not himself, but presence to himself, and that because of his consciousness. Freedom is the nothingness which is made-to-be at the heart of man, and which forces human reality to make itself be, instead of just to be. For men to be is to choose oneself. Freedom is not just a being: it is the being of man, that is, his nothingness of being. Obviously then the popular song must refer just to lions, not to men. Man is not born free. He has to make himself free. Each person is an absolute choice of himself from the standpoint both of the world of knowledge and the world of action which such a choice both assumes and illumines. Freedom is really the self in transcendence. It is the I insofar as it has to be outside of itself. As we have said, Sartre distinguishes the *en-soi* from the *pour-soi*. The *en-soi* is what a person is, what he has made himself be according to his free choices. The *pour-soi* is the self in transcendence: the projection of what a person chooses to be, the to-be-made of human existence. For the *pour-soi* to be is to nihilate the *en-soi* which it is. Freedom is essentially nihilation of essence. Through this nihilation the *pour-soi* escapes being an *en-soi*, escapes being its own essence. Through nihilation, as Sartre says, the *pour-soi* really is always something other than what can be said of it. We are not as a matter of fact free; we freely become free. The itch of the *pour-soi* is to transcend. One has to be outside of oneself. Radically this can be seen as a potential for freedom. If a person is to be a person in reality he has eventually to come to the point where he will nihilate his facticity. Otherwise he will remain just an essence; he will never become a person. At the point of nihilation he begins to establish for himself both his freedom and his personhood. He begins to have an individual identity. And his identity assures his freedom. One must nihilate what he is to be what he chooses to be.

The existentialist notion of freedom is reflected also in the definitions given by modern theologians. For Bultmann genuine freedom is escape from the motivation of the present. He brands as a delusion the freedom of subjective arbitrariness advocated by the scholastics. A person can become truly free only when he accepts the laws of his own being. And the law of human being is the law of self-transcendence.

Gustave Weigel describes freedom simply as the power of self-affirmation. Liberty in man does not mean absolute indifference to either of the two alternatives, though it does presuppose that one have the physical power to choose one or the other. Empirically it is simply the human capacity to develop in accordance with one's self-image. It is the power to become what one sees oneself to be. Weigel's definition of freedom jibes closely with the notions expressed by Rahner and Teilhard de Chardin.

While Christian theologians today tend to portray humanity itself as a structure of hope and as a result to dwell on the possibilities for good that freedom implies, the existentialist philosophers are usually more pessimistic. Sartre looks upon freedom as at one and the same time man's greatest glory and most horrible curse. Because man is free he can escape from being just what he is; his potential is virtually limitless within the scope of his own being. But because man is free he can never be true to his own being and at the same time indulge himself in rest or complacency. He is doomed forever to be not enough. He can never be satisfied with what he is. He is always urged on by his being itself to become more than he is. He has set foot upon the moon; but now he must look to Mars. He must continually nihilate himself and what he has accomplished. He must always live in *Angst*, in fear and dread of the terrible power and urge that he is. So Kierkegaard defines *Angst* as the reality of freedom as a potentiality, before this potential has been actualized.

If freedom is considered as the ability of a man to become a person, to escape being an essence, it is possible to distinguish two states or conditions of it. The first we might call antecedent or potential freedom. It is a given of consciousness rooted in the being of man himself. It is the basic openness of a person to the possibilities of his being, grounded in the perception of himself as not enough, as to-be-made within the limits of his mode of being in the world, and in accordance with what he sees himself to be. A person is born into the world prepersonally conditioned not only by the laws of his own being, but also by the circumstances of life in which he will eventually discover himself to be. But as his consciousness develops, he will come to a point where he will have to ratify the image of himself engendered by this conditioning. He will then realize his own nihilating power; he will begin to know that he has to be a choice of himself from the standpoint of what he knows and what he projects. This is the only way he can truly exist. He will recognize at least in a non-reflective way his potential freedom.

The second modality under which freedom can exist is quite different. It might be called consequent or achieved freedom, and is related to the *en-soi* more than the *pour-soi*. It could simply be defined as the thraldom of being what one sees oneself to be and has committed oneself to be. In the process of developing freely, of course, achieved freedom is the ground from which new potential freedom springs. It is one's self-concept that underlies the possibility of further self-definition. Consequent freedom can be considered as a plateau that one has reached in his self-explicitation through free choice. But it is better viewed as the springboard which will hurl a person to a new height where he will find another to propel him on in the endless ascending quest of his ideal self.

These two modalities of freedom are evidenced in the free act inasmuch as there is immanent in it the element of determination and the element of indetermination. The indeterminateness of the act reflects the fundamental openness of potential freedom, while its condition of being caused by and attributable to a definite individual, its note of being a responsible act, the element of determinism in it, proceeds from the thraldom of achieved freedom. But since it itself is the result of previous exercises of freedom, this type of thraldom, this type of determination, in no sense impairs the perfect freedom of the human act that has steadfastly been demanded by orthodox theology.

In the chapter on grace we explained how love necessitates a surrender of freedom. We also indicated how through love freedom is restored, validated, strengthened and augmented. We pointed out that by sharing in God's freedom the person who loves him comes to participate in his being. We said that grace could most appropriately be described as freedom as well as love. We are now in a better position to appreciate that statement. For the graced condition is no other than a state of achieved freedom where one's own self-image is rooted in and related to God through Christ by grace. Through the grace of espousal the prospective lover of God tries on, as it were, a new identity, a tentative one. He perceives that only this can fully dispel his existential *Angst*, afford him complete security in his life and being, and provide a mode of existence that is completely autonomous and free. In the grace of union he puts on Christ. He assumes the new identity that he tried on before. He has a new transcendental self-image. He achieves the condition of being other to himself and is totally free of being just an essence. He becomes a real human person, and not just a stereotype of man. He surrendered his initial freedom to acquire this perfect freedom; this is true. He endured kenosis to make room for pleroma. The more complete a surrender he made of his initial freedom, the firmer the love that he swore, the greater will be the consequent state of thraldom. Thus the unbeliever, the person who does not know, might from his casual observation consider the Christian to be the most unfree of all persons. He is bound by a tie more potent than law itself to please the one to whom he has committed himself. He can never give in to himself, never gratify himself at the expense of his beloved, never lapse in the promise he made. Such a person cannot see how the graced condition can be described as one of achieved freedom. He cannot see it as a true state of human existence, full of new and exciting possibilities. And very likely the reason for his failure to see is that he cannot accept grace as the loving presence of God. He views grace as an object, and as a result looks upon God, too, more under the aspect of a valuable object than of a person who has first offered his love and surrendered his own freedom.

The state of perfect achieved freedom is fully attainable only when there is a mutual surrender of basic freedom between two persons in love. Only when the freedom of one person is completely merged and identified with that of another can the ensuing state be one of total freedom. If the self is surrendered to an object, freedom is alienated, but the condition of the subject is not one of achieved freedom, but enslavement. Objects as such can command only a partial, only a reserved and conditional surrender of self without destroying freedom. One must always retain the ready possibility of withdrawing commitment to an object if one is to attain a state of achieved freedom in regard to it. When there is question of another person, however, the commitment can be total and complete, if from the standpoint of both persons involved it is perceived to be mutual. In this situation the state attained is still fully one of freedom, not indeed the original freedom of each of the individuals, but the common freedom of both. The thraldom of such a state is in no sense unfree.

The reason for the unbeliever's (and perhaps even some believers') tendency to look upon God as an object rather than as a loving person might well be sought in Hegel's phenomenology of *Herrschaft* and *Knechtschaft*. In the relationship between man and God, God has to be considered the master and man the servant. The master alone envisages himself as a fully conscious person, as a person in the fullest sense, independent and autonomous, while his servant is merely his tool. But according to psychological law, as the relationship develops the master is bound to be downgraded, deformed and reduced, even more damagingly so than the servant. Because he is the master he has to cut himself off from the servant. He must maintain his position, his status. He comes to view himself as an essence, a master-essence. His own self-concept is communicated to his servants who then begin to view him as an object, not as a person. Thus in the very attempt to extol his personhood in his own eyes he loses it in the eyes of his servants.

Of course, the orthodox doctrine on the Incarnation and grace precludes any such idea of God's mastery over man. But the person who is not fully acquainted with this doctrine could well conclude from the description of God given by some preachers and writers that he is no more than a master-essence.

Having set forth some viable notion of human freedom for today, we must now address ourselves to the other polarity in the dilemma of grace and free will, God's mastery over the process of salvation. We must consider the priority of divine freedom and personality over the human. This was expressed simply by St. Augustine when he claimed that God not only loves us, but also makes us his lovers. Theological tradition has passed it down as the somewhat terrifying doctrine of predestination. The very idea engenders disaffection in many people today, but since it is an important ingredient of the theology of grace we must consider it. In this chapter we shall accept it in its most generic sense as a time-honored belief of orthodox Christianity. We shall leave the last word about predestination to the next chapter of this book.

There is no doubt about the fact that despite its unpopularity today the idea of predestination has been one of the ma-

jor issues treated by a number of councils and ecclesiastical
documents. It is mentioned, for instance, in the Second Council
of Orange, the Council of Quiersy and the Council of Valence.
The Council of Trent was concerned with it in a number of
connections. While the profession of faith issued by Pope Leo IX
expressly refers to the fact that predestination is a matter to
be believed, it demands with less rigor acceptance of the idea
of a prevenient grace that in no way blocks the exercise of
human free will. The letter of Pope Hadrian I to the bishops of
Spain treats at some length Pelagianism and the orthodox doctrine of predestination.

Predestination can be defined as an act of the divine will
directing a person to salvation. This divine act is absolute and
ineluctable. It most assuredly produces its effect. It is irresistible. Moreover, it must be considered as prior to, as independent
of, any human act. It is not conditioned upon divine foreknowledge of a person's merit. Predestination is in no sense the result
of merit of any kind: rather merit is the result of predestination.
Predestination has to be clearly distinguished from foreknowledge. The former is the act of the divine will, the latter that
of the divine intellect. There really is no great problem about
divine foreknowledge. As completely independent of time God
sees all things in one act while for the creature who exists in
time events are played out in succession and are distinguishable
not only in themselves, but also according to the handy reference points that time provides. Pelagius, who, as we have seen,
held that God is a mere spectator in the drama of human salvation, also admitted the fact of divine foreknowledge. For him as
well as for orthodox theologians the fact that God's knowledge
encompasses all things in a constant now was indisputable. But
the heresiarch considered the divine knowledge open to human
choice, so that the resultant divine will acts directing a person
to salvation could be made with reference to his merits. Orthodoxy rejects this notion. St. Augustine clearly expresses the
truth when he states that the predestining decrees of the divine
will are infallible, not because God knows in advance that a man
will give his consent to grace; they are infallible because God

is omnipotent and accomplishes what he wills. The divine will act has essentially and necessarily to be prior to the human. In his *De correptione et gratia* Augustine teaches that there can be no doubt that the human will cannot resist the will of God which "has made all things in heaven and earth, whatsoever God wanted," (Ps. 134, 6) even "those things that are to come" (Is. 45, 11). Man's actions can in no way obstruct God's doing what he wants at the time he wants and in the way he wants. God has infinite power, and that means he can draw even human free wills withersoever he pleases. In some places in this work the Doctor of Grace seems so obsessed with this idea that he dares even to stretch the apparent meaning of Scripture to fit it. He writes that our willing or not willing is, to be sure, in our own power, but not in such a way as to impede or overrule God's will and power. If it has been written that God "wills all men to be saved" (I Tim. 2, 4), and the fact is that all men are not saved, an explanation has to be given to the statement of St. Paul. A number are possible; but one might very well be that the text refers only to those who are predestined, because all men are represented in them.

From this dialectical consideration of the omnipotence of God and the freedom of man in some of the Fathers, particularly in the works of St. Augustine, the teaching authority of the Church has issued a series of dogmatic propositions which have guided theologians in their discussion of this theological problematic. It will be useful for us to enucleate them here:

1. God wills all men to be saved. This will is truly operative. Thus:
   a. All men receive grace that is sufficient to bring about their salvation.
   b. There is no predestination to evil; evil is exclusively the result of the operation of the human will.
   c. Christ did not die to redeem just the predestined or the faithful; he died for all men.
   d. Grace sufficient for conversion is offered even to hardened sinners.

2. Grace can be resisted by man's free will. A human will-act at odds with grace is one that God permits to safeguard human freedom, but the concursus he offers to it is in no way a cause of the evil it implies. A grace that is foreseen by God as sufficient to bring about the intended result, but which as a matter of fact will be resisted is called a truly but merely sufficient grace.

3. From these dogmatic data, theologians have concluded that besides merely sufficient grace there is another that can be termed efficacious. This grace is assured of having its effect even before actual acceptance by the human will. Efficacious grace does not destroy human freedom, but irresistably draws the will to cooperate with it.

The traditional doctrine of merely sufficient grace must be held as a dogma pronounced by the Council of Trent against the Protestants who in their doctrine of grace appeared to have done away with real human freedom. The idea of efficacious grace is closely connected with Christian belief in divine providence and predestination, but some theologians regard it as only a conclusion from and not an integral part of dogmatic teaching about the operation of God's providence.

The core problem about the relationship of predestination to human freedom is centered in the idea of efficacious grace. For God executes his will to predestine precisely through efficacious grace. And of its very nature efficacious grace is such as will ineluctably have its effect even prior to any free acceptance of it on the part of the human will.

To reconcile freedom with the idea of efficacious grace various systematic explanations have been proposed by different schools in the course of theological history. It will be helpful briefly to present their basic principles before we offer our own tentative solution.

In general we can divide the opinions of theologians on this matter into two large groupings. The first offers what we might call an intrinsicist solution, the second an extrinsicist one. The intrinsicists say that the efficacy of an efficacious grace is a function solely of the grace itself. Grace is endowed with some internal element that makes it fruitful even before the free operation of the human will. The extrinsicist group on the other hand teaches that the efficacy of an efficacious grace, nonetheless real and absolute, stems not from something intrinsic to the grace itself (in itself every grace is essentially versatile) but from factors external to it. Internally an efficacious grace is no different at all from a merely sufficient one. It becomes efficacious even before the operation of the human will because it is supplemented by external graces.

A. The Extrinsicist School.

1. Congruism holds grace to be efficacious because of the circumstances in which it will operate. These are also the results of a divine will act, and are taken into account by God when he metes out his internal grace. The older members of this school regard these crucial circumstances as principally objective ones. If, for example, an equal amount of internal grace were given to two different men, one reared in an exemplary Catholic suburban home, and the other in the inner-city ghetto where religious values are not very much in evidence, the grace given to the first might well be efficacious, while that given the second would be merely sufficient. Stronger grace would have to be given to the second person if, in accordance with his circumstances of life, it is to prove efficacious. The external grace of a Christian environment in conjunction with a certain value of internal grace renders the operation of God efficacious in bringing about the results he desires. On the other hand, more recent followers of this way of thinking opine that the circumstances involved in the consideration of the efficacy of grace are chiefly subjective ones. That is, an efficacious grace becomes so before acceptance because it is exactly tailored to the subjective dispositions of the recipient at the time it is given. The circumstances crucial for the consideration of whether a grace is to be efficacious or not are not chiefly the objective, but rather the subjective ones. These may, of course, have arisen precisely because

of some objective conditions. These congruists maintain that
the freedom of the will under efficacious grace is assured by the
fact that a person has already disposed himself to cooperate with
it at least implicitly by either accepting or rejecting the circumstances of his life. God foresees this disposition and takes it into
account in meting out his grace. The difficulty with this system
is that, if the disposition of the subject results from an act of his
that makes reference to the morally good or evil quality of his
situation, it could exist as the effect of a meritorious act. Hence
efficacious grace would not be doled out independently of merit.

2. Molinism sustains the same basic principle as Congruism,
that is, that efficacious grace is that which is given in circumstances favorable to its operation. But it avoids the difficulty we
have noted through the theory of the *scientia media*. Theologians have always taught that God's knowledge extends to all
actual beings, past, present and future according to the human
reference point of time, as well as to all possible being. Molinists place in God's knowledge between the order of actual
being and that of possible being another of conditional being.
The *scientia media* is God's knowledge of conditional being. God
knows not only possible being and actual being, but also those
beings which would have come into existence had certain conditions or circumstances been verified. When compared to actual
being, beings in this conditional order of knowledge are only
possible, because as a matter of fact the conditions which would
have assured their existence were not verified. When compared
to merely possible being, beings in this order of knowledge participate more in the characteristics of actual being—inasmuch as
they lean toward, tend toward actualization—than merely possible ones do. So the knowledge that God has of them is neither
his knowledge of actual being nor that of merely possible being; it is a *scientia media,* a middle kind of knowledge. Of
course, there can be no such reality as an order of being between actual and possible being, but, according to the Molinists,
this does not preclude the possibility of a middle *knowledge*.
In the first instance then God foresees all possible orders of creation. In each he sees the persons he would create as well as

all the possible circumstances of their life and the amounts of grace he might bestow upon them. He sees how each would have reacted freely in all possible varying circumstances to all possible amounts of grace. Of course, there is no question of merit, because this consideration is still in the order of possibility, not of actuality. When he does actualize one of these orders with its concrete situations and realizations of grace of varying amounts, he automatically predestines, because he knows that some graces will be efficacious even before their actual acceptance. And his predestining act does not destroy freedom for freedom is taken into account in the *scientia media.* Nor is it dependent upon merit, as we just said, because as yet there is no merit. Thus God, leaving freedom intact, is the master of salvation, because out of all possible orders of creation, he gives actual existence to the one he himself selects.

This system is most attractive and obviously provides a good solution to the basic problem. It safeguards both divine control over the means of salvation and human freedom. There is only one major difficulty with it—the *scientia media.* Its opponents say there can be no divine knowledge corresponding to the unreal. The order of possible being is real in the sense that it is comprised of essences that can really be actualized. The order of actual being is obviously real. But between the actual and the merely possible there can be nothing that is real. So there can be no divine knowledge corresponding to it. Advocates of the system can only offer the rejoinder that rejection of it leaves no alternative but an intrinsicist view of efficacious grace, and human freedom is destroyed by that.

B. Intrinsicist Schools.

1. Banesianism teaches that the efficacy of an efficacious grace comes from a special entitative quality it possesses which predetermines its acceptance by the human will. This is called the *praedeterminatio physica.* The evident objection to this idea, that any predetermination does away with freedom, is answered through the use of a distinction between the *sensus divisus* and

the *sensus compositus*. If we consider the human will prescinding from the *praedeterminatio physica* it is perfectly free to sin. But it is not possible for the human subject in his exercise of freedom to bring into being an act adversative to the divine movement if we consider the operation as a whole. Man's contact with being is limited, though perfectly free in what it can attain. So with the *praedeterminatio physica* man freely attains what alone is physically possible for him: the good that God wants. He simply cannot attain what is physically impossible. But this is not precisely a restriction pertaining to the order of freedom as such, but rather to the order of man's limited being. Thus I am not able seriously to will to be transported now to the center of the sun. But no one would say that my freedom is impaired on this account. This impossibility merely reflects an essential modality of my being in the world; I cannot choose what is physically impossible for me to attain no matter how much freedom I have.

2. The school of Del Val proposes a similar idea. But it substitutes moral predetermination for the *praedeterminatio physica*. The ontological impossibility that a man experiences in placing an act adversative to the movement of an efficacious grace is not of the physical, but only of the moral order. But it is nonetheless a real impossibility. The *praedeterminatio moralis* like the *praedeterminatio physica* introduces a human limitation in the order of being as such, not precisely in the area of the exercise of his freedom.

3. The idea introduced by the Jesuit theologian Boyer might appear to some as of the same *genre* as that of the Banesians. Like them he wants to base his theory on what he thinks is the doctrine of St. Thomas. But rather than explaining it, his opinion seems to be more confusing than the doctrine of St. Thomas. He defines efficacious grace as divine premotion which does not physically predetermine. Perhaps the significance of his negative qualification is that he does not want entirely to exclude extrinsicist ideas. He seems to move the question of premotion out of the order of being as such and back into that of freedom. But in this order he has to maintain the priority of the divine action

over the human and thus runs afoul of the problem of liberty. His solution seems almost nominalistic to one who is not thoroughly skilled in the highly technical points of the issue.

4. The Augustinian school holds that efficacious grace is such because it offers man what he freely does not resist: a fully delectable allure that overcomes the opposite attraction to evil. One is ineluctably drawn by the delectation of a love that is clearly and cogently proposed. It is the very nature of a human being to respond to such an allure. He does so with utmost freedom and great joy. His freedom is in no sense restricted, but rather established and confirmed in such an act.

Augustinianism radically differs from Jansenism. Jansenists say that man is not free to resist delectation as such. The Augustinians say that he can be free only in embracing it. Here again in this view freedom is related to being. Man's being itself demands that he freely choose the perfect good when he clearly perceives it. By this choice his freedom is not restricted; rather his being is fulfilled.

The great merit of the Augustinian system is that it proposes grace as love, and focuses upon the ineluctable existential delectation that love can offer. Much of the difficulty about the scholastic ideas on efficacious grace stems from the fact that they do not regard grace as love, but as a display of divine power. God seems to force, not to draw. So through efficacious grace he seems to act in opposition to and not in accordance with what human freedom implies. Indeed the picture Scripture paints of the operation of God's grace engenders the notion that it is a power, a great power—but the power of love, not of brute force. And love is what man wants; love is what freedom is all about. Take for instance the words Hosea the prophet places in the mouth of the Lord: "With human lines I led them, with the cords of love" (11, 4). The Fathers too insist upon a fact that many think has been discovered only in our time. The only power that God uses is that of love. St. Peter Chrysologus, for instance, says in his seventh sermon: "When God changed his guise from that of a Lord to that of a Father, he manifested his will to rule rather in love than in power, and to be loved rather than to be feared." At the time of the heyday of the development of scholastic theology, however, the kingly archetype of God was still very much in vogue, and the Church's statal image of itself gave ample opportunity for seemingly ingenuous love to be regarded as weakness rather than strength. The problem involved when one considers that love takes a person as it finds him and does not produce a kind of instantaneous magical transformation left many theologians wary about using it to describe God's way of exercising his mastery over creation and salvation. Then again, as we know from our experience today, love in the concrete is hard to judge. The love of people long married sometimes seems like something else. They often get their way with their spouse by appearing crotchety, impatient, angry and disrespectful, by seemingly more forceful means than a display of affection. Finally the minimalist position with regard to charity always in vogue in theology seemed to weaken the idea of love and make it less apt for expressing the way in which God rules his creation. It is only in our day that the notion of love as a power greater than fear itself has taken full root in society and provides a better way in the judgment of most to explain the operation of God's providence. But it does happen to coincide very well with the biblical and more ancient theological views.

5. A very clever idea, one that is most commendable, is introduced by Thomassin in attempting to reconcile human freedom with efficacious grace. When we considered the theological doctrine on just what a man could and could not accomplish without the help of grace, we culled from textbooks on grace the proposition which states that without any kind of grace it is impossible for man to go for a long time without violating the precepts of the natural law. Theologians in this case, as we saw, were talking about an absolute moral impossibility. They regard man as not really free to observe the law. But we mentioned that a person's freedom as such actually was not impaired at all by maintaining this doctrine. While in each individual case he had both the possibility and freedom to observe the law, it was due to the added difficulty imposed by a whole series of en-

counters with the law that the lack of freedom and possibility arose. For more is required to resist a whole bombardment than a single shell. This idea is applied by Thomassin to the question of efficacious grace. No single grace as such is to be considered efficacious. God's intent in predestining is achieved not in one or other grace, but in the whole complex of graces that he gives to a person. Thus efficacious grace is a congeries of individual graces which will ineluctably produce the effect that God wants. When grace is given in great abundance and variety it will infallibly achieve its purpose. While man is free to resist each individual grace, he is not free in regard to the whole complex. More power is needed to resist a constant bombardment by grace than human freedom implies.

C. *The Intrinsicist-Extrinsicist School.*

An attempt to reconcile the extrinsicist and intrinsicist positions in regard to efficacious grace is undertaken by Tournely. He maintains that in the ordinary, relatively easy decisions of daily life an extrinsicist view of efficacious grace can be employed. Ordinary grace is efficacious because of the circumstances in which it is given. But in key decisions, those involving a total change of style in one's life, it is necessary to avoid Pelagianism that an internally efficacious grace be bestowed, for here precisely there is question about the goodness of the circumstances in which one is living themselves. Efficacious grace would be seen as the result of human merit, or else a *processus ad infinitum* with regard to circumstances would have to be instituted. At some point in life a grace which is intrinsically efficacious must be given. From then on circumstances can play a part in the consideration of how a grace becomes efficacious.

The explanation of predestination in relation to human freedom which we offer will have to be wide enough to allow for both an internal and external economy of grace. We have already stressed the importance for our time of external grace. But since external circumstances which can truly be called graces have to be eventually internalized to affect the operation of the human mind and will, ultimately the problem is always one of reconciling on the one hand the vectoring of a person toward his final destiny either through God's direct offer of love to him or an already interiorized self-image, which itself has to be the result of the person's contact with God's love expressed perhaps in some external circumstance of his life, with that person's freedom to reject that divine motion on the other.

The theory that we shall propose is based largely on the thesis elaborated by William G. Most in his *Novum tentamen ad solutionem de gratia et praedestinatione.* This exposition is couched entirely in scholastic terminology and follows closely the methodology of the Schoolmen. Accordingly it still conceives grace as a divine physical force. But it is, I think, readily translatable into terms more palatable to a modern audience. It can be fitted into an existentialist-personalist framework. There perhaps it will assume an even greater clarity and intelligibility.

In considering the question of predestination theologians usually distinguish three phases of divine operation. Of course, they do not indicate thereby any temporal progression in God. This is only our way of envisioning causal priorities. In the first stage God wills the salvation of all men. This act is not a mere velleity. God implements it by proffering his love to all in such a way that it at least suffices to obtain a response. To some he may offer efficacious grace and so predestine them. In the second stage God foresees the cooperation of those to whom he gives efficacious grace. By responding to it they merit. But he also foresees the rejection of his love by those who receive merely sufficient grace. They become guilty of sin. In the third stage he rewards those who have merited and punishes those who have sinned. When proposing these data theologians remind us that we cannot play God. The distribution of grace is essentially a mystery, and we cannot fully fathom it. It is certainly possible that God would give efficacious grace to all men and thus bring them to salvation. But when considering the case theoretically we must provide for all possibilities.

Most proposes two situations that may occur in the case of efficacious grace. The first he sees as an exercise of special providence in regard to those persons whom God signally loves and calls to be exceptional saints. Among these we can certainly list the Mother of God, and to a lesser degree, the Apostles. But there could very likely be others. The second situation is the ordinary one where no special kind of providence is in evidence.

First let us take the case of the person who is the object of God's special concern. Since God's personal love has of its very nature to be absolutely free and bestowed gratuitously, such an individual may receive graces in such abundance and with such frequency that he will not be able to resist in accordance with his humanity itself the delectation that is offered. Of course this person too is radically free; otherwise he could not merit. But as we said, freedom does not mean absolute indetermination. We are dealing here with the constant and clear proposal of God's love and the delectation it can offer to alleviate existential human *Angst*. Man, as we have said, will most freely and yet ineluctably give himself to such delectation. Neither in the case we are considering is there question of only one act. We can have recourse to the idea of Thomassin. While the individual retains perfect freedom to reject each and every single offer of love, he cannot resist a whole series of offers. Thus the efficacy of this kind of grace is assured in the very lavishness with which it is proffered. It is the constant persistence of grace that makes it efficacious.

The second case is that in which there is no extraordinary exercise of divine providence. Here a grace that is *per se versatilis* is given. In other words a grace is bestowed that can either be accepted or resisted not only in each and every distinct offer but in a complex as well. Whether a man will resist or not will depend upon his disposition. When God's offer of love is manifested to the person, if he resists, he does so by a positive act of his own. He cuts off God's love. If he persists in doing this until death he will be condemned. His condemnation is foreseen by God. But in no prior sense was it willed or caused by God. It occurs only as the result of his own demerits. All that

God did in the case was to proffer his love. The person by a positive act of his own rejected this love because it was not in accord with his self-image, and so became responsible for his own condemnation. Nor does the fact that a person can reject the love of God in any real sense limit God's mastery over creation and salvation. The act of rejection is subjectively a positive one, and so for it divine concurrence is necessary. But God cooperates with the action only inasmuch as it is a positive entity, not in any sense with its object. Subjectively the action is a positive being; but its object as such is a pure negativity. It is a rejection of, a denial of love. As tending toward a purely negative object it is an act of negating being. It is an act centered on non-being, on sin. Since God is the master only of being and not of sin or non-being, there is no question of man's freedom in this connection in any way restricting God's control over being. In creating man free God willed to permit sin. He allowed non-being to be mingled with being. But non-being in no way limits his own being or power. Non-being does nothing. As we have seen, this conception of a free human act as having the capability only to deny being is in perfect accord with the existentialist notion of man's power of freedom itself. Freedom is primarily a power to say no to what is. Man has no real control or power over being as such. He can exercise his freedom only by negating being or placing negative conditions on being by delimiting it in accordance with his designs. His freedom formally consists in his power to negate. According to Sartre's definition freedom is not a being; it is the being of man, that is, his nothingness of being, his ability to negate being.

In this case, then, the original *gratia versatilis*, that is, the offer of love that was open to resistance by the human will, was as a matter of fact a merely sufficient grace. It had the power to move the human subject to a loving response, but it was rejected by his free will. But what happens in the case of an efficacious grace? For the sake of clarity we can consider just a single act. What happens in one case can be extended to a whole series or a lifetime of encounters with God's grace. In the first phase of the operation when God wills the salvation of all men, the efficacious grace, too, is basically one that is able to be resisted by the human will. This grace as love tends to move a man to respond to God. It vectors him toward salvation. It draws a man only in one direction. And man is perfectly free in accordance with his self-image to reject it. In the first instance of our consideration of efficacious grace it in no way differs from that which is merely sufficient. But in the supposition of the case the fact is that man in this first instance does not resist it. Through his foreknowledge, to the human way of thinking, God takes note, as it were, of this fact of non-resistance. At this point he sees the grace as efficacious, and, if we consider all the graces of a person's life, predestination occurs. Predestination, therefore, takes place before any consideration of merit. At this point, of course, man can have no merit. He has not even acted as yet. Only God has acted in offering his love, foreseeing that in accordance with the self-image of the recipient there is no resistance to that offer, and finally predestining that person. If the person had resisted, of course, he would have acted. But non-resistance is not an act. It is only an indeliberate predisposition for a free act. Non-resistance is obviously nothing positive at all; it is a state of non-action in relation to an occurrence in the purely conceptual, and hence indeliberate, order. The human person becomes aware of God's offer of love and the possibility of accepting or rejecting it. He is conscious that it is not in opposition to his self-concept, to the way he grasps his own self at this moment. So he does not bring his freedom, his negating power to bear on it at this time. He has not and does not act as God predestines him. But a further reflection emanating from the first is that through this offer of love he can negate his own facticity. He can be more than he is. He perceives himself as not enough without this love. He negates himself as he is, and thus projects himself into the love that was offered to him. In negating his facticity he acted freely; he acted meritoriously. But in the ultimate analysis his whole action can be traced to the initial movement of divine love. In the final breakdown of this process up until the time man freely and yet ineluctably cooperates, God's movement of love is the

full and exclusive cause of the whole enterprise. So in the first
instance salvation is due to God, and to him alone. It becomes
due to man also only in the second instance, later on to the human way of thinking, when his free cooperation is irresistably
elicited. So the resulting merit is really the man's own, but due
to him solely because of a prior divine action. Thus Augustine's
idea that in human merit God merely crowns his own action is
fully verified in this system.

In short, then, we can describe the operation of efficacious
grace in this way: God offers his love. He foresees the non-
resistance of the human person in accordance with his own self-
concept. God foresees his grace as efficacious. He predestines
the man. Since predestination occurs prior to any human act, it
is totally independent of merit. The person then acts in response
to the love he has not resisted in accordance with his self-
image. He thus merits. He will be rewarded and God's predestining act will be realized in him.

The key to the whole conception is that non-resistance is
not an action, but only a purely negative condition of the human subject, while resistance is a free action: a positive action
if it is considered as a modification of the subject, but purely
negative if seen from the perspective of its object. Non-resistance as a non-action can in no sense be causative of anything. It
is merely a condition in divine foreknowledge. So in full agreement with the ideas of St. Augustine predestination in this system is not at all dependent upon merit or any act of man. Rather
merit and man's action is the result of predestination.

It seems necessary to me in the application of this system
to accept the existentialist notion of freedom. Most apparently
does not, but it seems that he ought to. Everyone, existentialist
or scholastic, will admit that human freedom is a positive reality,
an active power of man. As a modality of man's being in the
world, freedom is something most positive: the greatest power
man has. But the existentialists view its tendential energy as
primarily negative. As over and against an object, it can only
negate or delimit. If, on the other hand, freedom is regarded
as primarily positive also as a tendential force, I would have

great difficulty in defending the system. For if freedom attained objects primarily in a positive way, its ability to negate would then have to be regarded as a secondary alternative, as the obverse of its basic power to affirm. When two possible alternatives are offered an equivalence is set up between affirming the one and denying the other. To say yes to one is implicitly to say no to the other and viceversa. In accepting one of two possible courses of action a person would have implicitly but nonetheless positively denied the other. Now in the case we were considering, non-resistance, as well as resistance, would have to be viewed precisely as the result of a free choice, and not merely as a condition that precedes the exercise of freedom. For if the free act primarily tends in a positive direction non-resistance can be only an equivalent way of describing acceptance. But if the very essence of human freedom is placed in the power to negate this difficulty is avoided. If a person has not negated something, he has not used his freedom. To say yes to what is, is an act of reason, but not of freedom. To affirm an essence is to be unfree. Saying yes to what is not is only a secondary act of freedom, presupposing that one has already said no to what is. In this view there can be no equivalence between yes and no. They are not just different tendential perspectives of one and the same act. They are radically different.

The existentialist conceptualization is in better agreement too with the scholastic notion that man has no real power over being as such. At best man's action can only modify being. And this power of modification is basically negative. Man has the ability to limit being, to place negative conditions upon it, to cut it off, to separate it, to play the limitations of one being against those of another.

Were we to explain the process of predestination then with the presupposition that freedom is fundamentally a positive tendency, we would, it seems, fall into Pelagianism. We would have to present it in this way: God offers his love. He foresees that man will not resist. He predestines. Man acts in accordance with the offer of divine love. He merits. But resistance and non-resistance are only negative ways of looking at non-acceptance and acceptance. If freedom is primarily a positive tendential reality we can better describe the situation in positive terms: God offers his love. He foresees that man will accept. He predestines—thus if acceptance, saying yes, is the primary act of freedom, when a man accepts, he has already acted freely, and predestination is made dependent upon divine foreknowledge of a free human act. So we must say to preserve the system from Pelagianism that resistance and non-resistance are not just negative ways of looking at non-acceptance and acceptance. We have to say with the existentialists that they constitute the essence of human freedom. One may object that even in an existentialist philosophy non-resistance has implicitly to be acceptance. But upon further examination it is easy to see that this is not necessarily so. In scholastic terminology we would have to say that non-resistance is *potential* affirmation, but unless freedom is essentially a positive tendency, it is not implicit affirmation. For even in scholasticism freedom implies not only the ability to choose among alternatives, but also not to act at all. If one does not resist an alternative it cannot logically be concluded that by that very fact he has accepted it. The possibility of making no decision at all is still open to him. An example might be helpful. I was born an American. It occurs to me that I ought to review whether I can intellectually accept the American political philosophy. For the moment I do not reject it. But by that very fact no one can say I have accepted it. I may merely have deferred further consideration of it for the time being. If I decide to negate the possibility of existing under any other form of government, then and only then have I implicitly accepted it.

There may still remain in the minds of some readers a difficulty about the relationship of the original offer of God's love as a *gratia versatilis* and the human self-concept which will be instrumental in influencing resistance and non-resistance. It might seem that God has not retained mastery over this situation, because at least initially in the order of being, though certainly not in that of freedom, God's love may be dependent in some way upon a modality of human existence. It might be one's

self-concept and not the love which is the chief factor in swaying
the final decision. But this has simply to be denied. The human
self-concept will result either from previous free choices, and so
be dependent on grace as we have explained, or else, as it has to
in the instance of the very first choice, be the result of a prepersonal conditioning of the human person by the modalities of
his existence in the world. But this situation of the person in
the world is also the result of an exercise of divine providence.
We might resort again to the example used before to clarify this
statement. The fact that I was born in America is in the first
instance before I have had a chance to make a decision to accept or reject my citizenship a prepersonal situation of my being
in the world; it truly affects that being and conditions it in
many ways. It automatically becomes a part of my ego-synthesis just as my humanity itself does. As such it will influence the
free choices I make even if as yet I have not made a decision
about it. As we said, non-resistance to it does not necessarily
imply an acceptance of it. Provisionally I may act under its influence without having made a formal decision about it. It has
become a part of me not by an act of mine, but as it were by
an act of God's providence willing that I be born in America
rather than in Russia. I have not resisted it, and so as a positive
situation or condition of my being it can affect my decisions. But
I may have not as yet negated the possibility of moving, for
instance, to Russia. So I have not as yet really acted freely in
regard to it. It exists only as an act of God, and not as yet as
one that I have fully and freely accepted. So God's act has
to be regarded even in this case as prior to any of mine, and
my disposition, my self-image, itself as resulting from God's
exercise of freedom and love, not my own.

The explanation we have offered to the basic difficulty about
the priority of divine love over the human despite the existence
of true freedom in man seems to be adequate within the parameters we have laid down. Of course, it has not in any way solved
the basic mystery of divine love itself. We have not and cannot
address ourselves to the why of divine love. Why was I born
in America rather than in Russia? Why does God seem to love

some more than others? We are not always able to rationalize our own love, much less God's. As Jung has remarked, the basic problems of existence can never be solved, and if it looks like they are, something significant has been lost.

Nor have we really considered fully all the knotty problems of divine predestination. The idea of an arbitrary decision of God with regard to the eternal fate of man is one that still strikes us with bewilderment and fear. We mentioned that as Christians we have to hold some kind of predestination. It is a traditional doctrine not merely of theology but of faith itself. But can some interpretation of it be given that will make it more intelligible than it was in the past? Can predestination be seen in a better light by the world today? That is the question we shall treat in the next chapter.

CHAPTER VIII

Predestination

There are some Christians today who would consider the idea of predestination too fantastic to be taken seriously; a few have been driven to neurotic anxiety by it; but the great majority are totally irresponsive toward it. If the problem is brought to their attention this last group will console themselves with the thought that God will take care of them if they do their best, or that God will save all men, or that predestination is not really an issue today when few people believe in hell anyway. One detects a definite avoidance pattern in the behavior of many of these people, and that may well indicate that the notion of predestination is really too disturbing for them to bear.

The heart of the difficulty about predestination lies in the impression most people have about it. They project God as first deciding who is to go to heaven. This is the chief element in the process to their way of thinking. Out of some cosmic grab-bag God selects the souls who are going to be the winners in the game of life. No one can know his reason for choosing some and leaving others; it is a mystery. (Many people have a Pelagian outlook and think that the selection is made on basis of merit). Then after God has picked out the elite, he gives efficacious grace to them, and so assures that his will shall be carried out. This is a secondary element in the process: it can be called predestination, but only in a derived sense. If God wills the end, he must will the means to the end. God's purpose is to populate heaven; the means he uses is efficacious grace. The word "predestination" is applied primarily to the end, in a secondary sense to the means.

If we prescind from the theological sophistication evidenced by use of the word "efficacious" in relation to grace, we would have to admit that this modern textbook view of predestination is very similar to the idea of it presented by some of the early Fathers of the Church, particularly by St. Augustine. But what few people today realize is that, in the course of time, the notion of predestination has undergone a great metamorphosis at the hands of theologians. While these all admit it to be a matter of faith that predestination at least in the very general sense of God's mastery over the economy of salvation be acknowledged, they are by no means in any kind of agreement as to the theological specifics of it.

The Scriptural basis for the doctrine of predestination is to be found chiefly in the writings of St. Paul, particularly in his letters to the Romans (9, 6 ff.) and Ephesians (1, 4 ff.). Though the gospels hint at the idea, they propose very little explicit material on the subject. Guided mainly by the principles laid down by St. Paul, the great Doctor of Grace, St. Augustine, elaborated his theory about predestination, a theory that was to be considered the classical one, and was to remain in vogue down to Reformation times. To a certain extent Luther, but much more notably Calvin, relied upon Augustine's theory to bolster their own ideas about the sovereignty of God and the compelling power of his grace. This stance of the great Reformers forced Catholic theologians back to the tedious study of the monumental anti-Pelagian treatises of the Bishop of Hippo. They came up with distinctions galore to save him from being stigmatized as a forerunner of Calvinism. Practically all of these Catholic theologians defended the basic orthodoxy of the Augustinian notion of predestination by trying themselves to give a clearer presentation of his thought, or what they considered to be his thought. Only a few like the great historian of theology Denis Petau dared to challenge ideas of the African Father that had up to his time been sacrosanct. But once the gauntlet was down, others began unostentatiously to leave the Augustinian camp and to propose new theories about predestination and grace.

Of all the later schools the Thomists remained most faithful to the Augustinian idea as it was understood in the middle ages. God predestines some souls to glory before any consideration of their merits. To these souls he gives efficacious grace, that is grace embellished with the *praedeterminatio physica*, and so accomplishes his will. Grace thus is distributed in accordance with a previous divine plan to direct those who were predestined to the actual achievement of the end.

The Congruists reacted against this idea of predestination. Molinists agreed with the Thomists inasmuch as they held that there was a predestination of the elect to glory and consequently to efficacious grace. But they hedged in admitting that this occurred simply before any consideration of merit. Their notion of the *scientia media*, which we considered in the last chapter, allowed them to introduce a distinction: *ante praevisa actualia merita, concedo; ante praevisa futurabilia merita, nego.* In other words, they were willing to admit that predestination took place before any prevision of the actual merits of a person, but they denied that it could justly take place without any reference to futurable merits, that is, those merits foreseen in the *scientia media* as ones which would have accrued to a person in the different possible orders of creation. Without some such distinction, they contended, the positive will of God to save all men cannot be taken seriously.

Other Congruists like Toletus, Maldonatus, Lessius, Vasquez, Valentia and Suarez introduced a distinction in the very notion of predestination that reversed the emphasis of the classical view. God does not predestine a person before any consideration of his merits to both glory and grace. Before any consideration of his merits a person is predestined only to receive the kind of graces that God freely wills to give him. It is only after a consideration of his merits that a person is predestined to glory. Predestination is concerned primarily with heaven or hell in the traditional and popular view; it relates chiefly to grace or sin in the theory of these theologians. To be predestined means to receive efficacious grace. The prefix in the word "pre-destination" in every system, of course, refers to a priority of causality, or an independence in the order of causality in relation to some thing or event. And in this school as in the classical the prefix refers to a person's foreseen actual merits. God's distribution of grace is made totally independently of, causally prior to, any prevision of actual merit. But while the classical view insists on a predestination to glory, this is something that cannot be admitted by these Congruists. There is no such thing as *pre*destination to glory, for one is chosen for heaven only *after* prevision of actual merits. Predestination thus can refer only to the total series of graces that a person will receive in his lifetime, graces which, because they are efficacious, will ultimately bring that person to heaven.

It will be useful for our purpose to pursue the line of argument used by this group of Congruists to arrive at its conclusion, a conclusion which stands in such stark contrast to the traditional notion of predestination, certainly to that proposed by St. Augustine. For on the basis of it we may arrive at an idea of predestination that will be more acceptable to our own times.

For the adult in the present dispensation of grace there are only two possible final states: glory or condemnation, heaven or hell. If a man does not go to heaven, the only other alternative is hell. The obverse then of predestination is reprobation, or condemnation to hell. Now no orthodox theologian has ever held a positive antecedent reprobation: no orthodox theologian has ever proposed the idea that before any consideration of demerits (antecedent) God selects (positive) some people to send to hell. The strong reaction of the Church to this doctrine when it ap-

peared in the writings of Calvin evidences the disdain that
Catholicism has always entertained toward it. By explaining how
God predestines a man by removing him from the *massa damnata*, St. Augustine himself neatly avoids any possible accusation
of defending positive antecedent reprobation. The *massa damnata* is wending its merry way to hell on its own initiative, not
because of any positive act of God. To extricate an individual
from the *massa* a positive act of the divine will is required: this
is the act of predestining. But no special act is needed on the
part of God to leave a person in the *massa*. And every person
since Adam is born in the *massa* because of original sin. If he
is not removed from the *massa* by a special act of God, he will
be carried along with it to hell. As we said, it does not require
a special act of God to leave a person in the *massa*. So God
does not positively reprobate anyone before a prevision of death
in sin. But leaving a person in the *massa* is equivalent to some
kind of reprobation. Later commentators called it negative antecedent reprobation.

In the doctrine of St. Augustine then God acts positively to
predestine the elect. But in regard to those who are not predestined no action is taken at all. They are simply left in the
massa damnata. By that very fact they are condemned, for there
is no other alternative for them. If they are not selected to go
to heaven, they will have to go to hell. Now the action of God
in predestining the elect occurs logically and causally before
any consideration of their merits. Thus similarly it would seem
that those who are not called to glory are left in the *massa*
without any consideration of their merits or demerits. Those
summoned forth for heaven will produce good works in virtue of
the efficacious grace given to them; those left in the *massa* will
sin, because they will not cooperate with the merely sufficient
grace they will receive. Those left in the *massa* then are truly
reprobated, for they are actually and effectively condemned to
hell. They are antecedently reprobated because the condition
they find themselves in is not the result of any consideration of
their personal demerits, but exists prior to any such reflection,
as it were, on the part of God. But they are reprobated nega-

tively not positively, because their condemnation has not resulted from any positive action on the part of God, but rather from a non-action, from his failure to call them to eternal life for a reason known only to him. This, of course, is not to say that God takes no positive action whatsoever to save those left in the *massa*. He gives them sufficient grace. But since he has not actually called them to salvation, the grace he gives to them is one that is truly but merely sufficient.

In the course of history many theologians defended the notion of antecedent negative reprobation as the correlative of predestination before any prevision of merit. It was rejected by the Congruists we have mentioned for a reason that now should be quite apparent. In reality antecedent negative reprobation is tantamount to and easily reducible to antecedent positive reprobation. In effect the two are identical. The only basis for any kind of distinction lies purely in the subjective order. In positive reprobation God's will is accomplished by an act; in negative reprobation it is accomplished by non-action. But in either case a choice has been made. Leaving a person in the *massa* for one who holds the scholastic idea of freedom, that tendentially it is primarily positive, is the same as willing to leave him in the *massa*, at least in the circumstances of the case. For God's intention in not acting is not merely to *defer* action, but never to act. And if he decides never to act, by that positive intention he has equivalently condemned.

Again opponents of the idea of negative reprobation assert that it contradicts the universal salvific will of God, a will to which Scripture makes clear reference. The will of God to save all men, which the Council of Trent says is sincere and truly operative, can be preserved only if it is seen as a conditional one in relation to those who are negatively reprobated. But if God is really the master of the economy of salvation, the condition cannot emanate from the situation of the human person as such. Selection or non-selection for heaven has to be made prior to any prevision of merit or demerit. Any condition placed upon God's will to save all men has to originate in God's will itself. It is as if God would say to himself: "I will to save all men,

if I will to save all men." The absurdity of such a statement
is patent.

A third argument is evolved from the case of a person who
actually is negatively reprobated, but who at some time in his
life is in the state of grace. If he is reprobated he will certainly
die in the state of sin, but he could still live for a long time in
grace. Even advocates of the theory of negative reprobation
have to admit this possibility as real. According to Catholic doctrine during the time that the person is actually in the state of
grace he is a friend of God and his adopted son. But this very
state of being signifies clearly and sincerely God's will to save
him. If, however, through antecedent reprobation God's will has
already been set against him, how can God be regarded as truly
loving him, as willing for him all possible good, as drawing him
toward his final goal while he is in the state of grace? The whole
situation would by human standards be quite a mockery. The
system would evince God's will as rather arbitrary and capricious.

A final reason against the idea of negative antecedent reprobation is drawn from the works of St. Prosper of Aquitaine. A
most dutiful follower of the tradition of St. Augustine on the
question of predestination and grace, Prosper was moved to give
an explanation of it to people who had become seriously dis-
turbed in conscience because of it. He opined that it was not
only the authentic doctrine of Augustine, but Catholic teaching
also that no one could deny, that reprobation or a denial of predestination can take place only after a prevision of the death of
a person in the state of serious sin; in other words, after a prevision of a man's demerits. He brands the interpretation that
some commentators gave to the teaching of St. Augustine, namely
that some are excluded from beatitude solely on the basis of an
arbitrary divine decision, as a shocking lie and outrageous blas-
phemy.

Thus a reputable and considerably large school of theologians rejects entirely the idea of negative antecedent reprobation. Persons cannot in any way be excluded from heaven before any prevision of their merits or demerits. God reprobates

only those whom he forsees will die in the state of sin. To be consistent with themselves, then, many of these theologians have deemed it necessary also to reject the idea of predestination to glory before any prevision of merit. If God's action of determining the eternal fate of those called to glory occurs before any consideration of their merits, no objective norm is introduced into the process of selection. So it would seem to be completely arbitrary. Those not selected have to be reprobated; and since the process of selection has to occur prior to any consideration of merit or demerit, the reprobates are equivalently condemned before any consideration of their demerits. Perhaps, however, someone might say that first God considers the foreseen demerits of those to be condemned. He reprobates them. The others then are predestined. But of course, even in this view predestination would not occur before a consideration of merit, for the absence of demerit, if we can so speak, automatically implies merit. And in this view at least in the first instance predestination would not be a positive act of God. It would result from non-action. In this view the positive action of God is directed only to the reprobates. Those left over, those not touched by the first divine action, are to be predestined. So the whole of tradition would be turned topsy-turvy by such a perspective, and God would be seen as primarily concerned with the condemnation, and not the salvation of men.

So this school of theology says that no matter how one tries to extricate himself from the difficulty posed by the possibility of a predestination to glory before prevision, he succeeds only in involving himself more deeply in it. The only solution is to deny entirely the possibility of a predestination *praecise ad gloriam ante praevisa merita,* that is, a predestination before prevision of a person's merits that singles him out, marks him for salvation, and grants him grace accordingly. God destines a person for heaven or for hell only after a consideration of his merits or demerits.

Of course, these theologians have not repudiated the notion of predestination which is required by orthodox faith. But they maintain that faith requires the acceptance only of a *praedesti-*

natio complete sumpta before any prevision of merits. By this they mean that God predestines a person in the sense that, independently of merit, he provides for him a whole series of graces that will be instrumental in bringing him to heaven. In this view the primary object of predestination is efficacious grace, not glory. Glory is attained in consequence of efficacious grace and remains an element of the predestining act of God, but it is just a component of the complex, not the be-all and end-all of predestination.

So predestination, the *bête noire* of the theology of grace, has been really defanged by these theologians of the Congruist school. They have changed the nature of the beast. One of the most complex of all theological problems has become really a non-problem. For to say that before any consideration of a person's merits God predestines him only to a series of graces culminating in heaven is merely to say something we already know and accept. It signifies only that God is the master of the economy of salvation and distributes his graces in complete freedom. It means only that love has to be absolutely and perfectly free. It intends to say only that love and what it leads to, union, cannot be dependent upon merit or demerit or any other purely objective value. Love is cheapened if it is in any way conditioned by or subordinated to anything outside of itself. It denotes that the kind of love God offers to man, familial love, is totally in excess of man's desserts, and man is completely unable to make any demands upon God in regard to it. There is nothing that can correspond to such love, neither power nor need, excellence nor indigence, merit nor demerit. Realizing what this love implies, and how it would be demeaned by any other posture whatsoever, all a man can do in the fact of it is to express his desire to be loved, his willingness to be transformed in it, and to commit himself fully to it.

The larval theology expressed in the general insouciance of people today about predestination is telling us something about it. Today it may very well be a non-problem. But the questions we asked about the distribution of God's grace, about the direction of his love, are still vexing ones. Why does God apparently love some more than others? As we said, the obvious answer to this question is that we do not know for sure that he actually does. But theology must provide for the contingency that he does not love all persons equally. The warnings of Scripture about the possibility of condemnation may be only that, warnings about a possibility and not at all a statement of fact. But then again they do indicate a real possibility which theology must ponder. If human love is a reflection of God's own, we find in it both a verification of both the reality of the unequalness of love in respect to different persons and at least a partial answer to the problem that this mystery poses. For man is held to love all at least minimally to the extent that he will good and not evil for anyone, but at the same time to repudiate and punish evildoing, and this for the sake of love itself. And as a matter of fact men do love some people more than others. They ordinarily love husbands and wives, mothers and fathers, sisters and brothers more than they love strangers. Of course, since no one is a stranger to God, and according to the Christian way of life even sin may be regarded as a special title to greater love for the sinner, the parallel is by no means perfect. But it does stress a possibility that is inherent in the concept of love itself. Love is indiscriminate to the extent that it takes a person as he is in the hope of transforming him into something better. If the beloved resists such transformation, the intensity of love may be eventually diminished and reduced to the minimal level. Apart from the minimal bestowing of it which is owing to all, it has to be absolutely free, and as such defies total explanation. In the final analysis one has to say that he really does not know why he loves. He just does.

If we consider grace as love all the difficulties associated with it, predestination not excepted, are swallowed up in the tremendous mystery that love is.

CHAPTER IX

Epilogue

The purpose of this book has not been to expound new doctrine. On the contrary, its intent is strictly theological. It represents an attempt to investigate from an orthodox faith position theological perspectives largely hitherto unexplored. Recently the magisterium of the Church has voiced incessant pleas that basic Christian doctrine be explicated by theologians in terms that people today can more easily assimilate. This book represents an effort to respond to that request in an area of theology that seems to be increasingly neglected precisely because it is becoming less and less intelligible to modern man. As we said at the beginning, the ideas we have proposed are addressed to all who have sufficient training and background relative to the doctrine of grace to be able to handle them with at least a certain amount of discrimination. But the book is especially dedicated to those whose difficult task it is to teach theology or study it today. It is respectfully submitted to them for their criticism and counsel. But it is also directed to them in the hope that they will by their own efforts in helping to create a relevant theology of grace excel whatever worth it might be seen to have in the promotion of Christian truth for our time.

In these days of the knowledge explosion when data with relationship to time are multiplying at an exponential rate we are fully aware that by the time this book is published it is already out of date. But as we have not principally attempted to propose any doctrine as such, neither have we intended to say the last word on grace even for our time, much less to provide for the future a lasting framework in which theological ideas about divine love can be developed. Such a notion would be diametrically opposed to the basic principle that human life is essentially a process in which eventually old and worn-out forms must be superseded by newer and more vital ones without losing their direction.

We realize full well that the basis of romantic love in the light of which we have explicitated our larval theology of grace is sexual love. And ours is a time of sexual revolution. Here too there can be no permanence. Sexual liasons among young people today do not necessarily involve lifetime commitments. And yet the love affair with God in terms of which we have spoken about grace must be an enduring one. So the time will come and maybe is already at hand when we must abandon all attempts to describe the grace relationship by comparing it to romantic love, and seek some new vehicle of communication.

In writing this book we have tried to keep constantly in mind its many limitations. But we have also attempted to keep ever before us its real objective which we hope has not been lost to the reader in the maze of details, intricacies and subtleties that has been an unintended result of the writing of it, necessitated only by the complexity of the theological issues involved. Our only real ambition has been to set up for examination one possible model for the explicitation of the larval theology of grace.

Our intent has been chiefly methodological. We realize full well
that there are many other models possible if we consider the
ways in which Scripture speaks of grace. As we said, we could
have viewed it as life, or as light, as adoption or assimilation.
Perhaps one of the more pregnant models for consideration
would be the one suggested by the letter of St. James (1, 21):
grace as the *emphytos logos.*

The truth that we sought in this book then is the truth of
a model. It is a relational rather than an absolute truth. We
have not primarily attempted to present arguments for, or even
to document, any of our statements. We have tried only to explain them so that the reader himself will be in a position to
judge whether the model proposed corresponds to the reality
under consideration. We have tried sedulously to avoid what
St. Augustine calls a *veracitas homicida,* such an unrelenting and
absolute devotion to *Wissenschaft,* accuracy and logic that it
kills the spirit. Though we have tried to relate our ideas to the
traditional elements which any confessional faith must defend,
we have not at all felt defensive about the model we have proposed. We experienced no need to establish it by proof or documentation, but only to explain it.

The tentative nature of our enterprise, however, should not
belie the importance of the subject with which it deals. For the
person who really wants to be a Christian, a Christian in fact
and not in name or gesture only, there is nothing more significant. The term "Christian" cannot be a category or stereotype
—an essence. It has to be the designation of a mode of existence
in the world that is rooted in the very depths of the personality
of each individual as only love can be. Buber speaks of a saying
of Rabbi Zusya: "In the coming world they will not ask me:
'Why were you not Moses?' They will ask me: 'Why were you
not Zusya?'" But the Christian on the last day will have to con-
front two questions: Why were you not yourself? Why were you
not Christ? He will have missed the very purpose of his existence if he is not able to accept himself as he really is and his
life as a process of Christogenesis. His life will have no cosmic

meaning unless he views it in the light of the biogenetic principle: ontogeny recapitulates phylogeny. Only by running ahead of time through faith will he be able to experience his life as a mirror of the process of creation itself groping toward that Omega day when, as St. Augustine says: "There will be just one Christ loving himself."

BIBLIOGRAPHY

I. Ecclesiastical Documents:

The Sixteenth Council of Carthage (418)—Original sin and grace. DB101 ff.
The Council of Ephesus (431)—Indiculus on grace. DB129 ff.
The Council of Arles (c. 475)—Grace and predestination. DB160 ff.
The Second Council of Orange (529)—Original sin, grace and predestination. DB174 ff.
Adrian I, pope—Letter to the Spanish bishops on predestination. DB300 ff.
The Council of Quiersy (853)—Gottschalk on redemption and grace. DB-316 ff.
The Council of Valence (855)—Predestination. DB320 ff.
The Council of Constance (1418)—The errors of John Hus. DB627 ff.
Sixtus IV, pope—Errors of Peter de Rivo. DB719 ff.
Leo X, pope—Bull "Exsurge" against Martin Luther. DB741 ff.
The Council of Trent (1563)—Decrees and canons on justification. DB792 ff; 811 ff.
Pius V, pope—Errors of Michael du Bay. DB1001 ff.
Paul V, pope—The efficacy of grace. DB1090.
Innocent X, pope—The efficacy of grace. DB1097.
Alexander VIII, pope—Philosophical sins. DB1289 f.
Alexander VIII, pope—Errors of the Jansenists. DB1291 ff.

240   CONTEMPORARY THEOLOGY OF GRACE

Innocent XII, pope—The most pure love of God. DB1327 ff.
Clement XI, pope—Errors of Paschase Quesnel. DB1351 ff.
Pius VI, pope—Errors of the Synod of Pistoia. DB1501 ff.
The First Vatican Council (1870)—Constitution on the Catholic faith. DB-
    1781 ff.
Pius XI, pope—Bull "Infinita" on the recuperation of merits. DB2193.
Pius XII, pope—Encyclical "Mystici" on the Mystical Body, the salvation
    of infidels, inhabitation of the Holy Spirit and capital grace. DS3800 ff.
Pius XII, pope—Encyclical "Humani" concerning new ideas about the su-
    pernatural. DS3890 ff.

II. Recent Books.

Alszeghy, Z. **Nova creatura: la nozione della grazia nei commentari medie-
    vali di S. Paolo.** Roma, P. Università Gregoriana, 1956.
Baltasar, E. **Teilhard and the Supernatural.** Baltimore, Helicon, 1966.
Baumgartner, C. **La grâce du Christ.** Tournai, Desclée, 1963.
Bouillard, H. **Conversion et grâce chez S. Thomas d'Aquin.** Paris, Aubier,
    1944.
Brinktrine, J. **Die Lehre von der Gnade.** Paderborn, Schöningh, 1957.
Cuttaz, F. **Our Life of Grace.** Notre Dame, Ind., Fides, 1958.
Daujat, J. **The Theology of Grace.** N.Y., Hawthorn, 1959.
Dedek, J. **Experimental Knowledge of the Indwelling Trinity: an Historical
    Study of the Doctrine of St. Thomas.** Mundelein, Ill., St. Mary of the
    Lake Seminary, 1958.
Denis, P. **La révélation de la grâce dans Saint Paul et dans Saint Jean.**
    Liège, Pensée catholique, 1948.
Dhont, R. **Le problème de la préparation à la grâce.** Paris, Éditions fran-
    ciscaines, 1946.
Dockx, S. **Fils de Dieu par grâce.** Paris, Desclée de Brouwer, 1948.
Doolan, A. **Sanctifying Grace.** Cork, Mercier, 1953.
Dürig, W. **Imago: ein Beitrag zur Terminologie und Theologie der Römi-
    schen Liturgie.** München, Zink, 1952.
Ferguson, J. **Pelagius: a Historical and Theological Study.** Cambridge,
    Heffer, 1956.
Flick, M. **L'attimo della giustificazione secondo S. Tommaso.** Roma, P.
    Università Gregoriana, 1947.
——— **Il vangelo della grazia.** Firenze, Libreria editrice fiorentina, 1964.
Fortman, E., ed. **The Theology of Man and Grace: Commentary.** Milwau-
    kee, Bruce, 1966.
Fransen, P. **Divine Grace and Man.** Rev. ed. N.Y., New American Library,
    1965.
——— **The New Life of Grace.** Tournai, Desclée, 1969.

Galtier, P. L'habitation en nous des Trois Personnes. Paris, Beauchesne, 1949.
—— Le Saint Ésprit en nous d'après les Pères grecs. Roma, P. Università Gregoriana, 1946.
Gleason, R. Grace. N.Y., Sheed & Ward, 1962.
Goldbrunner, J. Individuation . . . Notre Dame, Ind., University of Notre Dame, 1964.
—— Realization . . . Notre Dame, Ind., University of Notre Dame, 1966.
Guardini, R. Freedom, Grace and Destiny: Three Chapters in the Interpretation of Existence. N.Y., Pantheon, 1961.
Johann, R. The Meaning of Love. Glen Rock, N.J., Paulist Press, 1966.
Journet, C. The Meaning of Grace. Glen Rock, N.J., Paulist Press, 1962.
Koch, R. Grâce et liberté humaine. Paris, Desclée, 1967.
Küng, H. Justification: the Doctrine of Karl Barth and a Catholic Reflection. N.Y., Nelson, 1964.
Lampe, G. The Doctrine of Justification by Faith Alone. London, Mowbray, 1954.
La Taille, M. de. The Hypostatic Union and Created Actuation by Uncreated Act. West Baden Springs, Ind., West Baden College, 1952.
Lepp, I. The Psychology of Loving. N.Y., American Library, 1963.
Letter, P. de. The Christian and Hindu Concept of Grace. Calcutta, Little Flower Press, 1958.
Lonergan, B. Collection. N.Y., Herder & Herder, 1967.
Lubac, H. de. The Mystery of the Supernatural. N.Y., Herder & Herder, 1967.
—— Surnaturel; études historiques. Paris, Aubier, 1945.
Mackey, J. The Grace of God; the Response of Man. Albany, N.Y., Magi, 1966.
Matthews, J. With the Help of Thy Grace. Westminster, Md., Newman, 1945.
McCarthy, T. The Eschatological Character of the Grace of Christ in Contemporary Theology; its Catechetical Implications. (microfiche) Ann Arbor, Mich., University Microfilms, 1969.
McLaughlin, B. Nature, Grace and Religious Development. N. Y., Paulist Press, 1963.
Meissner, W., ed. Foundations for a Psychology of Grace. Glen Rock, N.J., Paulist Press, 1966.
Meyer, C. The Thomistic Concept of Justifying Contrition. Mundelein, Ill., St. Mary of the Lake Seminary, 1949.
Moeller, C. The Theology of Grace and the Oecumenical Movement. London, Mowbray, 1961.
Morson, J. The Gift of God: a Study of Sanctifying Grace in the New Testament. Cork, Mercier, 1952.
Most, W. Novum tentamen ad solutionem de gratia et praedestinatione.

Romae, Editiones Paulinae, 1963.

Mouroux, J. **The Christian Experience.** N.Y., Sheed & Ward, 1954.

Mura, E. **L'humanité vivifiante du Christ.** Paris, Vitte, 1951.

Nicolas, J. **The Mystery of God's Grace.** London, Bloomsbury, 1960.

—— **Les profundeurs de la grâce.** Paris, Beauchesne, 1969.

Noël, L. **De natura gratiae operantis actualis.** Quebec, 1952.

Parente, P. **Anthropologia supernaturalis de gratia et virtutibus.** Romae, Marietti, 1946.

Piolanti, A. **Aspetti della grazia.** Roma, Ares, 1958.

Rahner, K. **Grace in Freedom.** N.Y., Herder & Herder, 1969.

—— **Nature and Grace.** N.Y., Sheed & Ward, 1963-4.

—— **Theological Investigations.** Baltimore, Md., Helicon, 1961.

Rito, H. **Recentioris theologiae quaedam tendentiae ad conceptum onto-logico-personalem gratiae.** Romae, Herder, 1963.

Rondet, H. **The Grace of Christ.** Westminster, Md., Newman, 1967.

—— **Essais sur la théologie de la grâce.** Paris, Beauchesne, 1964.

Scheeben, M. **Nature and Grace.** St. Louis, B. Herder, 1954.

Semana Espanola de Teología, XV, Madrid, 1955.

Shepherd, W. **Man's Condition: God and World Process.** N.Y., Herder & Herder, 1969.

Smith, G. **Freedom in Molina.** Chicago, Loyola University Press, 1966.

Sola-Brunet, G. **Tractatus de gratia Christi.** Barcinone, Balmes, 1958.

Stevens, G. **The Life of Grace.** Englewood Cliffs, N.J., Prentice-Hall, 1963.

Stöckel, B. **"Gratia supponit naturam:" Geschichte und Analyse eines theologischen Axioms.** Romae, Herder, 1962.

Terbovich, J. **The Faces of Love.** N.Y., Doubleday, 1966.

Torrance, T. **The Doctrine of Grace in the Apostolic Fathers.** Edinburgh, Oliver & Boyd, 1948.

Uricchio, F. **Grazia e peccato in S. Paolo; rapporti ed effetti sociali.** Padova, Il Messagero di S. Antonio, 1955.

White, V. **God and the Unconscious.** Chicago, Regnery, 1953.

Wild, P. **The Divinization of Man According to St. Hilary of Poitiers.** Mundelein, Ill., St. Mary of the Lake Seminary, 1950.

Willig, I. **Geschaffene und ungeschaffene Gnade.** Münster (Westf.) Aschendorff, 1964.

III. Current Articles.

Alfaro, J. "Persona y gracia," **Gregorianum,** 1960, p. 5-29.

—— English summary: **Theology Digest,** 1966, p. 3-7.

Aumann, J. "Love God and do what you will; you will not sin," **Cross and Crown,** 1966, p. 218-26.

Chatillon, J. "Quidquid convenit Filio Dei per naturam, convenit Filio hominis per gratiam, à propos de Jean de Ripa, Determinationes, I, 4, 4," **Divinitas,** 1967, p. 715-27.

Combes, A. "Le P. J. F. Dedek et la connaissance quasi-expérimentale des Personnes Divines selon s. Thomas d'Aquin," **Divinitas**, 1963, p. 3-82.

Cooke, B. "Personal Development through Grace," **Catholic World**, 1964, p. 371-7.

Coyle, T. "Some Post-War Trends in De gratia," **Proceedings of the Catholic Theological Society of America**, 1961, p. 161-70.

Cuskelly, E. "Actual Grace: Personal Attraction," **Australasian Catholic Record**, 1961, p. 195-206.

——"Grace and Person," **Australasian Catholic Record**, 1961, p. 114-22.

Davis, C. "The Christian Mystery and the Trinity," **Theology Digest**, 1964, p. 176-7.

Donnelly, M. "The Supernatural Person," **Irish Theological Quarterly**, 1963, p. 340-7.

Doolan, A. "Actual Grace for Hardened Sinners; Final Perseverance," **Irish Ecclesiastical Record**, 1962, p. 251-8.

Drinkwater, F. "What about Divine Life?" **Lumen Vitae**, 1963, pp. 726-30.

Fannon, P. "The Changing Face of Theology: Man in Nature and Grace," **Clergy Review**, 1967, p. 331-6.

Farlardeau, E. "The Personalist Approach to Grace," **Emmanuel**, 1964, p. 120-4.

Flick, M. and Alszeghy, Z. "L'opzione fondamentale della vita morale e la grazia," **Gregorianum**, 1960, p. 593-619.

Forshaw, B. "The Doctrine of Grace Today," **Clergy Review**, 1961, p. 449-62.

Fransen, P. "Grace and Freedom," **Homiletic and Pastoral Review**, 1965, p. 731-54.

—— "How should we teach the Treatise on Grace?" **Apostolic Renewal in the Seminary** (N.Y., The Christophers, 1965) p. 139-63.

Gillon, L. "La grâce incrée chez quelques théologiens du XIVe siècle," **Divinitas**, 1967, p. 671-80.

Greeley, A. "God's Rendezvous with Man," **Ave Maria**, Sept. 28, 1963, p. 5.

Hawkins, D. "Two Conceptions of Freedom in Theology," **Downside Review**, 1961, p. 289-96.

Hill, W. "Uncreated Grace; a Critique of Karl Rahner," **Thomist**, 1963, p. 333-56.

Hopkins, R. "Grace and Commandments," **Priest**, 1964, p. 37-40.

Hyde, J. "Grace; a Bibliographical Note," **Irish Theological Quarterly**, 1965, p. 257-61.

Kay, H. "Life in the Spirit," **The Way**, 1966, p. 212-18.

Kenny, J. "Grace here, Glory there," **Clergy Monthly**, 1963, p. 54-9.

Letter, P. de. "The Catholic Doctrine of Grace," **Guide**, April, 1963, p. 9.

—— "Eternal Graces," **Irish Ecclesiastical Record**, 1965, p. 8-17.

—— "Pure or Quasi-Formal Causality?" **Irish Theological Quarterly**, 1963,

p. 36-47. (Reply by B. Kelly, ibid. p. 272).

——— "Sanctifying Grace and Divine Indwelling," **Gregorianum**, 1960, p. 63-9.

Malone, E. "Some Apostolic Dimensions of the Doctrine of Divine Grace," **Apostolic Renewal in the Seminary** (N.Y., The Christophers, 1965) p. 164-73.

Meyer, C. "Grace as Freedom," **Chicago Studies**, 1968, p. 143-61.

——— "A Personalist View of Grace: the Ghost of Galileo," **Chicago Studies**, 1968, p. 283-301.

——— "The Status of Grace Today," **Chicago Studies**, 1968, p. 27-51.

Moeller, C. "Grace and Justification," **Lumen Vitae**, 1964, p. 719-30.

Motherway, T. "Supernatural Existential," **Chicago Studies**, 1965, p. 97-103.

O'Shea, K. "Divinization; a Study in Theological Analogy," **Thomist**, 1965, p. 1-45.

——— "Pure Uncreated Unity," **Irish Theological Quarterly**, 1963, p. 347-53.

Peter, C. "The Position of Karl Rahner regarding the Supernatural: a Comparative Study of Nature and Grace," **Proceedings of the Catholic Theological Society of America**, 1965, p. 81-94.

Rahner, K. "Die Ehe als Sakrament," **Geist und Leben**, 1967, p. 177-93.

——— "Philosophie und Theologie," **Kairos**, 1962, p. 162-9.

Rondet, H. "Divinization of the Christian," **Theology Digest**, 1959, p. 113-22.

——— "Notes sur la théologie de la grâce," **Nouvelle Revue Théologique**, 1961, p. 382-99.

Trethowan, I. "The Union of Grace; a Suggestion," **Downside Review**, 1963, p. 317-27.

Van Roo, W. "The Resurrection, Instrument of Grace," **Theology Digest**, 1960, p. 94-8.

Vasey, V. "Grace perfects Nature," **Cross and Crown**, 1960, p. 437-47.

Vignaux, P. "La sanctification par l'Ésprit incrée d'après Jean de Ripa, I Sent., Dist. XIV-XV," **Divinitas**, 1967, p. 681-713.

INDEX